CU00928298

THE
GREATEST
EMPIRE

THE
GREATEST
EMPIRE

A Life of Seneca

EMILY WILSON

OXFORD
UNIVERSITY PRESS

OXFORD
UNIVERSITY PRESS

Oxford University Press is a department of the
University of Oxford. It furthers the University's objective
of excellence in research, scholarship, and education
by publishing worldwide.

Oxford   New York
Auckland   Cape Town   Dar es Salaam   Hong Kong   Karachi
Kuala Lumpur   Madrid   Melbourne   Mexico City   Nairobi
New Delhi   Shanghai   Taipei   Toronto

With offices in
Argentina   Austria   Brazil   Chile   Czech Republic   France   Greece
Guatemala   Hungary   Italy   Japan   Poland   Portugal   Singapore
South Korea   Switzerland   Thailand   Turkey   Ukraine   Vietnam

Oxford is a registered trade mark of Oxford University Press
in the UK and certain other countries.

Published in the United States of America by
Oxford University Press
198 Madison Avenue, New York, NY 10016

© Emily Wilson

All rights reserved. No part of this publication may be reproduced,
stored in a retrieval system, or transmitted, in any form or by any means,
without the prior permission in writing of Oxford University Press,
or as expressly permitted by law, by license, or under terms agreed with
the appropriate reproduction rights organization. Inquiries concerning
reproduction outside the scope of the above should be sent to the
Rights Department, Oxford University Press, at the address above.

You must not circulate this work in any other form
and you must impose this same condition on any acquirer.

Library of Congress Cataloging-in-Publication Data
Wilson, Emily R., 1971—author.
  The greatest empire : a life of Seneca / Emily Wilson.
    pages   cm
  ISBN 978-0-19-992664-0 (hardback)
   1. Seneca, Lucius Annaeus, approximately 4 B.C.–65 A.D.   2. Seneca, Lucius Annaeus,
approximately 4 B.C.–65 A.D.—Criticism and interpretation.   I. Title.
  PA6675.W55   2014
  878.0109—dc23
  [B]   2014008888

9 8 7 6 5 4 3 2 1
Printed in the United States of America
on acid-free paper

The greatest empire is to be emperor of oneself.
(Imperare sibi maximum imperium est)

Seneca, Epistle 113.30

CONTENTS

Acknowledgments   ix

Timeline   xi

Maps   xiv

Introduction: "A Rough Road to Greatness"   1

Chapter I: "Parental Love Is Wise"   23

Chapter II: Nowhere and Everywhere   61

Chapter III: "Vices Tempt You by the Rewards
             They Offer"   103

Chapter IV: "There's No Easy Path from Earth
            to the Stars"   163

Epilogue   215

Notes   231

Further Reading   239

Bibliography   241

Art Credits   247

Index   249

ACKNOWLEDGMENTS

I would like first to thank Stefan Vranka at Oxford University Press, for suggesting that I write about Seneca. Thank you also to the Penn Humanities Forum, where the interdisciplinary discussions of violence in 2013–2014 provided a useful background for thinking about life in imperial Rome. I'd also like to thank my colleagues, graduate students, and undergraduates at the University of Pennsylvania, who have all helped provide a stimulating but safe environment in which to write—quite the opposite of barren Corsica or Nero's court.

TIMELINE

c. 54 BCE	Birth of Seneca the Elder, father of the philosopher, in Corduba, Spain.
44 BCE	Assassination of Julius Caesar.
43 BCE	Assassination of Cicero (opponent of Mark Antony).
31 BCE	Battle of Actium, in which Octavian, later Augustus, defeated Mark Antony and Cleopatra. This marked the end of the Roman Civil Wars and the beginning of one-man rule (the Principate).
19 BCE	Augustus completed the conquest of Roman Spain (Hispania).
c. 8 BCE	Birth of Lucius Annaeus Novatus (later known as Gallio), elder brother of our Seneca, son of Seneca the Elder and Helvia.
c. 4 BCE	Birth of Lucius Annaeus Seneca, in Corduba, Spain.
?1 BCE	Birth of Marcus Annaeus Mela, younger brother of our Seneca.
c. 5 AD, or earlier	Seneca's aunt took him to Rome for education in rhetoric and philosophy (the latter subject taught by Attalus the Stoic and Sotion the Sextian).
14 AD	Death of Augustus; accession of Tiberius, his adopted son.
c. 20 AD (or a little later)	Seneca, suffering from bad health, went to Egypt for a long visit with his maternal aunt and uncle.
31	Seneca returned to Rome. His uncle died in a shipwreck en route back from Egypt. Seneca began to campaign for his first magistracy.

c. 37–41	Seneca wrote *On Providence.*
37/8	Death of Tiberius, accession of Caligula.
37	Birth of Nero, son of Gnaeus Domitius Ahenobarbus and Agrippina the Younger
38–40	Conflict between Caligula and Seneca; Seneca was spared execution due to bad health.
c. 38–39	Seneca's father died.
c. 38	Wrote *Consolation to Marcia.*
c. 40	First marriage, birth of a son. Built up connections in court, including friendship with Agrippina and her sister, Julia Livilla.
40–41	Seneca's son died.
41	Claudius became emperor. Seneca, at behest of his wife Messalina, was banished to Corsica on a charge of adultery with Julia Livilla.
c. 43 or 44	Wrote *Consolation to Polybius.*
c. 46–48	Wrote *Consolation ad Helvia,* to his mother.
c. 48–55	Wrote *On the Briefness of Life.*
42–49	Composed the first two books of *On Anger,* addressed to his elder brother, Novatus.
49	Won recall from exile thanks to intervention of Nero's mother, Agrippina, who hired him to be tutor of rhetoric to the young prince, age twelve.
c. 51–53	Novatus (=Gallio), elder brother of Seneca, acted as Roman governor in Achaea; there he dismissed charges brought by Jews against the apostle Paul.
October 54	Death of Claudius, after eating poisonous mushrooms. Nero, age seventeen, became emperor, with the support of the military and Burrus, leader of the Guard. Seneca composed speeches for Nero on his accession, including a funeral speech for Claudius and a speech to the Senate on the new regime.
December 54	Wrote *Apocolycyntosis (Pumpkinification),* a satirical account of Claudius' deification. Nero appointed Seneca and Burrus as advisors.

55	Murder of Britannicus, Nero's stepbrother, son of Claudius (presented as death by epilepsy).
55/56	Wrote *On Mercy*, addressed to Nero.
?55	Novatus (Gallio) attained the consulship (highest position of political power in Rome).
56	Seneca's consulship.
59	Murder of Agrippina, Nero's mother (and Seneca's patron).
c. 55–62	Wrote *On the Happy Life*, essay addressed to his brother Gallio.
c. 56–62	Composed *On Benefits*.
60/61	Seneca and other Roman financiers called in loans from the province of Britain; Queen Boudicca (Boadicea) led her people in a failed attempt at revolt against Roman rule.
62	Death of Burrus; Tigellinus took over the Praetorian Guard. Seneca tried in vain to retire from Nero's court; withdrew from most aspects of public life. Death of Seneca's great friend, Serenus.
62–64	Wrote *Natural Questions* and *Letters to Lucilius*.
64	Seneca again attempted to retire, claiming to be ill. Great Fire at Rome.
65	Pisonian Conspiracy, attempted assassination of Nero. Seneca was accused of involvement and forced to commit suicide. His nephew Lucan and many others were also killed or forced to kill themselves.
66	Forced suicides of Seneca's brother Mela, the writer Petronius, the senator Thrasea Paetus.
68	Coup forced Nero out of office; he fled Rome and killed himself, leaving political chaos in his wake.
69	Year of the Four Emperors, in which four successive contenders took power and were each ousted in turn.

Map 1: The Roman Empire in Seneca's Time.

LOWER
PANNONIA
DACIA
RICUM
MOESIA
Black Sea
Sea
THRACE
BITHYNIA – PONTUS
MACEDONIA
CAPPADOCIA
GALATIA
ASIA
CILICIA
PAMPHYLIA
ACHAEA
LYCIA
SYRIA
CYPRUS
CRETE
PHOENICIA
JUDAEA
n   *e*   *a*   *n*   *S*   *e*   *a*
CYRENAICA
ARABIA
EGYPT

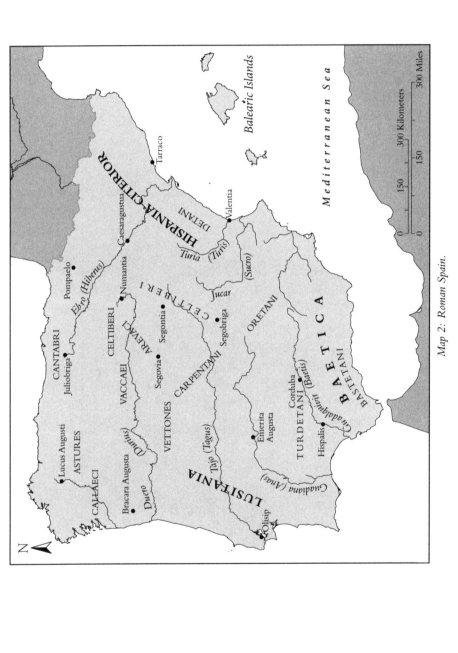

Map 2: Roman Spain.

Map 3: Roman Italy.

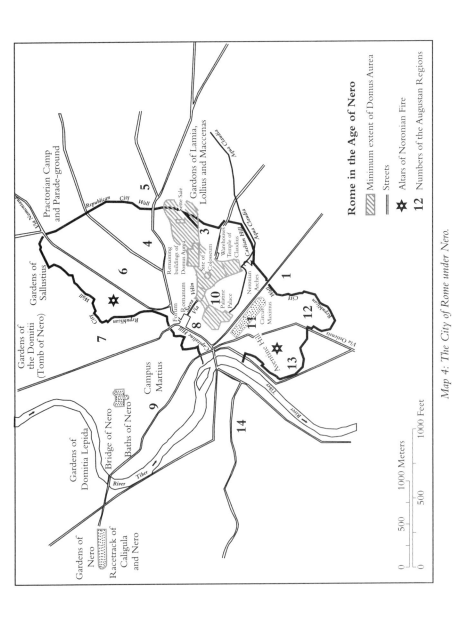

Map 4: The City of Rome under Nero.

INTRODUCTION:
"A ROUGH ROAD TO GREATNESS"*

L ucius Annaeus Seneca died in an extremely dramatic fashion in 65 CE.[1] He was forced to kill himself, having been accused of involvement in a conspiracy to kill the emperor Nero. A generation after his death, the historian Tacitus gives a vivid account of the scene, telling us that he died surrounded by his friends and in the company of his wife, who was willing to kill herself at his side. He was a man of around sixty-five or seventy, his body strong from regular exercise but skinny from his frugal diet of bread and fruit and weakened by lifelong chronic bronchitis and asthma. Cutting his wrists failed to do the trick, as did the traditional dose of hemlock. He died only once he stepped into a hot bath and managed to suffocate in the steam.

Seneca's death raises many of the puzzles and paradoxes that we will encounter in his life. He modeled his conduct in these last hours on that of Socrates in Plato's *Phaedo*, who spends his last afternoon on earth discussing philosophy with his friends before calmly drinking the hemlock and calmly passing away.[2] But Seneca's death was harder to achieve. He failed to die by the hemlock, or from the less philosophical wrist-slashing, and had to resort to the innovative use of a steam bath to stop his breath—a more fitting end for a man who suffered from life-long breathing problems, and a mark of his distance from the Socratic model.

* Confragosa in fastigium dignitatis via est (Epistle 84)

Moreover, Seneca is a Socrates without a Plato willing to tell his story. Instead, he is surrounded by a group of nameless, undifferentiated "friends," whose main purpose is to admire the great man and to record his words and deeds for posterity: Seneca had created for himself a mirror-image of the imperial Roman court, with the Philosopher as equivalent to the Emperor. Tacitus slyly tells us that he will not transcribe Seneca's last words in his narrative, since they are already part of his public works. He hints that Seneca's own self-publicizing may make him less admirable than his old Athenian model.

Socrates' life and his death were intertwined with his philosophical activities. He invented new gods and corrupted young people by his teaching. Seneca followed Socrates in claiming that a wise man spends his whole life learning how to die (*tota vita discendum est mori*—*On the Shortness of Life,* 7.3). But he died for reasons that seem to have very little to do with his philosophy, or indeed, might seem to be antithetical to his intellectual pretensions. He was closely entangled with the intrigues of Nero's court, having served both as his tutor and, later, his advisor and speechwriter. Nero wanted Seneca dead because he suspected, probably rightly, that Seneca wanted him dead; the details of Seneca's philosophical views (on ethics, the gods, or anything else) had little or nothing to do with it. His death had political causes, even if he managed to give it a philosophical turn. The paradoxes of being both "a philosopher in politics" and a politician in philosophy are central to his life (Fig. I.1).[3]

The story of Socrates' death, as told by Plato, gives an impression of complete calm, total control, and cohesiveness. Not a word, not a gesture, not a limb is out of place; the whole thing is beautifully choreographed and utterly harmonious. Seneca's death, on the other hand, seems haphazard and full of mistakes. Nothing goes according to plan. He fails to die by the suicide method he had picked and fails again on his second attempt. It is a story of hesitations, reversals, and multiple changes of mind. When juxtaposed with the death of Socrates, Seneca's death looks like a failed version of the philosophical end. This Roman philosopher cannot manage to die easily, even after a long life devoted to preparing for it; there is tension, to the last minute, in his attenuated, skinny tendons. The painter Rubens, deeply influenced by Seneca, viscerally makes this point in his famous painting of the death scene.[4] Seneca died in a state of struggle against the political powers

Figure I.1 Seneca modeled his death, and to some extent his life, on those of Socrates.

that were. The attempt to die, and to attain philosophical calm, takes every nerve and muscle in his body. "Living is fighting," he declared (Epistle 96.5), and dying, too, involved a battle, as well as a long process of trial and error.

Seneca's legacy, in both literal and metaphorical senses, is also ambiguous. He promised to leave behind, as his best achievement, the "image of his life." But he also vowed to leave money to his friends in his will, to show his gratitude to them for their "services" to him. The image of a philosopher who has amassed enormous amounts of money to leave behind him, and one who is obviously obsessed with his own postmortem reputation (rather than, say, with the immortality of the human soul), seems to fall rather short of the Socratic ideal. Moreover, there is no particular reason to believe that Nero honored Seneca's will: probably he seized the estate back for himself. His wife, who had planned to die with him, was saved by the soldiers and ended up outliving him. Seneca's dying words are not recorded, at least by Tacitus, our only source. Seneca's time of power and influence was necessarily brief. It was a compromised death, full of second and third guesses, that follows a life of compromises and complex negotiations, between ideal and reality, philosophy and politics, virtue and money, motivation and action.

The story of Seneca's life raises a broader, indeed universal question, which has particular resonance in our time: What counts as success? This is an issue that runs through all Seneca's literary output. He constantly stages conflicts between different models of the good or successful life. He rose from a provincial background and suffered exile and disgrace, but in middle age Seneca found himself suddenly one of the most powerful men in Rome, and eventually right-hand advisor to the emperor himself. He felt increasingly trapped, alienated, and terrified by his position. After begging in vain to be allowed to retire, he gave back some of the wealth Nero had given him and withdrew from court in 64 CE. But retirement was not enough to save him. His condemnation on the charge of conspiracy represents the emperor's final word against his teacher, counselor, and one-time friend.

Seneca was deeply engaged with the philosophy of Stoicism and knew that an ideal Stoic wise person ought to be free, tranquil, and happy at all times, even while dying, even in agony, even in the depths of grief, humiliation, or loss. But Seneca was also, as we shall see, highly conscious of his own distance from the Stoic ideal. He presented himself as one who is only setting out on the philosophical journey (*proficiens*), not as one who has achieved it. His awareness of his own imperfection is perhaps the most likeable aspect of this endlessly fascinating character. The account of Seneca's death-scene in Tacitus shows us a philosopher who is, at the end of his life, still straining towards calm, not one who has already found all the answers. In his writing, Seneca imagines death as the easy exit that is always available: "I have made nothing easier than dying," declares God in Seneca's essay *On Providence* (6.7). He insists that we ought always to be able to rise above fortune, both good and bad, and that we can, through our own strength of will, overcome any challenge with ease: "It is not because things are difficult that we don't dare do them; our lack of daring makes them difficult" (Epistle 104.26). But for Seneca himself, despite his courage, both dying and living were far from easy.

THE SOURCES

There are particular difficulties surrounding a book that focuses on the life of Seneca. Some of these are endemic to the study of any ancient or premodern person's life. We have none of the rich fields of evidence—letters, diaries, photographs, surviving possessions, oral testimony from friends, students, enemies, lovers, spouses, publishers, or students—which are often available to biographers of the more recently deceased. In Seneca's case, over half of his vast literary output is lost, including all his political speeches, all private letters, and much of his poetry, as well as works on India and Egypt, an early study of earthquakes, a book about his father, and a treatise on marriage. We also have very little evidence of any kind about his earlier years: this biography, inevitably, has little about its subject's childhood and youth and focuses disproportionately on a couple of decades in his life—the years in which most of his extant work was produced, and for which we have references to Seneca from other authors, because of his involvement with the court of Nero.

But the challenge is not simply due to lack of evidence. The nature of the evidence we do have is problematic in itself. Seneca's surviving work is voluminous, a far larger extant *oeuvre* than most ancient authors. We have his tragedies, his essays on a wide range of subjects, philosophical letters, one political satire, and an extensive treatise on scientific issues (the *Natural Questions*). Unlike most ancient writers, Seneca often uses the first person and has much to say about the details of daily life and how to live it. Yet none of these works has a direct, uncomplicated relationship to the author's own life. None of Seneca's works comes as close to autobiography as the private letters from Cicero to his great friend Atticus. All are carefully constructed works of public performance, even the most apparently personal (such as his letter to his mother on his own exile). Every apparent report of biographical fact is slippery and often untrustworthy. As we shall see repeatedly in this book, Seneca's literary work plays a fascinating dance with the reader's desire for information about his lived experience. For instance, Seneca was sent into exile and also wrote a great deal about exile, including his own. But the few details he provides about the material conditions of life in exile on Corsica are all literary fictions, modeled on the writings of that earlier famous exiled Roman writer, Ovid.[5] Still more complex versions of the problem arise

when we try to use Seneca's writings to reconstruct his domestic life
(with parents, wives, and children), his friendships, or even, most desirable but most difficult of all, his relationship with the emperor Nero. We
can gain some access to Seneca's perspective on his life through his writings, but it must be emphasized right from the start that the enterprise is
peculiarly difficult.

We might hope, at the very least, to construct from Seneca's writings a
set of coherent, "Senecan" beliefs about abstract philosophical topics, or
even about more practical issues, such as whether a person ought to participate in politics, or whether wealth contributes to human happiness.
Or, on the assumption that his views may have changed over time, perhaps we could reconstruct at least what he believed about a particular
question at a particular period of his life.[6] But even this is often an impossible task. Many of Seneca's extant works cannot be dated with any certainty, although some can. Many contain not only contradictions with
one another, but even internal tensions and contradictions. Moreover,
many of the attitudes struck in the extant works are entirely incompatible
with what we know of Seneca's life story. It is hardly surprising to find
the ancient historian Dio (in the early third century CE) accusing him of
downright hypocrisy.

The charge of hypocrisy against Seneca is generally dismissed fairly
quickly by modern scholars, who tend to regard it as implying a simplistic and even anachronistic set of expectations about how life ought
to relate to literary work, and also about what it is to be a consistent
person.[7] But such dismissals often go too fast and sometimes imply an
even more simplistic assumption: that good writers must be nice people.
The most interesting question is not why Seneca failed to practice what
he preached, but why he preached what he did, so adamantly and so effectively, given the life he found himself leading. The extant works enact
a fascinating, prolonged struggle for constancy, the power that implies an
ability to stand still while the world revolves around one. *Constantia* and
inconstantia are rather different from the modern, post-Romantic terms,
"hypocrisy" and "integrity." Whereas "hypocrisy" (from the Greek word
for "acting") suggests a mismatch in a single moment of time between a
person's external behavior and the internal reality, "inconstancy" suggests
a failure to remain the same at every moment, across time. "What is
wisdom?" Seneca asked, and answered his own question: "Always wanting the same things, and refusing the same things" (Ep. 20). The Stoic

ideal of constancy (*constantia*, on which, as we shall see, Seneca wrote a highly influential essay) is the wise man's ability to be firm, always the same, always stable, even as the world changes all around him. Seneca longed to find a coherent identity, whether dining in the court of the emperor or moldering in exile on a rocky island, far from the center of power. But he also knew how difficult it was to attain the ideal.

Both the life of political power and the life of philosophical counseling emerged from the same deep place in Seneca's psyche: in a desire to be safe at home, and able to look out on the changing world around him—rather than being hurled constantly around the periphery. He was, throughout his life, very deeply both an insider and an outsider, and his life story was a series of swings toward and away from Rome and the center of Roman power: from Spain to Rome; from Rome to Egypt and back; from Rome to Corsica, and back; and finally a long, painful set of vacillations and attempts to get out from Nero's court—if only to the safety of the grave.

This book traces the paradoxes that emerge in Seneca's life and work through his attempt to gain "control" or "empire" (both covered by the Latin term *imperium*) in both the public and personal senses: to be influential over other people within his society, and also to be stable in himself. The phrase I use as my title, "the greatest empire," comes from a passage in Epistle 113 (113.30) dealing with the problematic relationship of these two kinds of empire. Seneca insists that those who attempt to conquer the world and attain political, military, and economic power are far inferior to those who manage to achieve the empire of control over themselves: *imperare sibi maximum imperium est* ("The greatest empire is to be emperor of oneself"—or, "The greatest kind of power is self-control"). Seneca's intellectual activities as a writer and a philosopher allowed him to grasp toward an alternative to the life of politics and ambition, creating his own, distinct model of what "real" power should look like—an empire inside his own head.

But it is revealing that the image used to describe this alternative is drawn from the external political world. Philosophical control is described in terms of political control, and political control of a particular kind (an empire). Seneca's attempts to draw a sharp contrast between the empire of Nero and the empire of philosophy were never consistently maintained, and each informed the other. Seneca's intense awareness of, for example, the emptiness of luxury was not independent of his own experiences in luxurious living. Rather, he knew of what he wrote. He understood first hand that wealth cannot buy peace of mind; if he had not been so rich, he would have been less conscious both of the dangers and the advantages of having money. He was neither a monster nor a saint; he was a talented, ambitious, deeply thoughtful man, who struggled to create an uneasy compromise between his ideals and the powers that were, and who meditated constantly on how to balance his goals and his realities. His work is deeply preoccupied with the question of how to create and fully inhabit an authentic self, and of what it might mean to be authentic. This is one of many ways in which his work seems particularly relevant to contemporary anxieties and concerns.

Seneca wanted to be the most popular, most powerful man in Rome, and also to live in perfect calm, at peace with himself, away from the gnawings of fear and guilt that were also constant features of his adult life. Seneca was exceptional in his intelligence and in his literary and political prominence, but his apparently contradictory desires were in many ways characteristic of the high pressures facing the Roman elite at this period. After a long and exhausting period of civil wars, the Roman Republic had ended at the Battle of Actium (31 BCE) with the victory and accession of Octavian, later Augustus, as one-man ruler of the empire. But Augustus claimed to be not a monarch (a *rex*—always a problematic word in Roman culture) but the "first among equals" (*princeps*, hence principate, the name given to his and his successors' reign); not the sole ruler of the empire, but the "restorer of the republic." It became increasingly clear, under Augustus and his successors in the Julio-Claudian family (Tiberius, Caligula, Claudius, and Nero), that the old power of the Senate, the ruling body under the Republic, was in fact much diminished, and power had shifted toward the emperor himself, his court, and the military—without whom the empire would collapse. But the old families of the Roman elite still paid lip-service to the concept of republicanism and still wanted to believe that they held on to real political power. The conflict between the institutions of government and the political imagination put the upper-class Romans of this period in a deeply problematic position. There was a disconnect between political realities and acceptable forms of speech, which led to a culture characterized by dissimulation; being fake was a prerequisite for social success.[8] Elite Roman men were eager to assert their masculinity (or *virtus*— "virtue" or "manhood") in a political system that robbed them of the old kinds of power. They constantly spoke and wrote in a kind of double-speak, making verbal gestures that could always be interpreted more than one way. The fashionable style of speech and writing piled up aphoristic polished witticisms, a bombardment of the most "truth-y" kind of sentence, as if to compensate for an underlying fear of falsehood. Rhetoric was not only a style but a way of being in the world. Seneca was the master of this style, which was one of his most important literary legacies. Any list of the most referenced Latin quotes will include a great deal of Seneca's aphorisms—lines like "Necessity is usually more powerful than duty" (*Trojan Women* 581), or "Nature takes revenge on everybody" (*Phaedra* 352), or "Crime must be hidden by crime" (*Medea* 721). The aphorisms often speak to recurrent preoccupations of Seneca's, with fortune and its many reversals ("A man that dawn sees proud, dusk sees laid low," *Thyestes* 613–614); with the dangers or emptiness of wealth and material greed ("Wealth doesn't make a king," *Thyestes* 344); with kingship and authority ("A king is one who fears nothing," *Thyestes* 388); with the mechanisms of ambition and power ("One who asks fearfully teaches us to say no," *Phaedra* 593–594); with virtue and willpower ("It's never too late to choose the path towards goodness," *Agamemnon* 242); and with death ("If you can be forced, you don't know how to die," *Hercules* 426).

All these concerns, and the punchy, mannered mode that Seneca uses to articulate them, were very much of his time, although nobody formulated them better. We can get a good glimpse of the ways that times had changed by glancing back to an earlier Roman writer whose life and work bear comparison with that of Seneca, namely Cicero.[9] Both were voluminous authors, deeply influenced by rhetorical training, who composed both poetry and prose, including philosophical works, and both were also key figures on the political stage in their times. Both were controversial figures who were accused of various forms of duplicity (indecision and flip-flopping in Cicero's case, or a failure to practice what he preached in the case of Seneca) and who aroused deep enmity as well as deep friendship. Both were exiled but succeeded in making a comeback. Both died by force when the political tide turned against them. Seneca was forced to kill himself by Nero, while Cicero was assassinated in 43 BCE thanks to the enmity of Mark Antony. Cicero's death could be seen as marking the beginning of the end for the Republic, while Seneca's marked the end of the dream that an intellectual could guide Roman politics.

The similarities and differences between these two life stories provide
a good way of seeing how much Rome had changed, and also of seeing
what was distinctive about Seneca's intellectual and political allegiances.
Both rose from a relatively modest equestrian background (knight's class,
the second tier within the upper class), trained in rhetoric and philosophy, and eventually became consul (the highest office in the land, held
for a single year by a pair of men who were, thereafter, in the highest
possible social rank). But their early years were spent very differently.
Cicero worked as a hugely successful lawyer and also zoomed up the
official career-ladder (the *cursus honorum*), taking up each office at almost
the youngest possible age. Seneca had a very late start, due both to illness
and (probably) lack of commitment to the political career, especially,
perhaps, in the uncongenial atmosphere of the reign of Tiberius; he
wanted to spend more time on philosophy. Cicero delivered his own
speeches, both in the law-courts and the Senate, and saw himself as an
orator, not merely a rhetorician. Seneca was, as we shall see, Nero's
speechwriter and never showed any particular interest in delivering
speeches himself. This difference can be connected to the so-called
"death of oratory," much lamented in the ancient sources, whereby oratory lost its power to enact political change after Cicero and the death
of the Roman Republic.[10]

Moreover, Cicero and Seneca were on opposite sides of the political
spectrum. Cicero (despite repeated acts of hedging and compromise)
struggled to stand up for the old ways of the Republic. Seneca, by contrast, belonged both to the empire and to the emperor. Despite deep
hostility to particular emperors (such as Caligula and Claudius—at least
after his death) and a degree of covert resistance to his ward and patron,
Nero, Seneca had no interest in restoring the Republic and no particular
hostility toward the institutional structure of the Principate.

Not coincidentally, Cicero and Seneca had different visions of the relative importance of philosophy and politics. Cicero turned to the writing
of his works of philosophy only in the interludes between his political
engagements; philosophy was, for him, a means to an end, the primary end
being the renewal of the Republic. For Seneca, philosophy was an end in
itself. His rhetoric aims to achieve a change in the reader's individual
psyche, not in the institutions of government. In Cicero's time, there was
still a sense that political action could make a difference: Cicero hoped
that he really could bring down Caesar and Mark Antony. Seneca, by

contrast, had no hope that he could achieve anything by direct opposition to any of the emperors under whom he lived. His best hope was to moderate some of Nero's worst tendencies and to maximize his own sense of autonomy.

Cicero was an essential precursor to Seneca in a literary sense, since he was the most important earlier writer who had attempted to convey the ideas of Greek philosophy in the Latin language. But Cicero's philosophical affiliations were very different from those of Seneca. He had eclectic interests in a number of different schools, and he combed through all branches of Greek philosophy in search of consolation in hard times (for instance, in his desperate grief after the death of his daughter Tullia). But he sometimes expressed disappointment that no philosophy seemed able to solve the most important problems he faced. His primary sympathies throughout his life lay with the Academy, the school originally founded by Plato, which had evolved, by Cicero's time, into a form of Skepticism. Cicero also had an interest in Epicureanism and Stoicism. The influential *Tusculanian Disputations* is a vivid Latin summary of Stoic-influenced arguments in favor of peace of mind, designed to help the reader (and the author) overcome grief, pain, and fear of death. In *On Duties,* Cicero draws on the version of Stoicism mixed with Platonism that had been developed by the second-century philosopher Panaetius. His most extensive discussion of Stoicism and Epicureanism comes in *On Ends,* in which he summarizes and criticizes the thought of the Epicureans and the Stoics before offering an account of his own position.

Cicero's central disagreement with what he perceived to be standard Stoic ethical belief was that he saw it as entirely unrealistic. He suggested (in the *Pro Murena* and elsewhere) that the ideal of the Stoic wise person had no relationship with lived reality. Moreover, the Stoic ideal is not even ideal, since the Stoic wise person is far too cut off from emotional engagement with the world around him. Cicero strongly disagreed with the Stoic goal of *apatheia,* or "being without passion." He argues at length in the *Tusculanian Disputations* (Books 3 and 4) that it is neither possible nor desirable for a person to be rid of all feelings of grief, rage, or fear.

Seneca, unlike Cicero, saw Stoicism as an absolutely useful model for a pragmatic political person in the center of Roman political power, and this difference is, again, a mark of how fundamentally times had changed. It was more important than ever to hang on to an ideal of tranquility in a world where it was so terribly difficult to achieve.

STOICISM

Stoicism, the intellectual movement with which Seneca most closely associated, was designed to create a possibility of individual happiness in times of vast social unrest. The ideal person in Stoic theory is the Wise Man (the *sapiens*), who is able fully to realize the truth that nothing except virtue really matters. He thus becomes fully aligned with the real nature of the universe.

Stoicism was an intellectual movement that had been in existence for over three hundred years before Seneca's birth and had undergone many important changes and developments in that time. Like most philosophical histories, the tale begins with Socrates—in particular, with the Socrates who wore the same cloak both summer and winter, who was guided by a divine sign, and who taught that it is better to suffer wrong than to do it, and that nobody willingly does wrong. The combination of asceticism (or "voluntary simplicity"), providentialism (being guided by a mysterious but entirely reliable divine force), and some kind of intellectualism (all wrongdoing is due to mistaken thinking), along with an insistence that being good is the primary, or indeed only, component of human happiness—all of these are ideas articulated by Socrates and developed by the Stoics.

The next element in the story is the Cynics, whose name means "dog-like." This movement was initiated by a man called Diogenes in the fourth century CE, who notoriously spent most of his life like a homeless person on the streets of Athens, living in a barrel with no possessions. One story goes that after he saw a poor boy drinking water from his hands, he threw away his single wooden bowl, realizing that it, too, was unnecessary. The Cynics presented themselves as followers of Socrates and were notorious for their eagerness to endure and celebrate poverty, on the grounds that material possessions distract one from life in accordance with virtue. True happiness and peace of mind could be achieved only by self-sufficiency. Self-sufficiency itself is possible only through indifference to the material world and to the false norms of human culture. The ideal Cynic philosopher—like the founder of the school, Diogenes—would spend his life in rags or naked, defecating and fornicating in the street without shame, like a dog. There is an ancient story that Alexander the Great once came to visit Diogenes and asked him if there was anything he would like from him. "Get out of my light," the sage replied. Alexander was not offended: he recognized a kindred spirit, somebody with as much ability to ignore human convention as he had himself. The world-conqueror remarked, "If I were not Alexander, I would like to be Diogenes."

Cynicism was a philosophical movement that only a fairly limited number of the population were willing to embrace wholeheartedly, for obvious reasons: most people do not want to defecate in the street. But the central impulse of Cynicism—its recognition that material wealth and social status do not always bring happiness—was appealing to a huge number of people, and increasingly so. In the third and second centuries BCE, with the fall of the great Greek city-states and the rise of great empires (first Macedon, then Rome), in a time of enormous, and terrifying, alterations of the cultural, military, and political landscape of the Mediterranean area, more and more educated people were searching for peace of mind. People sought comfort not in large-scale social change but in their own individual spiritual healing. All the great philosophical movements of the period—including Cynicism but also Stoicism, Epicureanism, and Skepticism—promised to provide the state of "untroubled-ness," *ataraxia*, to their practitioners. Happiness (in Greek, *eudaimonia,* "blessedness") was associated not with the extremes of joy or exhilaration, nor with external achievements or events, but with an individual's capacity to maintain a calm disposition no matter what.

Stoicism can be seen as a more socially acceptable version of Cynicism, one that had deeper intellectual credentials and was more compatible with the normal behaviors of not only slaves and working people but also elite inhabitants of Hellenistic or Roman cities—those who did not want to live half-naked in a barrel but still hoped for spiritual calm and a sense of self-worth, virility, and autonomy in a vast and bewildering world. It is not surprising that Stoicism proved extremely popular.

Stoicism was founded around 301 BCE by a Greek called Zeno, living in Athens. Zeno acknowledged his debt to Cynicism: he was taught by a Cynic named Crates in his youth. It is difficult to reconstruct exactly what Zeno's version of Stoicism was like, since none of his work, or indeed that of any of the original Greek Stoics, survives. But Zeno is the person who gave Stoicism its name, by teaching in the location of the *Stoa Poikile*—the Painted Porch, an area of the Athenian marketplace.

Stoicism was developed in a systematic way by a slightly later leader of the Stoic school, Chrysippus.[11] Chrysippus' philosophy is recognizably a development of Cynicism. The Stoics, like the Cynics, believed that nothing was truly valuable except virtue; that virtue was both necessary and sufficient for human happiness; and that such happiness involves living a life in accordance with Nature. But Stoicism was different from Cynicism in two crucial ways. The Stoics, unlike the Cynics, placed enormous value on human reason. They also, again unlike the Cynics, placed a high value on action in the world, including political engagement. Whereas Diogenes the Cynic dismissed Alexander, Chrysippus the Stoic would have engaged with him and tried to advise him on his public policy.

Stoicism, like the other major ancient intellectual movements of antiquity, is dubbed a "school." The word "school" implies a shared tradition of belief and practice, not necessarily a shared physical location, but it does not necessarily imply total agreement on every point of doctrine. Our (fragmentary and inadequate) evidence for Greek Stoicism suggests that there were a number of shifts of focus and belief over the course of the movement's history. Scholars usually distinguish between the early period and the Middle Stoa (although there is less of a gap between the early and middle periods than was once thought), and then the Roman period, characterized by an increased interest in ethics. Moreover, adherents to Stoicism often held different views from one another even in a single period. Seneca was an eclectic thinker; despite identifying primarily with Stoicism, he draws on many other traditions. Adherence to a school did not imply that a person would take all aspects of dogma as already predetermined by that school's traditions: a philosophical movement was not a faith. Seneca was also an original and creative thinker who made significant new contributions to Stoic views of psychology.

Despite all these caveats, some central notions were common to Stoic belief throughout its history and among all its adherents, including Seneca. The Stoics believed that the whole world is governed by universal Reason or Fate or God or Providence, also identified as Jupiter or Zeus, and associated with primordial Fire, which guides all of nature. "Any name for him is suitable," as Seneca says: "You can't go wrong" (*Natural Questions* 2.45.2). According to Stoic physics, the cosmos has a cyclical pattern: at regular intervals everything is destroyed by fire (*ekpyrosis*) and then remade again (*palingenesis*). Nature was not merely inert or purposeless; rather, the whole universe followed a fixed, predetermined, and always benevolent pattern. It is always in the best interests of humanity to follow nature, because nature is always good. Despite a firm belief in Fate, the Stoics emphasized individual decisions, since we always have a choice about whether we conform our will to the will of the universe, or resist. In Seneca's imagery, the wise person, who conforms his desires to those of God, becomes the follower of God; the foolish person, who fails to conform to what must be, is merely His slave (*On Providence* 5.6–7).

Virtue and knowledge are thus closely connected. The Stoics challenged the view common among other philosophical movements in antiquity (such as Platonism) that the human soul includes both rational and irrational elements. For them, human beings are a complete whole, not a collection of diverse parts, and that whole is entirely rational—although people are prone to false reasoning and mistaken beliefs. It is a failure of reason that makes us liable to unhappiness and wrongdoing. For the Stoics, if we always thought properly and managed to perceive the truth, we would never do wrong or be unhappy. This helps to explain the central place of logic in the Stoic system. The Stoics believed that humans are entirely capable of understanding the universe, and also that human happiness depends on our ability to think properly. The ideal is to align our own minds with the rational will of the universe. The Stoics were sophisticated logicians who made many advances in formal logic; in antiquity, those hostile to the school often mocked them for their abstruse reasoning and fondness for paradox.

Ethics was and is the most challenging area of Stoic philosophy—the most inspiring or the most infuriating, depending on one's point of view. The Stoics had, as we have seen, a notion of the "wise man." I use "man" deliberately because for most Stoics and Stoic-sympathizers, including Seneca, there is a strong assumption that the ideal wise person will be male, and that there is a correlation between virtue (in Latin, *virtus*, "manliness"—from *vir*, "man") and masculinity—although a few Stoics, most notably Musonius Rufus, a younger contemporary of Seneca, seem to have questioned this association and argued that women are quite capable of learning to be philosophers.[12]

The wisdom of the Sage consists in the fact that he knows, fully and at every moment, that virtue alone is sufficient for happiness: everything else, including pleasure, pain, health, wealth, and freedom, is "indifferent." This virtuous wisdom is an all-or-nothing proposition: the Sage is always, at every single moment, acting virtuously and in possession of all the virtues. Even when doing apparently normal things that might not look especially virtuous—eating dinner or taking a bath—the sage is always acting with wisdom, courage, temperance, and justice. Conversely, those who are not sages can never act virtuously; even when they may seem to be doing something good (like saving a child from a fire) or neutral (like eating dinner), the non-sage is always in a state of vice. Moreover, only the Sage is free and self-sufficient; everybody else, even when they seem to be making their own choices, is actually in a constant state of meta-physical enslavement. The Stoics cited the metaphor of a person drown-ing: it makes no difference whether his head is ten feet under water or only an inch; any amount of water above your head is enough to stop the breath (Plutarch 61T).

All this is, of course, very paradoxical, and it is not hard to see why Stoic ethics were widely mocked. The Stoics themselves acknowledged that the true Sage is very rare, possibly nonexistent; it is, after all, difficult for a human being to be perfectly virtuous and perfectly wise. One may well wonder, then, what practical purpose is served by the ideal. If a person who is utterly depraved is no worse in relation to true virtue than one who has just a few faults, then why would one ever try to improve? What would improvement even mean, if virtue is something you either have or you don't?

But the Stoics allowed a great deal of room in their system for im-provement and education in the path toward virtue. Crucially, they distinguished between performing a "correct function," *kathekon*, and performing a "fully correct action," *katorthoma*. The former includes any kind of action that is in accordance with nature (such as eating or breath-ing or exercising in appropriate ways); correct functions can be per-formed by plants and animals as well as non-sage humans. The non-sage can train himself (perhaps with the help of a philosophical tutor or teacher) to perform more and more correct functions and to come closer and closer to full realization of the true nature of the universe. He may still die before attaining the status of a sage, but the attempt to come somewhat closer to the surface of the water is itself a worthwhile goal.

Many complained (as did, jokingly, the satirist Lucian) that Stoics were entirely out of touch with the practicalities of daily life.[13] One may accept in theory that it is more important to be a good person than to have a lot of money, but, given the choice of wealth or abject poverty, most of us would rather be rich. The Stoics took account of this in their theory and allowed for a category in between the things that are absolutely good and bad: the "indifferent things." The Stoics were able to acknowledge that, all things being equal, it is preferable not to be tortured, imprisoned, enslaved, impoverished, dishonored, die, have one's loved ones die, or suffer a painful or debilitating illness. Epictetus tells us, "Of things that exist, some are good, some are bad, others are indifferent. Good things are virtues and everything that shares in virtues; bad things are the opposite; and indifferent things are wealth, health, reputation" (*Discourses* 2.15). The indifferent things are incommensurable with the value of virtue, such that any amount of torture would be better than any amount of vice. The Stoics insist that, even under torture, even while having his limbs cut off, even while being enslaved, even under the greatest humiliation, the Stoic Sage will be happy and free, living the ideal life as long as his virtue remains intact. The promise of Stoicism, in which lies much of its attractiveness, is that one can be guaranteed a life of pure joy, if only one can attain the correct attitude toward the universe. The Stoic—unlike the "stoic," in contemporary, nonphilosophical usage—will not repress feelings of anxiety, rage, or pain: he will not feel troubled by any of them, and indeed, he will be objectively unhurt by any of them. He is, in Seneca's terminology, not merely above bad feelings but immune from all actual injuries (see, e.g., *On Constancy*, 3.1–4).

There were some significant differences within Stoicism on how exactly we should view the "preferred indifferents."[14] The issue became increasingly important in the school's thinking, as more Stoics took an active part in public and political life: it is an essential issue in Seneca's life story. Panaetius of Rhodes, writing in the second century BCE, had made certain essential adjustments to traditional Greek Stoicism, making it more flexible, more eclectic, and more focused on the practicalities of ethical behavior, with less focus on logical and metaphysical abstractions. He spent time teaching in Rome and became a major influence on Roman Stoicism (including the work of Cicero and Seneca). Roman Stoicism is often considered to be different from earlier forms of the movement in its (Panaetian) interest in pragmatic choices, psychology, and natural human impulses.

Seneca clearly saw Stoicism not as an abstract intellectual interest but as a practical guide to the big decisions and small daily habits of his life. He made a series of choices between preferred and nonpreferred indifferent things: he chose Rome over exile, vast wealth over modest means, and enormously high social status at court over a humble life in the provinces. His work is haunted by the question of whether indulging in the "pre-ferred indifferents," like money and honor, may get in the way of the journey toward the true value of virtue. Stoicism allowed him to justify choosing, or preferring, things like health, wealth, and luxury—and not preferring exile or torture or death. But he remained strikingly anxious about the fact that indifferent things may muddle one's thinking, since they are all too easy to confuse with real goods.

When considering why Seneca identified primarily as a Stoic, we should be aware that Stoicism was not the only philosophical option for an elite man in Rome at Seneca's time period, and not even necessarily the most obvious choice. There were the Peripatetics (followers of Aristotle); the Academy (founded by Plato); the Cynics (whom Seneca quotes with admiration); the Pythagoreans; and the home-grown Roman school of the Sextians, with whom Seneca felt a particular affinity. An especially influen-tial movement was Epicureanism (named for its founder, Epicurus). The Epicureans believed that not virtue, but pleasure, was the most important value for human beings. But unlike the Hedonists (also called Cyrenaics, from Aristippus of Cyrene)—with whom they were often unfairly con-flated—the Epicureans did not advocate a life of sensual physical indul-gence. Rather, Epicurus taught that physical pleasure is best attained by a life of moderation (since, for example, eating and drinking too much will ultimately cause more pain than pleasure). He also argued that the most important pleasures and pains are mental, rather than physical. One can achieve maximal mental pleasure and freedom from mental pain only by ridding oneself of the fear of death, by acting with kindness and justice toward others, and by avoiding the turbulence of public, political life. In-stead, the Epicurean ideal is to live quietly with one's close friends and contemplate the random movements of the atomic universe.

Seneca's choice of Stoicism as his major intellectual framework has important political implications, since the Stoics, unlike the Epicureans, had a strong tradition of political engagement. Epicurus, in contrast, had advocated a life of withdrawal: "Hide away while you live your life." Seneca chose, rather, a life of political involvement. But he read Epicurus and other Epicureans and took their views seriously, often quoting Epi-curus favorably in the *Letters to Epistles* (at a time when he was particu-larly concerned with the attempt to withdraw from politics).

Seneca's presentation of Stoicism is distinctive in a number of ways. He writes constantly about suicide, death, and the briefness of life—apparently much more than the Greek Stoics had done. He is also focused on practical, as opposed to theoretical, advantages of the Stoic way of life. Seneca made a number of original contributions to the Stoic analysis of psychology, for instance in his careful distinction between involuntary impulses and actual emotions. Seneca's philosophical writings are important for being composed in Latin—as opposed to Greek, which was traditionally the language of philosophy—and for the virtuosic literary and rhetorical skill with which he explores philosophical and quasi-philosophical ideas. Seneca was at least as much a writer as a philosopher.

The Writer, The Man

Seneca would be an important figure in cultural and intellectual history even if he had not become so closely attached to the court of Nero. He was exceptional in his ability to compose in a highly original manner, in a far wider range of genres than most ancient authors. He developed a distinctive, hugely influential literary style, full of wit and paradox, and flexible enough to accommodate multiple turns and points of view. His pragmatic, psychologically acute version of Stoicism had a huge influence on later Western culture, as did his tragic depictions of ambition and revenge.

But Seneca would also have been famous as a historical figure, the tutor and advisor to Nero, even if he had never written a word. Few other writers in history have had quite so much political power and influence. The relationship of Seneca's literary output and his philosophical life to his dizzying, fragile rise to the pinnacle of social success is one of the most fascinating aspects of his story. Seneca struggled to combine the life of the mind with the life of active political and social engagement and was always deeply aware of the dangers, paradoxes, and compromises that the combination might involve.

This book teases out the relationship of his literary output to the events and actions of his life. I am highly conscious of the dangers of circularity, both in deducing life from art and using the art to illustrate or investigate the life. But I hope to show how each side of this binary illuminates the other. Seneca's writing constantly resonates with the events of his biography, without ever providing a perfect mirror for it. We can read these texts more richly by understanding the social, historical, and personal contexts in which they were produced. Conversely, Seneca's literary work makes us see more clearly what it was like to live through these interesting times—to suffer through illness, exile, and social exclusion, to rise to the very top of Roman imperial society, and to grapple with the constant dangers and challenges of life in the court of the emperors.

My first chapter traces Seneca's origins in provincial Spain; his journey, at a young age, to the capital city of Rome; and his parentage, son of an elite and educated mother and a father whose work on rhetoric and education still survives. I look at the work of Seneca the Elder here, which provides valuable insight into the relationship of this dominating father to his young sons—our Seneca and his brothers—and into the education Seneca the Younger received. He was trained both in literary and rhetorical technique and in philosophy, and I discuss the early influences of his philosophical teachers. We also glimpse Seneca's bad health from a lung ailment, which haunted his early years. In the second chapter, we encounter a series of journeys: first a long trip to Egypt for a period of convalescence from his bronchial problems; then back to Rome for the beginnings of his political career, under Tiberius, Caligula, and Claudius; then the scandal in which Seneca was accused of a high-profile adulterous affair, and consequently his exile to the island of Corsica. In Chapter III, we move back to Rome: Seneca, now a middle-aged man of about fifty, was recalled from exile thanks to the emperor's new wife Agrippina and became tutor to her son Nero. I focus on the fascinating tensions and contradictions created by Seneca's position as the educator of the young prince, including the paradoxes of being an ascetic philosopher who achieved vast wealth in the imperial court. In Chapter IV, we turn to the life and work of Seneca's last years, his repeated attempts to disentangle himself from Nero's service, and eventually his long-awaited death. The Epilogue traces some key moments in the reception of Seneca's life and work in the later Western tradition. I point to the ways that Seneca's yearnings for wealth and wisdom, for death and time, for power and kindness, for flexibility and constancy, even in the most terrifying and tempestuous of circumstances, have provoked both shocked resistance and desire to emulate him, in the early Christian period, in the Renaissance, and into the twentieth and twenty-first centuries.

Seneca's life and work have been a source of fascination, although not always admiration, ever since his death. Seneca's Rome was, like modern

Britain, Europe, and especially the United States, a place of vast social inequality. The inhabitants of the early Empire were—like ourselves—struggling to come to terms with huge political, cultural, and economic changes. Rome had emerged from a series of devastating civil wars and transitioned uneasily from a Republic to an Empire under the rule of one man (with the help of the army). Through Rome's extraordinary military success, the world had quickly become more centralized. The gap between rich and poor was vast, and the elite class had gained wealth undreamed of by their ancestors, including an array of luxury products imported from the distant reaches of the empire. But these upper-class men had, at the same time, lost much of the political power they had had under the Republic and had lost much of their sense of security and identity: the display of wealth was used as an inadequate substitute for self-respect. Seneca's work is brilliantly articulate about the psychological pressures created by consumerism. "Being poor is not having too little," he declares: "it is wanting more" (Epistle 2). One of his great themes is the way that people surrounded by an excess of material wealth, and in a culture characterized by competition for status, may become obsessed with striving for unreal or actually damaging "goods" (like new clothes or furniture or houses, elaborate food, thrilling and violent entertainment, or titles, promotions, social power, and the admiration of others), which provide no real happiness or satisfaction. And yet our desires for these unsatisfying things remain, as Seneca also recognized, almost impossible to eliminate; and Seneca constantly suggests that complete withdrawal from the social world is not the solution to the problem. As both a Stoic and a pragmatist, he constantly sought to be engaged in the world without losing integrity. He was deeply aware of how difficult this quest is. This is one of many reasons why his work and life story remain so relevant for us.

"PARENTAL LOVE IS WISE"*

I t is conventional to begin a biography with an account of the subject's birthplace, parents, childhood, and early adolescence. But according to Seneca himself, none of these things are of any importance whatsoever. He insists:

> As for the fact of my birth: consider what it really is, in itself. Being born is a trivial thing, uncertain, with equal chance of turning into something good or bad. It's certainly the first step to everything else, but it's not better than everything else just because it came first.
>
> (*On Benefits*, 3.30.2)

The context here is a discussion of favors and gratitude; Seneca is challenging the conventional Greek and Roman view that parents, and especially fathers, bestow an enormous debt on their children by giving them life in the first place, such that nothing the child does in later life could ever repay the father's first gift of life. Seneca suggests, on the contrary, that it is perfectly possible for sons to outstrip their fathers and to give their parents—and the world—far more than they were ever given by them: "Seeds are the causes of all growing things, and yet they are the tiniest parts of the things which they produce" (*On Benefits* 3.29.4). The father, then, need not overshadow the son. Moreover, the first part of a life is not necessarily the most important element in a person's story: "There is a great deal of difference between what is first in time, and what is first in importance" (*On Benefits* 2.34.1). To take Seneca at his

---

* Sagax parentum est cura (Phaedra 152)

word, we might judge him only by his later public and professional life and cast a veil over all his early years.

But this would be a mistake, since there are discernible biographical and psychological reasons why Seneca was drawn to this particular rhetorical gesture. As the son of a rich, successful, and domineering father, a well-born and well-educated mother, and the middle child of three bright, well-loved, and well-educated brothers, he had a good reason to work hard to define himself as a self-made man, and indeed, to suggest that all humans are the products of something other than family heritage. Through philosophical training, thinking, and writing, Seneca could emerge from the shadows cast by his parents and brothers. Moreover, as somebody who rose to extraordinary prominence from a wealthy but provincial family, Seneca had a motive to downplay the importance of heredity and up-bringing in a person's life. He often challenges the conventional Roman belief in "nobility" (*nobilitas*), which suggested that excellence comes by inheritance from one's fathers or forefathers. Seneca argues for a far more egalitarian model in which every person, or at least every man, is the source of his own success. His philosophical writings constantly revert to the theme of autonomy. The Stoic wise man, Seneca's ideal, is dependent on nobody, always free, always happy, and in need of nothing and nobody.

But the very fact that he makes so much of the possibility that a son can exceed his father, both in moral and in social and financial worth, tells us a great deal about how Seneca presented himself to the Roman public in his later years, and perhaps even about his vision of himself. His meteoric rise was both an irrelevance—"being born is a trivial thing"—and also a source of both pride and anxiety.

Seneca the Younger—so called because his father's name was also Seneca—was born around 1 BCE (or a little earlier), in Corduba, in the Roman province of Hispania, in southern Spain, a city geographically distant from the center of Roman power. The ancient accounts of his life make much of his meteoric rise from a peripheral background to the heights of Roman society, as tutor, advisor, and speechwriter to the emperor, and from an economically modest family to a position of enormous wealth. But Seneca was hardly unusual in being a Roman writer who did not come from Rome. Most of the famous Roman writers of the classical period (first century BCE to first century CE) came from places other than the capital: Virgil was from Mantua, Ovid from Sulmo, Horace from Venusia—all Italian towns at some distance from

Rome. Cicero, in the previous generation, was born in Arpinum, a small hill town south of Rome. Other Spanish Latin writers include the main Roman authority on agricultural practices, Seneca's contemporary Columella, and Seneca's own nephew, the epic poet Lucan; a generation later came the Hispanic epigrammatist Martial and the Hispanic rhetorician Quintilian.

Among Seneca's contemporaries, it could be a source of pride to have climbed up the social ladder from modest beginnings to high rank (and even to association with the emperor).[1] Seneca's own father makes a speaker note, in one of his debate speeches (*Controversiae*), that the city of Rome itself emerged from humble origins, and uses this point to defend the central position of people who emerged from rural peasantry to the aristocracy of Rome. The context is a speech defending the idea that an aristocratic man could marry out of his station (focused on a typically lurid example: a fine man who has been captured by pirates marries the pirate chief's daughter, to the disapproval of his own father).

> What do you think of those who came from the plough to bless the republic? Unroll any aristocrat you like; you will come through to humble origins. Why should I mention individuals, when I could show you the city itself? Once, these hills were bare, and among the far-flung walls, there was nothing grander than a little hut. Now above it shines the Capitol, with sloping roofs and gleaming with pure gold. Can you blame the Romans for touting their humble origins, although they might cover them up? They think nothing big unless it seems to have risen from something small.
>
> (*Controversiae* 1.6.4)[2]

The passage uses a metaphor based on ancient books, which were always scrolls: to flip back to an earlier part of a book and rediscover the previous part of the story, one had to "unroll" it. The image is used to assert that biographies of the elite are always easy to tell, because they are always the same. When we roll back the scroll of an aristocratic life, we read always the same story: a rise from humble origins to social greatness.

All cities were once nothing. But in many cultures, it is not common to mention the fact. In Roman society of the first century BCE, by contrast, the idea of social change was a constant preoccupation. Rome itself had risen particularly quickly to prominence as a world power, and for Rome's inhabitants, with the sudden acquisition of empire, social change

was a fact of life. We can see from this passage that there was a certain
anxiety as well as pride in Roman attitudes toward social climbing.
Those who had gained new positions of power tended to boast not of
their precipitous rise to prominence but rather of their lost days of humility. The speaker in Seneca the Elder's account acknowledges the possibility that somebody might want to criticize these upstart Romans
who fail even to cover up their peasant past. But the passage can be read
as much as a boast as a gesture of anxiety: the Romans are proud of their
humble origins, and unlike other, hypocritical cultures (such as Greece—
often seen as suspiciously dishonest), they acknowledge the real truth
about where they came from. The speaker thus manages to have it both
ways: on the one hand, the Romans are good (read: honest) for their res-
olute unwillingness to hide their (potentially shameful) lowly origins;
and on the other, they have nothing to be ashamed of, no skeletons in the
closet. On the contrary; the ones who "came from the plough to bless
the republic" are the most illustrious members of the Roman political
and moral canon—most obviously Cincinnatus, the Roman nobleman
of the fifth century BCE, who worked his own farm, who was summoned
to rule Rome single-handedly in order to fight off invaders to the city,
but who insisted on returning to his farm after just sixteen days in
power.[3] Rising from humble origins to the center of imperial power was
thus a biographical structure that went deep in the Roman cultural
imagination. But few Romans rose so meteorically as Seneca or became
so deeply entangled in the heart of the empire.

Seneca must have been formed in childhood by the experience of
growing up in a city where the native Gallic languages and cultures were
being edged out by the dominant culture of Rome.[4] Seneca's writings
suggest a sense of tension and dialogue between multiple voices, a trait
that some scholars have seen as essentially "theatrical." One might just as
well see this as a deep awareness of cultural and ideological difference,
which likely developed in childhood. Corduba was a place divided
along multiple fault lines in the first century BCE. It was divided between
native Roman and native Hispanic inhabitants (*Hispani* and *Hispanienses*) and also between sympathizers with Julius Caesar and sympathizers
with Pompey, since the civil wars made an enormous impact on the
region.

But Corduba was no provincial backwater: it was in many ways just
as close to the centers of Roman power as the smaller Italian towns.

Figure 1.1 The modern city of Córdoba. The main tourist attraction is now the Great Mosque (built in the tenth century, when the Iberian peninsula was under Islamic rule), but marks of the long period of Roman occupation are still visible in the Roman bridge and remains of the Roman temple.

Corduba in the first century BCE was a flourishing Roman colony (Fig. 1.1). Indeed, it was the leading city of the Roman province of Lower Spain (*Hispania Ulterior*), and it was one of the earliest Roman colonies to have been established in the region.[5] The city had great natural resources: it was built just below the Sierra Nevada range of mountains, on the Guadalquivir River, and just above a rich, flat plain, ideally suited for agriculture. It was also at a crucial trading location, in the southernmost part of Spain, just north of the Strait of Gibraltar and the ancient city of Carthage.

The city of Corduba was originally founded not as a *colonia provinciae* but as a *colonia Latina*, a title with a different legal implication: the inhabitants of a *colonia Latina* did not have Roman citizenship. But by the lifetime of our Seneca, the city's status had been upgraded, and at least the elite class of Corduba—such as the Annaeus family—were full Roman citizens, with the same rights as any other Roman citizen in the empire.[6]

The inhabitants of the new city were a combination of native Iberians with Romans, drawn from the ranks of veteran soldiers. One might assume that a city founded by an imperial overlord government would be necessarily a place of enormous social tension. One might also assume that the native inhabitants (the *Hispani*) would be of a lesser social status than the Romans shipped in from Italy (*Hispanienses*). But the evidence suggests a surprisingly harmonious conjoining of the two populations, at least among the elite classes. The Greek historian Strabo tells us that "the Turdetani . . . who live around the Guadalquiver, have so entirely adopted the Roman life-style that they have even forgotten their own language. They have mostly become Latins, and received Roman colonists; so that in a short while they will be all Romans" (3.2.15). Names found on inscriptions in the early period of the city's history are Latin and Iberian in roughly equal numbers, suggesting that the Iberians and their Roman overlords shared power and may well have intermarried.[7] The Annaeus family from which the Senecas came is likely to have been the result of such an intermarriage: the name *Annaeus* seems to be non-Roman.[8] Compromise between diverse social groups was thus an essential habit in the Annaeus family background.

Spain was fraught territory within the Roman empire. Gaul had been conquered by Julius Caesar in just ten years, but it took closer to two hundred before Spain was fully under Roman control. As one historian puts it, for most of the period from 218 to 16 BCE, "Spain was a war zone" (Keay 1988, p. 7). Spain was a highly desirable territory, rich in natural resources: as Pliny says in his *Natural History,* "Whatever life ought to contain is nowhere more present; grain, wine, oil, wool, flax, tissues, and oxen." He goes on to compare Spain to Gaul and notes that, while both provincial areas are perhaps equally good at producing oil and wine, Spain outdoes Gaul in producing both luxury goods, such as dye for clothes, and in the "natural" resilience of human capital to be found there. He acknowledges that Spain is dry in certain areas, but in the parts that are near the coast, Spain exceeds Gaul and is almost as good as Italy itself

… in rope, in mica, Muscovy-stone [a kind of transparent stone used for the luxury of windows], in the charm of its paints and dyes, in the workmen's diligence, in the slaves' good training, in the toughness of the people's bodies, and in the strength of their hearts.

(Pliny, *Natural History* 37.77 [37.203])

Pliny clearly sees Spain as a rich source of material and human capital, which can be shipped to the urban capital. Its specialty products mentioned here include a plant used to make rope and rugs, "Spanish broom"; mica, a transparent stone that was used for making windows that could actually let in light, an important item in elite houses; colorful paint to adorn the walls and statuary of the rich; and workers and slaves, with usefully strong bodies and biddable minds, who could extract and manufacture the products. As Pliny suggests, Spain was an essential component in the visible wealth of the Roman elite.

But those who lived in Hispania could also enjoy the natural wealth of the country in a more direct way, through farming and viticulture. An almost exact contemporary, Columella (4–70 CE), was born and raised in Roman Gades (modern Cadiz). After a stint in the army, he returned to the Spanish countryside and eventually produced one of the most influential Roman handbooks on agriculture, the still-extant *De Re Rustica* (*On the countryside*). Columella and Seneca probably knew each other and bonded over their shared love of viticulture; Columella praises Seneca's erudition and his skill in estate management in his villa at Nomentum, writing that "the neighbourhood of Nomentum is very famous, especially the part owned by Seneca, a man of exceptional talent and learning, on whose estates we gather that every part-acre (*iugerum*) of vineyard has usually yielded eight sacks."[9] Seneca himself presumably spent his early childhood on an estate that grew both olives and vines, probably managed by his competent mother Helvia.[10] He developed a lifelong love for, and interest in, gardening and viticulture, and grew vines on his own Italian estates in later years.

The people of Corduba may well have been proud at the success of Seneca and his brothers once they left Spain, were educated in Rome, and became famous. A Latin epigram laments Seneca's exile as the worst disaster to have befallen the city in its whole history, worse even than the times when Pompey, Caesar, and others attacked the town in the various battles of the civil wars:

Corduba, loosen your hair, let your face be sad,
weep and send gifts for my ashes.
Now lament, Corduba, far at a distance, for your poet,
Corduba, this is your saddest time ever.[11]

The sense of loyalty (if it was indeed felt by the Cordubans to Seneca) may not have been entirely mutual. Seneca includes few references to Spain in his writings but occasionally hints at a particular nostalgia for the province of his birth. In Epistle 66, he recalls the attack of the Roman general Scipio on the Spanish city of Numantia—which he razed to the ground in 133 BCE, in the course of the Third Punic War— and comments that there was enormous courage on both sides: "Great is Scipio...but great also the spirit of the defenders" (66.13). Seneca had reason to sympathize with the provincials, who were taxed and some- times, as in the Siege of Numantia, slaughtered by their Roman over- lords. But he lived much of his life as the servant of those same Roman overlords, and there is little in Seneca's writings to suggest more than glimmerings of such sympathy. Seneca shook the dust of Spain off his sandals fairly fast, and as we will see, he was accused of financial abuse in his economic relationship with the province of Britain, lending the natives money and calling back the loans suddenly, at a huge rate of interest. If Seneca was sympathetic to the provinces, he did not let such feelings get in the way of a profit.

MOTHER AND CHILD

Boyish joy at seeing his mother (Matre uisa semper puerilis hilaritas)

—Helvia 15.2

Nothing specific is known about Seneca's childhood. He would have had the normal upbringing of any elite Roman of his time and place. He must have spent much of his time playing with his brothers; presum- ably the three were fairly close in age, although the exact age gaps are not known. The boys would have had toys to play with: dolls, blocks, figu- rines, beads, toy carriages, and weapons (Fig. 1.2). Seneca in old age notes how highly children value their toys, treating this fact as an illustration of the vanity of human wishes: "children regard every toy as valuable, and

Figure 1.2 Seneca in childhood would have played with toys like this painted wooden horse.

they reckon necklaces bought for a penny as just as important as their parents and brothers" (Epistle 115.8). He suggests, too, that all of us who have not yet reached the condition of perfect wisdom are still like little children playing with their toys:

> Children are greedy for knuckle-bones, nuts and coppers, but grown-ups are greedy for gold, silver and cities; children play at being magistrates, and pretend to have bordered togas, the rods of a civil servant, and a court-house, while adults play at the same thing, in the Campus Martius and Forum and Senate.
>
> (*On Constancy*, 12.2–3)

Elsewhere, Seneca vividly evokes the heedless, innocent roughness of children to their parents:

> Children hit their parents' faces, and mess up their mother's hair, and a baby scratches, or drools on her, or pulls her dress to expose to the family's view parts that ought to be kept hidden; and the infant doesn't hold back from bad language. Yet we don't count any of their actions as an insult.
>
> (*On Constancy*, 10.2)

Childhood is here figured as a time that requires indulgence—children cannot help their clumsiness and their sticky drool. But it is not senti-mentalized: it is a state that one ought to try to escape as soon as possible, by studying philosophy.

Whom did Seneca scratch and curse at in his babyhood? Much of his day-to-day care and supervision would have been in the hands of slaves: babysitters, nurses, teachers, musicians, entertainers, and doctors. He would have been taught to read by a slave or freedman tutor, probably using wax tablets and perhaps blocks to trace out the alphabet. Since he had a lifelong propensity to bronchial infections and probably asthma, he is likely to have spent more time than most being tended by doctors, who would usually have been Greek slaves or freedmen. The experience of being sickly was one of many factors that made Seneca later so readily attracted to philosophy, and especially to ascetic forms of philosophy. He would have grown up accustomed to the regimens associated with chronic sickness: the constant vigilance and the close attention to diet, exercise, and daily routine that were, in antiquity even more than today, a crucial element in the practice of medicine. The habit of paying close attention to himself, and of attempting daily to make progress toward an unattainable ideal of perfect health, is one that Seneca continued his whole life long. In the writings of his adulthood, the main focus has shifted from literal, physical health to the spiritual health that is the aspi-ration of the Stoic philosopher. But the structures of practice are much the same, involving self-restraint, careful attention and time management, and daily practice.

Seneca would have spent a lot of time in early childhood with his mother. Roman fathers typically left their children in the care of the women of the house until they had survived toddlerhood and were at an age to begin their "real" education, in rhetoric and philosophy. Helvia may have breastfed him herself—a practice associated with old Roman virtues, against the newfangled trend towards using wet nurses. Seneca's mother was an essential figure in his early years, and she continued to have an important influence on his later life.[12]

Helvia may have been a Roman from Italy, whom his father might have met on one of his many trips to the big city. But it is perhaps more probable that she was a member of the Corduban Hispanic-Roman elite. She was a well-born, well-educated woman from a well-connected and wealthy family. Helvia's mother had died when the girl was born, so she had grown up under the care of a stepmother. She managed to behave so nicely that she transformed this notoriously difficult relationship, such that the stepmother became like a real mother to her. Presumably the stepmother had at least one biological daughter, a stepsister who became like a real sister to Helvia; this is the easiest way to explain the puzzle that Helvia is described by Seneca as an "only child" (*unica*), but he also tells us that she had a sister, Seneca's aunt. This aunt would later become an important patroness of her nephew in his early adulthood, as we shall see. The house of Helvia's childhood was, so her son said, "old fashioned and strict," and she carried those traditional values with her in later life.

This was a period in which more elite Roman women were receiving a literary education. The practice was controversial: a generation after Seneca, the satirist Juvenal declares that women "should not know all the tales from history" and claims, "I really hate the woman who checks up and leafs through Palaemon's grammar, always preserving the rules and laws of language, and who, with her love of archaism, remembers poetry I don't know" (*Satire* 7.434–456). Like many of Juvenal's satirical poses, this declaration rebounds to the discredit of the speaker, presented by the poet as an idiot whose complaint is only that women are capable of an intellectual rigor that he himself cannot muster. But such idiocy was not unusual.

Seneca, by contrast, expressed great respect for his mother's intellectual capacities as well as for her good character. Throughout his life, Seneca developed friendships with strong and well-educated women (including, most importantly, Nero's mother Agrippina and her sister Julia Livilla). His relationships with his mother and aunt prepared him to see women, if not as equals, at least as worthy of deep respect. Probably Helvia was the first to introduce him to history and poetry, sowing a lifelong love for the works of Virgil and Ovid (whom Seneca quotes constantly). He expresses regret only that she was not allowed to pursue her education further—a sentiment that involves implicit critique of his then-dead father (*To Helvia* 17: "If only my father, who really was the best of men, had resisted the tradition of his ancestors and let you make a thorough study of philosophy, rather than just a smattering!"). Helvia probably married very young: it was common for girls in the highest classes of Roman society to marry soon after puberty. At the time of marriage, she would have already been able to read and write, and had basic knowledge of literature and history. Helvia managed to make the most of her limited education. "Thanks to your keen intellectual appetite, you learned more than one could have expected in the time" (*To Helvia* 17).

Most of the evidence we have about Seneca's mother comes from the only published work he addressed directly to her, *To Helvia,* composed to console the mother for the son's own exile. It is essential to realize that this highly artificial and essentially public document is quite different from a private family letter, of the kind that might be available to a modern biographer. Seneca was engaging in this text with the long-established ancient genre of the "consolation," a public essay in which the author is expected to set out the traditional modes of overcoming grief and other kinds of emotional disturbance—and ideally, to display his virtuosic rhetorical artistry in doing so (a task at which Seneca certainly succeeds). Moreover, Seneca had personal motives for presenting his mother herself, and his own relationship with her, in the rosiest possible light. A major purpose of the *Helvia* was to assure the Roman reading public of the moral and, especially, sexual integrity of the whole family, in the wake of his own adultery scandal (on which, see Chapter II). There was therefore a clear motive for presenting the addressee as a particularly upright person. In the same piece, he praises his mother to the skies, emphasizing not only her intellectual capacities but also her extraordinary chastity. She was, her son insisted, always modest in her dress, "not tempted by gems or pearls." She never dressed to hide her pregnancy, or wore clothes that clung too tightly to her body, or wore makeup: "your greatest glory has been your modesty" (*To Helvia* 16). We can take all this with a pinch of salt. Seneca presents his mother in stylized terms here, as the ideal chaste Roman matron.

Despite all these caveats, there is no reason to doubt that Helvia was indeed an intelligent, educated, respectable, and well-respected woman, who may indeed have been relatively restrained in her style of dress, and who was—as Seneca's essay also implies—devoted to her sons and eager to see them flourish. It is plausible that Seneca had a close relationship with his mother, which included intellectual conversation as well as emotional closeness. He writes—in self-promoting but perhaps also truthful fashion—of his mother's pleasure in his company, and his in hers, painting himself as the confidant and comforter to whom she turned in times of trouble, and also suggesting that she took a serious interest in his studies and writing (*Helvia* 15.1–4). He emphasizes, too, his own pleasure at spending time with his mother, evoking the "boyish joy he always felt at seeing his mother" (*Helvia* 15)—a phrase that speaks to the continuity between boyhood and adulthood that was maintained by the close bond between mother and son.

SENECA'S FATHER AND BROTHERS

We learn not for school, but for life (Non vitae sed scholae discimus)

—Epistle 106.12

Seneca's relationship with his father was marked less by joy (a term that does not come up in any of his references to the father) than by pressure. The father clearly hoped to see all three of his sons succeed, both in their careers (and the concomitant wealth and social status) and in adherence to traditional Roman values. Seneca's father was the major force behind the son's early education in both rhetorical training and philosophy.

Seneca wrote a biography of his father, which is lost. But despite this, we know quite a lot about Seneca the Elder, since much of his own work survives. He came from a wealthy family of the equestrian rank. The Roman upper class was divided between senatorial and equestrian classes, with equestrians (or "knights") being the lower tier. The equestrian class was lower-upper-class, not middle class: the bourgeoisie did not exist in ancient Rome, and there was a vast gap between the wealth and social position even of equestrians, and that of the workers and tradespeople. The Annaei were not at the absolute top tier of Roman society, but they were rich and privileged, even before the son's stratospheric rise to the heart of the court.

The father's name was Lucius Annaeus Seneca, like his middle son (or perhaps Marcus Annaeus Seneca: the first name is doubtful). He was born around 54 BCE and died around 38 or 39 CE, in extreme old age—over ninety. He thus lived through the civil wars, as well as the early years of the principate. He would have been a child in the crucial conflict between Julius Caesar and Pompey, which culminated in Caesar's victory and brief term as Dictator for Life, before his assassination in 44 BCE. The Annaeus family probably supported Pompey, although they presumably switched over quickly and kept their old allegiances carefully under wraps in later years; they clearly did not suffer financially from the wars. The ability to bend with the political winds was one that Seneca the Younger mastered early, and it ran in his family.

It was traditional for elite Roman boys from the provinces to come to the city of Rome to be educated in rhetoric and philosophy. Seneca the Elder had a delayed start on his education because the civil wars made it dangerous to travel. But he was in Rome by 44 BCE, when he was around ten years old (he calls himself a preadolescent, a *puer,* at this time). He trained in rhetoric, and the experience of listening to the celebrity orators of the day was one that stayed with him all his life: he claimed to be able to remember, word for word, what was said by each speaker on those occasions, even recalling the debates some eighty years later. He suggests (in the preface to *Controversiae* 1) that even now, he can pluck out of it anything he entrusted to memory as a boy or young man. This claim has been doubted for obvious reasons, but even if it is not literally true, it is clear that the intellectual climate of the debating halls, with their fascinatingly diverse personalities, made an enormous impression on the boy and shaped his views about education and literature even in adulthood and old age. His idol was Cicero; he disliked the florid Asiaticism (a fancier style of speaking that was becoming fashionable).

His actual career was not in rhetoric (so that the usual title for him, "Seneca Rhetor," is rather misleading); we do not know exactly what he did for a living, although it is likely that he made money from his various estates, and he probably also profited from moneylending (as his son was later to do) and other forms of trade. He had inherited money and increased his wealth by his successful business ventures. It was likely thanks to his wealth that he was able to marry Helvia, whose family may have been of somewhat higher class than his own; he may also have increased his wealth through marrying her. He also had literary aspirations: he was engaged, at the time of his death, on a work of history. His extant works are two compositions made ostensibly for the benefit of his three sons, although with a larger readership in mind. They consist of evocations of the declamations he had enjoyed so much in his youth: the *Suasoriae* (*Persuasions*) and *Controversiae* (*Debates*). Both these works are concerned with rhetoric, or rather, declamation.

"Declamation" (*declamatio*) was a kind of debating exercise in which a group of elite boys or men each in turn tried their hand at coming up with the best phrase or line of argument to take on a particular fictional topic. It played a central role in the Roman educational system, preparing boys for a career in politics or the law, but it was also practiced by adults (like Cicero) just for fun, or to keep their wits sharp for the real thing. Declamation was somewhat similar to the debating contests that are popular in some modern high schools and colleges in the United States and the United Kingdom, although it was far more culturally dominant. Declamation had a clear pedagogical and social function: it trained students for political and legal life, since—in our society as in ancient Rome—lawyers and politicians wield a great deal of social power, and to succeed in these fields, a person has to be competent at persuasive speaking.

But declamation had a larger cultural function as well. In a world without television, declamation was a form of middlebrow entertainment; it had something of the elements of modern soap operas. The popularity of declamation is easier to explain if we see it not as a prototype of C-SPAN but as the ancient equivalent of legal drama shows (like "Law and Order," with all the salacious pleasure of contemplating sensational and violent crimes). It must have owed as much to the public performance spectacle as to the (inevitably very formulaic) topics that were actually discussed. There were celebrity declaimers, who gained the hearts of the audience as much by their skills in improvisational acting and gesture as by their fluent tongues.[13]

A group of speakers, all of whom would probably be well known to the gathered crowd, assembled in the center of the Roman Forum, the meeting place in the middle of town where almost all public business took place. Surrounded by the noise and bustle of street vendors, entertainers, lawyers, politicians, and shoppers, the display of declamation began. First came the premise of the day's debate:

> A wife is tortured by a tyrant to find out if she knew anything about her husband's plot to kill him. She persisted in saying that she did not. Later, the husband killed the tyrant. He divorced her on the grounds of her barrenness when she bore no child within five years of marriage. She sues him for ingratitude.
>
> (*Controversiae* 2.5)

Then each speaker in turn spoke, first for the wife, then on the other side. Often, the speakers would fully inhabit the various roles, speaking as if in the persona of the characters in the case: "Put her on the rack!" cry the torturers; "Apply the fire! The blood is almost dry right there! Cut her, whip her, tear her eyes—make sure she no longer pleases her husband as breeder of his children!" It is easy to see the melodramatic appeal of this kind of thing.

Roman declamation emerged out of a Greek tradition of public speaking for purposes of entertainment and education. Quintilian claims that it goes back to Demetrius of Phaleron (fourth century BCE: Quintilian 2.4.41), while Philostratus traces it somewhat earlier, to the first sophists of Greece like Gorgias of Leontini (Philostratus 481). The theory and practice of Greek rhetoric flourished in the third and second centuries BCE, the period after the death of Alexander the Great (323 BCE), when Greek cities were under the power of the Macedonian empire. The growth of rhetoric was closely associated in the minds both of Greeks and Romans with a decline in real political power for individual Greeks. At a time when Greek cities were relatively disenfranchised and cut off from real centers of political power, Greek men (always men) retained or gained a sense of cultural autonomy and masculinity through developing rhetorical and literary skills. Rhetorical display thus had much the same social and psychological function as Stoic philosophy, which, not coincidentally, grew in popularity in the same period. Both philosophical and rhetorical training allowed men who felt disempowered to hang on to a sense of control and self-worth. Elite gentlemen now found their "empire" not in government but in smaller social or intellectual worlds.

The Romans copied Greek models of education, including the practice of debate on set themes as both an essential feature of elite education and as a warm-up exercise for people in political and legal life. Cicero, as Suetonius tells us, "declaimed in Greek up until his praetorship, and in Latin even as an old man" (Suetonius, *Gr. Rhet.* 25.3). But Roman declamation in the time of the empire became something significantly different from its Greek predecessor. Seneca the Elder treats declamation as an entirely new phenomenon: "the thing itself was born after me: that is why it is easy for me to have known it in its cradle" (1. preface 12). Declamation in this time, if not entirely invented from scratch, became far more restricted in its scope (limited, in its primary usage, to purely educational contexts rather than including any loud speech on a specific topic). New technical terms were invented, including *controversia* ("controversy," or "debate," an exercise based on a legal case), *suasoria* ("persuasion," an exercise based on the premise of giving advice at a public meeting, some-times to historical characters, such as Alexander the Great), and various terms for components of the speeches, such as *color* ("color"—a particu-lar angle taken on the topic) and *sententia* ("sentiment" or "opinion," but usually used for aphorisms).[14]

Presumably declamation gained some of its peculiar cultural power in this period from the fact that political institutions were being steadily curtailed. At a period when the emperor—first Augustus and then his successors in the Julio-Claudian line (Tiberius, Caligula, Claudius, Nero)—was taking more and more power for himself, the Senate became increasingly impotent, and as a result, public political speech lost much of its potency. The real power of speech lay in the mouth of the emperor himself, which makes it particularly important that, as we shall see, Seneca the Younger would build on his father's educational legacy by becoming speechwriter for Nero.

Even if rhetoric no longer had the same political power that it had had under the Republic, declamation still had a central cultural position throughout the lifetimes of Seneca the Elder and his sons, for entertain-ment as well as a training for politics or the law schools. Moreover, Seneca the Elder suggests that all professions, including philosophy, may benefit from a thorough training in rhetoric. Roman culture in this period was thoroughly implicated in the style of writing, speaking, quick thinking, and feats of memory that were cultivated by declamation. The challenge was to come up with convincing arguments on both sides of any given topic. Almost all elite young men were trained in this style of speaking and thinking, so that those who were uneducated in declama-tion would have been seen as socially alien.

The elder Seneca's work preserves for posterity the voices of his dead intellectual heroes. One of the most important of these is a Spanish-born declaimer named Porcius Latro, his "dearest friend" (1. preface 12), who (on Seneca's telling) always came up with the best possible approach to any topic set up for debate. Seneca sets Latro up as an example for his sons to follow: he can throw himself into any pursuit (in work or play), shows incredible feats of memory and a vast knowledge of history, and can perform beautifully well-organized, fluent, and always well-judged speeches.

The poet Ovid was a declamation student at the same time as the elder Seneca, and he vividly evokes the boy's struggle to conform to the constraints of the declamatory genre: he was, we are told, a natural-born poet, such that even when he tried to imitate the best lines of Latro, he found himself converting them into verse (2.2.8). He was an excellent declaimer but undisciplined, and unwilling to perform except on the subject of love. In his poetry, Seneca tells us, Ovid enjoyed indulging his faults, of which he was well aware: at one point, his friends asked him to suppress three lines of his poetry, and he agreed only on the condition that he could choose three lines of his own to retain and write them out in secret. When all was revealed, Ovid and his friends had chosen exactly the same lines (2.2.12). Seneca tells the story without explicit comment, but with a hint of admiration as well as disapproval for one who managed to follow his own vision so stubbornly. But it is clear that he hoped his own sons would stay much more firmly under his own thumb. Ovid—who was exiled by Augustus for his indecent literary output and for some kind of involvement in the adultery scandal of Augustus' daughter—would remain for the younger Seneca a literary inspiration and a tantalizing model of literary and intellectual freedom, and its dire consequences.

Seneca the Elder was keen to defend declamation itself as a way of training young men in good Roman values—and as an endlessly fascinating way of exploring and telling stories. This case was worth making, since there were already rumblings of hostility to declamation in Roman society. A character in Petronius (a contemporary of our Seneca) describes it as "trivial and inane" and—worse—conducive to the "weakening and death of the substance of oratory" (Encolpius, in Petronius 1–2). Tacitus, writing a generation later, complains that the "highly rhetorical style is used to present this subject matter, divorced from reality" (Dialogus 35). Tacitus also laments that, once upon a time, young men would be instructed by observing or "shadowing" a real orator as he went about his daily experience in court or public assemblies; he was taught "in the open air," not in the fake indoor rooms of declamation halls; he got to see "an opposition and adversaries who fought not with fake swords but with the real thing" (Dialogus 34). Pliny, similarly, bewails the loss of real power in education and in speech (Pliny, Natural History, 8, 14.8). Juvenal denounced the displays for being horribly boring: "rehashed cabbage" is the term he uses (7.155). Seneca the Elder was defending a form of education that was seen by others as a marker of cultural decline—while also suggesting that the best declaimers (like Latro) were long dead.

The criticism that declamation was entirely divorced from cultural realities was somewhat unfair, although it picked up on the dramatic qualities of the exercise. Implausible premises allowed for explorations of genuinely important points of cultural tension. Here is one example: "A sick master asked his slave to give him poison; he refused. The master put a provision in his will that the slave should be crucified by his heirs. The slave appeals to the tribunes" (3.9). To deal with a premise like this, the speakers had to consider how to characterize both master and slave, as well as how to negotiate the complex Roman ethical and legal nexus surrounding slavery and the relationship of slaves and masters. Declamation provides a historical lens into Roman cultural preoccupations and helps us see not just how the Romans of this period argued and performed, but also what kinds of behavior patterns they thought were either plausible or admirable.

Anxieties about the relationship of fathers and sons, and about female sexuality as a dangerous, potentially disruptive force, were absolutely central to Roman cultural life. Declamation allowed practitioners to work through these issues. Common topics included conflicts between fathers and sons over inheritance, extravagance, or betrayal; many dealt with chastity, seduction, or rape. There is little about the relationship of mothers and daughters. Declamation was an entirely male sphere, such that women figure as topics for discussion (mostly as priestesses, prostitutes, wives, and rape victims) but not as participants. The *Suasoriae* and *Controversiae* are highly artificial texts, whose purpose is not to reveal the father's deep feelings about his family but rather to showcase the skills involved in declamatory oratory. But in reading them, we can catch at least a glimpse of how Seneca's father saw fatherhood in general, and perhaps his own relationship with his sons in particular.

The Preface to *Controversiae* Book 2 provides a particularly interesting glimpse of the father's relationship with his three sons.[15] It also gives us clues as to the father's attitudes toward the relative values of political, financial, and social success, and philosophy. The passage suggests a very competitive family structure in which the three sons are played off against one another and in which a dominant father tries, with a great deal of psychological ingenuity, to maintain control over even his adult children.

The "boys" were probably all in their late thirties at the time their father was addressing them, although he pretends for rhetorical purposes that they are only just on the point of embarking on their careers in life. He addresses all three: "Seneca, to Novatus, Seneca and Mela, his sons: greetings!" But the focus shifts to single out just one of the three: the youngest, Mela, who is keen to pursue philosophy rather than a public political or legal career. "I see that your heart shudders at public office and shrinks from all ambition: you have just one desire—to have no desires." The father is quick to suggest that he is not disappointed that Mela has renounced worldly ambition and insists that he is not pressuring him in any way: "I am no obstacle to a good mind! Go where your inclination takes you! Be happy with your father's social position [i.e., there is no need to rise above the equestrian rank], and put most of yourself out of the reach of fortune" (2. Preface. 3).

Seneca establishes himself here as a real old-fashioned Roman patriarch: by law, the Father of the Household (*paterfamilias*) had the power of life and death over his whole household, including his wife and even his adult sons. By insisting that Mela is allowed to do as he wishes, Seneca is also underlining his own power to give or withhold permission. Moreover, there are some fairly obvious strings attached to the freedom granted. He encourages Mela in his desire to pursue philosophy, but also insists that he must be trained first in the father's favorite skill: declamation. The passage begins with an account of a man called Fabianus, who became a well-known philosopher in the Sextian school (and may have influenced the middle son, our Seneca), but who—as Seneca triumphantly emphasizes—trained in declamation in his youth. The explicit lesson is clear: "the practice of declamation will help you in the goals to which you are so wholeheartedly committed—just as they helped Fabianus" (2. Preface. 4).

The passage uses the stereotypical Roman trope of the *exemplum*: the "example" of some earlier historical (or, sometimes, mythical) person is invoked to point to a moral lesson in the present.[16] But Seneca never gives any actual reasons why declamation might be useful as training for the future practice of philosophy. In fact, the story about Fabianus shows exactly the opposite: Fabianus' early training in declamation was something he had to fight against. His teacher, Arellius Fuscus, taught him a highly florid, "effeminate" style of oratory, which he then had to struggle to cast off. Despite his efforts, his work even in philosophy remained tainted by the influence of bad declamation: he succeeded in becoming less long-winded, but "he couldn't escape [his teacher's] tendency to obscurity." Fabianus, we are told, counteracted his teacher's tendency to bloviate by cultivating a highly controlled, aphoristic style, but he is sometimes so concise as to be incomprehensible, and "some sentences stop so suddenly as to be abrupt rather than concise."

The story bears two incompatible interpretations. Firstly, perhaps Fabianus' interest in philosophy helped him become a better orator and declaimer. We are shown how Fabianus managed to curb some of the bad impulses of his teacher and become a more precise speaker and writer, and the suggestion of the narrative is that what makes this possible is not declamation but his philosophical interests and training. Alternatively, skill in philosophy has absolutely nothing to do with skill in declamation—and indeed, that early training might have inhibited his later professional development. Fabianus managed to become a good declaimer and a good philosopher despite bad early education.

The natural inference is that Seneca the Elder was not really concerned with constructing a story about the proper modes of education and intellectual training that made either logical or narrative sense. Rather, he was interested in promoting his own favorite practices. Declamation itself did not encourage clear thinking. Instead, it trained the memory and created facility in coming up with neat, aphoristic turns of phrase and, especially, a skill in telling a vivid set of stories from multiple points of view—regardless of whether they were consistent. The point of invoking Fabianus is to bless declamation by vague association with philosophy, and vice versa, without any intention of teasing out a precise relationship.

Anxieties about the moral status of rhetoric go back at least to the time of Plato, whose *Gorgias* indicts the moral turpitude of oratorial skill in favor of philosophy. But Roman intellectuals tried to defend oratory against philosophical attack by conjoining the two disciplines. They suggested that good moral character is an essential feature of the best orators: Cicero famously defined the orator as "a good man skilled in speaking." Both elements in the definition are necessary for Cicero's conception: unless the declaimer or orator has a good character, all the skill in the world will not make him a real orator. As we have seen, Cicero made significant contributions to philosophical writing in Latin. Philosophy provided an escape from the stresses and anxieties of political and legal engagement, but it also provided ways of approaching and understanding public life. Cicero had shown how it might be possible to combine the life of political engagement with the life of the mind—a possibility that clearly haunted Seneca the Elder and was of even more concern to his middle son.

Philosophy had once been seen as a foreign, Greek import, which had the potential to threaten good old Roman values associated with Roman traditions, examples, and the ways of the ancestors (the *mos maiorum*). Cato the Censor, also known as Cato the Elder, notoriously recommended dismissing from Rome an embassy of three philosophers who came from Athens in 155 BCE to spread philosophical education to the city (see Plutarch, *Life of Cato*). By the adulthood of our Seneca, Roman attitudes toward philosophy had mellowed as the discipline had assumed a central place in elite education, but it still was viewed with some suspicion, as a potential threat to old Roman moral values.

Seneca the Younger presents his father as an old-fashioned patriarch. He suggests that he was religious, traditionalist, and very hostile to philosophy. But this does not fit what we learn from the father himself.[17] He expresses particular admiration for the "lofty and manly teachings" of Stoicism (2. Preface. 1). If he had hated philosophy, it is hard to explain why he encouraged his middle son to study it.[18] We might also note that Seneca says nothing in his extant work about his father's interest in rhetoric, nor does he comment on his successful career in business and finance. The obvious inference is that Seneca fictionalized his own relationship with the father, for two main reasons. First, the son bolsters his own claims to moral decency by presenting himself as the offspring of a man who was the salt of the old Roman earth. It would have looked bad for the author of the *Moral Epistles* to acknowledge himself as the son of a *nouveau riche* provincial, one who encouraged his sons to be highly ambitious, who enjoyed rhetorical exercises as a leisure-time activity, and who had some interest in (Greek!) philosophy, especially as a tool for social advancement.

The second reason for the fudging is more personal. Seneca was presumably comforted by presenting himself as the beloved son of a devoted father. This was a particularly important fiction since the father's own writing suggests, quite to the contrary, that Mela, the youngest boy, was the favorite, and that Seneca the Elder may have been rather less impressed with his two older sons. In a complex and important passage, the father puns on the name "Mela," suggesting a (false) etymological connection with *melior* ("better"): to be "Mela" is to be inherently superior to one's brothers:

> You [Mela] had greater natural talent than your brothers. You were the most competent in all the best fields of study. This is in itself a sign of your superior talent (*melioris ingenii*): not to be spoilt by its power into abusing it. But since your brothers have ambitious goals, and are preparing for the forum and a political career (fields in which one has to fear even the things one hopes for), even I, who am otherwise eager for such advancement, and encourage and praise such efforts—it doesn't matter if they are dangerous, as long as they are honorable—even I keep you in port while your two brothers venture out.
>
> (2. pref. 4)

The attitude expressed here toward public success is deeply ambivalent. Seneca acknowledges that politics and the law courts carry all kinds of hidden and even obvious dangers: the claim that in public life, "even those things which are hoped for, ought to be feared," carries an extra resonance in retrospect, when we remember the middle son's later position as tutor and advisor to the emperor. A wish come true can also be a fear come true, and Seneca's father recognized the danger clearly at the start of his career. He warns his sons of the possibility that success, in politics at least, might come at a terrible cost of lost moral or social identity. But the father pressures the sons toward worldly success even while warning of its dangers.

We might have guessed that the middle brother, our Seneca, would be seen by his father as the most talented of the three, especially in philosophy. What should we make of the fact that the father here identifies the youngest as the one with most natural genius? One might conclude that Mela really was much more talented than Lucius, and the father recognized the truth. If so, an interesting further possibility is that our Seneca, the middle brother, may have been motivated in his own lifelong pursuit of philosophy by a desire to compete with his brother in his chosen field, and thus finally win his father's wholehearted approval. Mela, who became father of the poet Lucan, makes no appearance in Seneca's extant work, and it is impossible to tell how well or badly they got along—although the fact that he addresses no writing to him and says nothing about him, in contrast to his positive account of his elder brother, in itself suggests that his younger brother was not dear to Seneca's heart. It is

likely that at least part of Seneca's recurrent preoccupation with the possibility of withdrawal from public life, into a quiet life of philosophy, was
figured for him as a question of whether he should, after all, have been
more like Mela.

The father puts the elder sons in an impossible situation here: he
admits (or claims) that he himself has driven them to compete in the
public goals of law and politics, but he also suggests that there is greater
moral and intellectual value in not pursuing these things. He has created an imperative that is impossible to fulfill. Mela's talent, the father
notes, is incorruptible: he refuses to apply his mind to anything but
philosophy. By implication, the elder sons have already (thanks to
their father's urging them on) spoilt their moral purity by applying
their minds to the world of law and political ambition. All this complex
pressure must have been an important formative influence for the
middle son, for whom fear and guilt remained ever-present emotions,
and whose writings are marked by the sense that he must always aspire
upward toward an unattainable, and mutually incompatible, set of moral
and social ideals.

Seneca the Elder is also here putting a good public face on what might
look like a failure—Mela's apparent stagnation in his career. We are being
assured that this is due not to laziness or lack of natural talent, but the
opposite (a claim that one might well mistrust). The talents of the elder
brothers must have been fairly obvious by the late thirties CE, when the
passage was written; family honor was salvaged by the claim that the
younger brother, though unknown to the public, was actually the best of
the three. In fact, Mela was not quite as purely philosophical in his interests as his father presents him here. Tacitus suggests that he was more of
a strategist than a pure intellectual. He avoided politics because it was
dangerous and wanted its perks without its hazards: he tried to "get
power equal to an ex-consul, while remaining a Roman knight," and he
figured the best way to make money was through procuratorships, linked
with the administration of the emperor's business interests (*Annals* 16.17).
Of the three brothers, only the eldest, Novatus, had a regular political
career (including, as we shall see, a provincial governorship in Achaea).
The other two, our Seneca and his younger brother, became rich and
powerful by unconventional means. Their lives represent two different
responses to the ambivalent attitudes toward public life that their father
had taught them.

At several moments in later life, Seneca expresses his love and admiration for his two brothers, although he only mentions the elder, Novatus, by name. Middle children often find themselves trying to imitate both their older and their younger siblings, and stretched between the two. Like his younger brother, Mela, Seneca wanted to be an unworldly philosopher, above the fray of political ambition—and to be praised for it by his dominating father. But like his older brother, Novatus (later Gallio), he also aspired to be a successful career politician—which was another avenue by which to gain praise from his father, and probably his mother as well. Like Novatus, Seneca hoped to combine political success with integrity. There are several passages of admiring commentary on Novatus in Seneca's work. For instance, he says that "I'm accustomed to telling you that Gallio, my brother, who is not loved as much as he deserves even by those who could not love him more, is innocent of other vices, and hates flattery" (*NQ* 4. Preface. 10) Seneca goes on to emphasize his brother's extraordinary charm as well as his rock-solid honesty. There is a only a shadowy hint of envy in Seneca's account of this perfect older brother, who never descends from his moral high ground, who is impervious to either praise or blame. He remarks finally that if you tried to flatter Novatus, he would refrain even from pointing out your dissimulation: "he would not catch you out, but he would reject you" (*NQ* 4. Preface. 12). Seneca presumably felt keen anxiety that his beloved older brother might not admire his superior political and economic status but instead might judge and condemn him in his heart for the means by which he achieved these ends.

In his *Consolation to Helvia*, he notes how much both his brothers have each achieved, in very different ways: "the one has gained high office by attention to business, the other has philosophically despised it." He goes on to argue that both have made their choices primarily in order to please their mother: Novatus has chosen high office to bring glory to her, and Mela has withdrawn from society in order to have more time with her. The result, he tells her, is that "you may be protected by the authority of the one, and delighted by the literary leisure of the other. They will compete with one another in love shown you, and the loss of one son will be supplied by the love of two others. I can confidently promise that you will find nothing wanting in your sons except their number." Seneca thus manages to ensure that he himself retains his mother's attention, even in exile, by the virtuosity of his literary composition.

EDUCATION, PHILOSOPHY, SICKNESS

My studies were my salvation (Studia mihi nostra saluti fuerunt)

(Epistle 78.3)

Seneca was brought to Rome as a young boy, in the "arms" of his aunt, his mother's stepsister (*Helvia* 19.2). They were also presumably accompanied by her husband, although Seneca does not mention him. His father was apparently already in the city, perhaps having taken his older brother on ahead. The phrasing suggests that Seneca was very young at the time (small enough to be carried), but he was old enough to understand when his father showed him the great orator, poet, and politician Pollio, who died around 5 CE. It is likely, then, that Seneca came to Rome with his aunt in approximately 4 or 5 CE, at the age of about five. They would have traveled in springtime, and begun the journey by carriage along the well-built Roman roads leading from Corduba to the Mediterranean Sea. They would have taken a *raeda*—a type of large, solid coach, pulled by a team of horses, mules, or oxen, which could fit several people and a good amount of baggage; such coaches could carry as much as a thousand Roman pounds (=327 kg) (Fig. 1.3). The family group would have been accompanied also by a large retinue of slaves as they made their way over the hills toward one of the coastal ports on the eastern coast of Spain—perhaps Tarraco or Barcino (modern Taracino or Barcelona). There would have been daily stops in dirty, bedbug-infested inns along the way. From the coast, they would cross the sea in a boat, perhaps pausing for a night in Sardinia or Corsica, until they finally reached Ostia, the port town nearest to the big city of Rome itself. The whole journey would have taken a little under three weeks.[19]

For a provincial child coming to Rome for the first time, the city would have seemed imposing and unimaginably huge. The population of Rome under Augustus has been estimated at around a million, although exact numbers are impossible to reconstruct.[20] Augustus, who had been emperor since 27 BCE, had established an ambitious building program of public monuments. In his account of his actions, composed to be inscribed on his (marble) tomb, *Res Gestae* (*The Accomplishments*), he boasted that he found the city brick, and made it marble. A grand new marble altar to Peace, the *Ara Pacis,* had been set up in 9 BCE to celebrate

Figure 1.3 Seneca's first journey to Rome, as a child traveling with his father and other family members, would have taken place in a coach like this one.

Augustus' victories over both Hispania and Gaul (Fig. 1.4). There were new hot baths (the Baths of Agrippa, named for Augustus' favorite advisor and friend), new theaters, and many magnificent new temples, including the Pantheon. There was also a new civic center joined onto the main Forum: the Forum of Augustus. The need for an extra public space is a mark of how busy life in the capital was at this period. Most of the business of government still took place in the old Roman Forum, but the Forum of Augustus, adjacent to it, provided another area for public ceremonies and for legal discussions: the law was a growing industry in Rome in this period. The new forum was built around a new temple to Mars, god of war and father of the Roman people.

This would have been where Seneca first assumed his *toga virilis*, "manly toga," a symbolic moment roughly equivalent to a Bar Mitzvah. Elite Roman citizens wore the toga for important public occasions. It was a long garment worn over a light tunic, consisting of a single woolen cloth, folded in half and worn over one shoulder. The toga was highly impractical: it required constant tweaking so as to keep it from flopping

Figure 1.4 The Ara Pacis ("altar of peace") was built in 13 BCE to celebrate Augustus' return to Rome in triumph after his campaign to subdue Hispania and Gaul under Roman rule.

off; nobody could run or do any kind of manual work wearing it; and the white wool took enormous amounts of (slave) labor to keep clean. The impracticality was at the root of the toga's symbolism. It represented the wealth and power of the male elite, as well as Rome's distinction from foreigners (since no other culture would adopt such an odd style of dress), and it was the garment of peace (since one could not possibly ride to war wearing one). At the age of around fourteen or fifteen, Roman boys stopped wearing the toga with a purple stripe around its border and put on their first pure white toga. The ceremony represented their accession into manhood and simultaneously into the upper elite class of Rome.

This moment must have been one of the major highlights of Seneca's youth. In looking back on the ceremony, in an epistle written in old age, Seneca tells his friend Lucilius, "I'm sure you remember how happy you felt when you put off your boy's toga for the man's toga, and were taken to the forum." But he goes on to insist that this merely external mark of maturity is never what really matters: "you can expect even more joy when you put off the mind of boyhood and when philosophy has enrolled you among men. For it is not childhood that still stays with us, but something worse: immaturity" (Epistle 4). People wear out their bodies and even their togas in the pursuit of things that do not really matter at all: "It is the superfluous things that wear our togas bare." The toga itself, he insists in the following letter, must be simple, neither sparkling white nor conspicuously dirty, since wisdom is on the inside, not in a person's dress. But he also acknowledges that clothing can be an important marker of one's inner state.

Seneca's intellectual growth from childhood to maturity was shaped by two main modes of education: rhetoric and philosophy. He would have begun from early boyhood to listen to the declamations of the type celebrated by his father, and soon would have learned to compose and perform his own. We know nothing in detail about Seneca's rhetorical education, because—revealingly—he himself says nothing about it. He is keen to present himself as a philosopher (albeit one with a highly rhetorical and carefully crafted Latin style), as opposed to a rhetorician who happens to write on philosophical topics. But Seneca made extensive use of the rhetorical training of his day, transforming and exaggerating the kind of witty tropes used by his father and teachers into a barbed, pointed style, in which every line or two has a punch line. Declamatory training also helped Seneca hone the ability to see multiple sides to every question and to insert multiple voices into his prose. Moreover, even the desire to write in Latin—as opposed to Greek, the traditional language of philosophical prose—may have been influenced by Seneca's early glimpse, in the halls of declamation, of the power and potential of the Latin language, which could make even a provincial like the Hispanic Latro into a major star in the big city. Seneca learned Greek in boyhood, presumably from a tutor who would have been a Greek slave, but he was not interested in writing in the language.

It was common for elite Roman teenage boys to be educated in philosophy. Many elite fathers sent their boys to Athens to study, which Seneca's father did not do—perhaps because it was too expensive, but also because he wanted his sons to learn about Roman culture at the same time as studying the intellectual heritage of the Greeks. Roman attitudes toward philosophy had changed a great deal since the time of Cicero.[21] As we have seen, there was a tendency to view it as a foreign and frivolous or dangerous pursuit, but philosophy had gradually begun to take hold in Rome, thanks in part to the work of Cicero himself, who labored, especially at times when he was excluded from active political life, to write up detailed summaries and assessments of Greek philosophy. Cicero hoped these would create an ethical synthesis between Greek theory and Roman moral practices. By the time of Seneca, philosophy was a reasonably well-respected field of study, and even profession; a career in philosophy was now a viable alternative to the life of politics (as the case of Mela shows).

In contrast to his silence about his rhetorical training, Seneca gives us a vivid picture of how eagerly he plunged into the study of philosophy— all too eagerly, he suggests with the wisdom of hindsight. He recalls being "the first to arrive and the last to leave" among the boys attending his philosophy class, and he paints a gently humorous, self-mocking picture of his relationship, as an obsessive and demanding adolescent, with his patient tutor in philosophy, the Stoic Attalus. Attalus was a Stoic philosopher chosen as the boy's teacher by Seneca the Elder; the father makes many admiring remarks about the man's eloquence and intelligence. None of Attalus' work survives, although he obviously took an interest in natural science as well as in ethics; apparently he wrote a book about lightning.

The young Seneca was thrilled by Attalus' lectures and greedy for more. He tells us that he used to pester Attalus with questions and demands for more and more discussion, and Attalus would respond with a mixture of encouragement and reproach, suggesting that the boy, like all students of philosophy, needed to go slowly, taking things step by step, and not try to acquire a total knowledge of everything all at once. Seneca repeats to his own addressee, Lucilius, the advice supposedly given to himself by Attalus: "Don't absorb all you want, but all you can hold. If your mind is good, you'll be able to take as much as you want. The more the mind takes in, the more it opens" (Epistle 108.2).

So far, so commonsensical: eager young learners are often urged to walk before running. But Seneca in the same epistle also suggests that Attalus inspired him, in more specific and potentially rather more challenging ways, to practice lifelong abstinence, in diet especially. "When I used to hear Attalus speaking out against various kinds of sin, errors, and the evils of life, I often felt sorry for the human race, and saw Attalus as a sublime being, existing on a super-human level. He called himself a king, but I thought he was more than a king, because he was allowed to pass judgment on kings" (Epistle 108.13). The claim that the wise man is

a king was more or less a Stoic cliché, but it acquires a particular resonance in the context of Seneca's life, since he was to find himself in the
position of having to negotiate between these two quite different and
apparently incompatible kinds of control or quasi-royal power (or *imperium*): the kind represented by Roman emperors and the kind displayed
by the Stoic sage.

Seneca goes on to tell how inspiring he found Attalus' praises of poverty and moderation and asceticism and how eager he instantly became
to live his own life in defiance of the luxury-loving consumer culture
that was an essential strand among the Roman elite of his time. The real
key to happiness, Attalus insisted, was to be free from cravings. This was
a lesson Seneca struggled with all his life and one to which he often
returns. He comments, with partially self-deprecating irony, that he was
so inspired that he even managed to keep some of his ambitious resolutions toward moderation, even when he moved away from philosophical
study and began a political career:

> I gave up oysters and mushrooms forever. Actually they are not really
> food; they are just relishes designed to make the sated stomach go on
> eating—the favorite of foodies and people who stuff themselves
> beyond what they can digest: quickly down, and quickly back up
> again! For the same reason I have also, throughout my life, avoided
> perfumes, because the best scent for the body is no scent at all. That is
> why my stomach keeps its distance from wine. That is why throughout
> my life I have stayed away from baths, and have believed that the prac-
> tice of boiling down the body and sweating it thin is both pointless
> and effeminate. Other resolutions have been broken, but in such a way
> that, for the areas where I gave up abstinence, I have maintained a
> moderation that is very near abstinence; perhaps it is even a bit more
> difficult, because it is easier for the will to give things up completely
> than to use them moderately.
>
> (Epistle 108.15–16)

The accomplishments that Seneca learned from Attalus, and that he feels
the need to boast of even in old age, are all associated with the details (or
trivia) of daily lifestyle choices: "Attalus used to recommend a pillow
which would be hard against the body, and now that I'm an old man,
I use one so hard that no pressure marks it" (108.23). Seneca prided himself, all his life, on his ascetic habits, including an avoidance of over-eating

and over-drinking. Physical moderation became absolutely central to his understanding of himself. Being a philosopher was not simply a matter of theoretical understanding; it influenced, first and foremost, his daily life—including, especially, his eating habits. He returns here to the issue of whether the outside and the inside are entirely separable, and whether the physical practices of the body are mere externals, mere indifferent things, or have some real moral value. It is important not to show off by wearing a dirty toga and scraggly beard, like people who are trying to parade their "philosophy," but Seneca himself boasts of his capacity to behave moderately, to pass on the oysters even while living at court.

Seneca characteristically combines the exalted philosophical motivation with notions that seem far more aesthetic than moral, and with the purely practical. Giving up mushrooms is presented as a real moral or "philosophical" triumph. But it is also a pragmatic choice (it helps avoid stomach upsets). Long baths and saunas are both useless and effeminate—again a characteristic conflation of practical and quasi-moralizing forms of value judgment. The evasions here are as striking as the positive claims. Seneca does not specify which "other resolutions" he has broken, preferring rather to dwell on his lifelong success in steering clear of perfume, and of mushrooms and oysters, those foods so symbolic of luxury within Roman culture. The focus on consumption allows for a comforting sidestepping of the other issue raised by Attalus' teaching, as described by Seneca: politics. Who is the real king, and where does his authority come from? If the Stoic philosopher can call himself a "king" and become able to pass judgment on merely worldly rulers, what implications might this have for Seneca's relationship with the emperor Nero, whose power went far beyond that of kings? Seneca's interest in policing the boundaries of his own body springs from his implicit recognition that the relationships of power in the body politic are far more difficult to control.

Seneca picks up the theme of his own broken resolutions in the same epistle when discussing his other main teacher of philosophy, Sotion. Sotion was a Sextian, a specifically Roman sect developed from the work of Sextius and his son. Seneca was inspired by the work of Sextius throughout his life, commenting in the Epistles on how uplifting he still finds it to read him: "He is alive; he is strong; he is free; he is more than a man; he fills me with a mighty confidence before I close his book" (Epistle 114.3). The Sextians, like the Stoics, insisted that virtue and an

avoidance of consumerism were essential for happiness, although the
Sextians had a more practical bent than many Stoics: they mocked some
of the more obscure and abstract discussions favored by Greek practitioners of Stoicism. The central difference between the Sextians and the
Stoics was that unlike the Stoics, Sextians favored withdrawal from the
political arena.

The Sextians rejected the consumerism and luxury of contemporary
elite Roman society. They were vegetarians: they believed that eating
meat was unnecessary and unhealthy. This was just one mark of the
pragmatism on which the school prided itself. Seneca read Sextius
with attention and admiration and followed in his practice of daily self-
examination. The Sextians saw themselves as quite distinct from the Stoics,
although Seneca conflates the two schools; unlike the Stoics, they favored
withdrawal from political life, and unlike the (Greek) Stoics, they had no
patience for logic or any abstruse abstract thinking. They rejected the
Stoic idea that the perfect wise man may never really exist. It was partly
from Sextians like Fabianus that Seneca drew his model of philosophy
grounded in basic common sense—a notion that he also viewed as specifically Roman.[22] Moreover, Sotion may have written a treatise on
anger—an inspiration for Seneca's own work on the subject.

Seneca tended to fudge the differences between his two major tutors
in philosophy, describing the Sextian Sotion as just a kind of Stoic. In
studying philosophy with these tutors, Seneca learned the importance of
the philosophical life, including a respect for multiple versions of that
quest. Seneca is willing to use arguments that are not Stoic, or are even
anti-Stoic. Moreover, he includes arguments that come from no philosophical school at all but are simply common sense or folk wisdom.

Sotion inspired in Seneca a brief flirtation with vegetarianism, when he
was a young man of around twenty-two. Sotion told the young Seneca
about two earlier philosophers who practiced vegetarianism. Pythagoras forbade eating meat on the grounds that all living beings are related,
and the souls of animals migrate back and forth with the souls of
humans. Sextius, Sotion's own preferred model, recommended vegetarianism on the very different (and Sextian) grounds that consuming meat
encourages a "habit of cruelty," since it trains a person to consider unimportant the suffering and death of another living thing. Sotion, ever the
pragmatist, suggested that it hardly matters which of these reasons one
chooses: even if Pythagoras' theory of transmigration is false, then

vegetarianism is still a good idea, because it helps one avoid brutality and cultivate purity (by not sharing the "food of lions and vultures"); anyway, it is cheaper not to eat meat. The pragmatism and the focus on cultivating psychological health by avoiding habits of cruelty were teachings that stayed with Seneca long after the vegetarianism had lapsed.

Young Seneca kept up a meat-free diet for a whole year, finding it increasingly easy and even enjoyable. But then he met an obstacle and immediately abandoned the cause:

> Some foreign rites were at that time [19 CE] being inaugurated, and abstinence from certain kinds of animal food was set down as a proof of interest in the strange cult. So at the request of my father, who did not fear prosecution, but who hated philosophy, I returned to my previous habits; and it was no very hard matter to induce me to dine more comfortably.
>
> (Epistle 108)

The "foreign rites" in question included both Jewish and Egyptian dietary customs. We learn from Tacitus that there was in the year 19 CE a resolution in the Senate to expel four thousand freedmen-class people who were "infected with superstitions and of military age" and to transport them to Sardinia "to reduce piracy in the area, or act as a cheap sacrifice if they died from the awful climate." All other practitioners of these rites were expelled from Italy or ordered to quit the practice.[23]

The episode reveals how deeply intertwined were politics and philosophy in this period. Even the apparently entirely personal decision to avoid eating meat had a political dimension and carried political risks. Any cult or group that involved a loyalty perceived to be "higher" than the citizen's loyalty to the empire was likely to be seen as a threat, and that included both religion and philosophy. Certainly, Seneca was not practicing vegetarianism through any particular sympathy with Judaism. But Seneca's father obviously felt that his son would be in danger in the contemporary political climate if he were even imagined to be in the same category as those dangerous practitioners of foreign cults. The Annaeus family had a particularly strong motive to try their best to fit in with the customs of Rome, since they were, after all, foreigners, or at least provincials.

Seneca declares here that his father "hated philosophy," but as we have seen, this can hardly be taken at face value. Seneca's own attitude is hedged with irony. He is giving a somewhat self-deprecating account of the ease with which he was induced to return to his old, meat-eating ways. But he is also mildly ironic about his father: claiming to be motivated by an abstract hatred for philosophy is, of course, what any self-respecting person who actually feared prosecution would claim as his motive. Moreover, the whole notion of "dining more comfortably" has a double resonance. It is more comfortable to eat whatever one wishes, without worrying about rules. But it is also more comfortable to eat without worrying about being prosecuted and subsequently exiled, tortured, or executed.

Physical discomfort was a major theme of Seneca's teenage years and throughout his twenties. He was a lifelong sufferer from some kind of lung condition, which he describes primarily in terms of "snuffling": "the snuffling of catarrh and short attacks of fever which follow after long and chronic catarrhal seizures" (Epistle 78). It is likely that Seneca had pulmonary tuberculosis, which would also help explain why he became thinner and weaker as the disease advanced, and why his contemporaries did not expect him to live long. The experience of living with chronic illness must have done much to inform Seneca's constant sense that death was always just around the corner. If he did not die at the hands of an emperor or an assassin, his lungs would finish him off. Every breath he took was a mark of his limited time on earth.

The condition was apparently bearable in childhood and early adolescence, but it became worse later, when Seneca was in his late teens and early twenties—perhaps as a result of the move from the relatively low pollution of Spain to the built-up, dusty, and dirty big city of Rome. Seneca tells us at one stage, apparently in his late teens, he felt so miserable that he contemplated suicide. Again, his story goes that it was his father who held him back from the brink:

> I finally gave up, and was reduced to dripping away in snuffles, and became totally emaciated. I often had the impulse to end my life. It was the old age of my most loving father that stopped me. You see, I didn't focus on how capable I would be of showing courage in death, but on how incapable he would be of showing courage if he lost me. So I ordered myself to live.[24]

(Epistle 78.1–2)

Seneca boasts of his own capacity to face death by suicide bravely, even as he assures his readers that his own courage was not his primary

concern. Moreover, the relationship between father and son is deeply
ambivalent. The father is "most loving," "most kind," "most indulgent"
(*indulgentissimus*): the son depends on the father's protective love. But the
father protects the son only by his weakness, not his strength, and the son
is not given orders by his father, but by himself, a mark of his accession
to manhood: "I ordered myself to live."

Seneca goes on to suggest that the father was not the primary factor
that prevented him from suicide—despite what he just suggested. Actually, what saved his life was philosophy: "My studies were my salvation.
I ascribe it to philosophy that I recovered and got stronger. It is to her
that I owe my life, and that is the least of what I owe her" (78.3). Philosophy takes over from the biological father as his inspiration and cause
of recovery. His old human parent's weakness prevents him from actually
dying, but it is philosophy, his foster mother, who inspires him to live.

As often in Seneca's prose, just as we think we have reached an end
point, there turns out to be another twist. Seneca then assures his reader
that the abstraction of philosophy alone was not all he lived for: it was
his friends who "helped me greatly towards convalescence." He tells that
it was they (not the father or other family members) who sat at his bed-
side while he was sick: "I was comforted by their words, by their presence at night by my side, and by their conversation" (78.4). "Nothing,"
he assures Lucilius, "refreshes and helps a sick person as much as the love
of his friends; nothing is so good at taking away the dread and the fear of
death." The passage veers between three quite different reasons why
Seneca felt able to pull through his illness: the pressure of obligation to
his old father competes with philosophical studies and the joy of spending time with loving friends. Philosophy comes back again as the final
motive, when Seneca sums up the moral. The best prescription for sickness, he tells us, is to despise death. That will cure all other human ailments (78.3). If you can stop being afraid of death, nothing else need
bother you. We may remember, however, that Seneca initially described
his wish to kill himself rather than suffer from his sickness. It is hard to
see how despising death can be much help, if death itself is longed for
but unavailable.

Seneca emerges in this self-presentation as preoccupied with some
unspecified fear whose nature and solution are constantly shifting, even
in the course of a single paragraph. Death mutates from cure to disease and
back again, but the constant is fear. In Freudian terms, Seneca's attitude

toward death is a form of "neurotic fear," in which the negative emotional affect is related only symbolically, not empirically, to the object of the fear.[25] Seneca's pathological manifestations of obscurely motivated anxiety suggest his desperate yearning for some place of safety and psychological relief in multiple locations—family, friends, and philosophy (and later, as we shall see, political power, money, and social status)—despite the fact that they offer incompatible kinds of comfort.

The feeling of unlocalized dread is powerfully expressed in a number of Seneca's works. Perhaps its most memorable expression comes in the tragedies, the earliest of which may have been composed when Seneca was still fairly young: the sense of dread was something he carried with him all his life. Seneca's Oedipus declares,

> *This fear drove me away from my father's kingdom.*
> *For this I fled and left the gods of my hearth.*
> *I mistrusted myself, but kept safe your laws,*
> *Nature! When your dread is vast, you must feel fear*
> *even at things you think impossible.*
> *I feel terrified at everything, and do not believe in myself.*

(*Oedipus* 22–27)

The specific fears of Oedipus—told by an oracle that he was fated to kill his father and marry his mother—were not applicable to Seneca's situation; despite his obvious admiration and affection for his mother and his difficult relationship with his father, there is no particular reason to think he had a classic Freudian Oedipus complex (at least, no more than for anybody else). But the psychological state of constant dread that cannot be fully articulated, involving mistrust of the self as much as of any external object, was a central component of Seneca's experience. Like Oedipus, Seneca was constantly trying to get away, to withdraw, to find a place safe from the nameless horror. Like his own Oedipus, he seems to have repeatedly suspected that he might carry the objects of his fears away with him, however far he ran.

NOWHERE AND EVERYWHERE*

They stand around as judges of my words and deeds.[1]

Seneca's account of his illness and recovery in the Epistles suggests that it was his anxious father, his devoted male friends, and his own intellectual interests that drew him back from the brink of death. But a quite different picture is painted in the treatise to his mother, *To Helvia*. Here we learn that when Seneca's illness became crippling, his mother's kind "sister" (presumably a half-sister) stepped in and whisked him off to Egypt, where it was hoped that the warm climate would cure his affliction. This aunt, like Seneca's mother herself, was a highly educated and well-connected woman. The reason she herself was going to Egypt was that she was married to the Roman prefect of Egypt, Gaius Galerius.

Egypt was agreed to be the best possible cure for those afflicted by lung disease. Pliny tells us that the reason it is so beneficial is not so much for its own sake as for the length of time it took to get there: the sea voyage is good for the chest, since seawater dries out congestion from the lungs, and even seasickness can be healthy for the head, eyes, and chest. Other good cures for this kind of medical condition included leek

---

* Nusbquam est, qui ubique est (Epistle 2.2). More literally, "One who is everywhere is nowhere. It happens to those who spend their lives traveling that they have many acquaintances but few friends."

juice (Pliny, *NH*, 20.22), or, even better, the blood of wild horses, or failing that, a potion made of asses' milk mixed with leeks, with the whey mixed up with nasturtium and honey (Pliny, *NH*, 28.55). Also good for asthma or any kind of shortness of breath was the liver of a fox mixed in red wine, or the gall of a bear taken in water (Pliny, *NH*, 28.55). Seneca, who was under the care of expensive doctors all his life, presumably tried them all.

Seneca spent as much as ten years in Egypt, from the age of around twenty-five to his mid-thirties. He would have spent the time mostly in Alexandria, which was a large, multicultural metropolis that had been under the rule of the Roman empire since Octavian (later titled Augustus) defeated Cleopatra in 31 BCE. Presumably he was laid low by sickness for some of the time but recovered enough to continue his studies and his writing. A particularly appealing feature of Alexandria for Seneca would have been the presence of the famous library, which had been established in the reign of the Ptolemies (Greek-speaking Macedonian rulers of Egypt from the third century BCE onward). The library was said to have been burned by Julius Caesar, perhaps only partially, but this may be a myth; in any case, there were plenty of books available in Alexandria. Seneca studied the local culture, customs, and history and composed a treatise about Egypt, which is lost. He also had the leisure to continue in his philosophical studies, and it is quite possible that other writings date from this period; unfortunately, none can be dated with certainty, and it is impossible to say more about these formative years.

The health-cure seems to have worked, albeit rather slowly. Seneca notes that, by his aunt's "affectionate and motherly nursing, I regained my strength after a long period of illness" (*Helvia*). He sailed back from Egypt to Rome in 31 CE. The voyage would have taken at least three weeks, first crossing the sea from Alexandria to Crete, then on to the north of Sicily, then sailing round the island and up the coast of Italy to Rome. It is possible that he was traveling on the same boat as his uncle, who drowned while making the crossing at this time. Or, perhaps more likely, Seneca traveled separately, on a more seaworthy vessel. In any case, Seneca and his aunt survived and reached Rome safely.

By this stage, Seneca would have been around thirty-five, rather late to begin a political career by traditional Roman standards. But Seneca was fortunate that his aunt was both able and willing to help him get ahead. As he reminds his mother, she used her influence to get me a quaestorship, and although she was very shy of talking or greeting people in a visible way, her love for me overcame her nerves. Nothing got in the way of her even being proactive on my behalf, despite her withdrawn mode of life, her modest country manners amid so many brazen women, her quietness and her habit of living a retiring life, far from bustle.

(*To Helvia* 19)

The quaestorship was the first official rank on the standard career ladder for ambitious Roman elite men, the *cursus honorum* (the sequence of offices). In normal circumstances, a man was expected to serve ten years in the military as a general before attaining this rank. Seneca entirely skipped this step, thanks no doubt to his aunt's influence.

Seneca had shown no interest in entering public life until this point. Perhaps he was so disabled by sickness during his twenties that he felt unable to aspire to any future except death. Perhaps he did not even want a career in his youth; he may have hoped for a quieter life as a philosophical writer and teacher. Perhaps, too, he shrank from climbing the political ladder in fear of the particular dangers of life in the court of Tiberius (Fig. 2.1). But presumably by the time he arrived back in Rome, he was ready to begin his political career. Seneca works hard to present his aunt's ambition on his own behalf as a becoming kind of paradox: she pushed him without being pushy, she helped him succeed in the big city despite being not at all a big-city kind of woman. The rhetoric works to dispel any suspicion the reader might otherwise have, not only about the aunt, but also about Seneca himself. He implies that he, too, was a shy country boy, devoid of all personal ambition, who just happened to find a good career landing in his lap. There is no reason to believe that this pose corresponded to reality, although it shows how fluently Seneca had already mastered the social gestures necessary for success.

The year in which Seneca arrived back in Rome, 31 CE, was an interesting and terrible time in the city's history. The emperor Tiberius, Augustus' adopted son, had taken over power in 14 CE but had little active interest in governing the empire; he hoped to let the wheels of government turn without having to intervene. From 26 CE onward, he left the capital altogether and lived full-time in retirement on the island of Capri—supposedly entertaining himself with constant sex orgies. In the meantime, there were other people who very much did want to take an active part in government. The most important of these was Sejanus,

*Figure 2.1 Tiberius, emperor from 14 to 37 CE, was a reclusive and bitter emperor whose
court had an atmosphere of fear and suspicion.*

who had been appointed consul in 31 and used the position as leverage
in his attempt to seize complete control of the empire. But Tiberius
found out about the plot and sent a letter to the Senate ordering that
Sejanus be executed immediately. He and his followers were killed
within days, and in the weeks that followed, the previously inactive Tiberius is said to have woken up enough to conduct a series of further
executions of all those associated with the plot.

Seneca's life under Tiberius must have been defined by fear. The earlier
years of the rule were relatively good, comparable to the good years of the
Divine Augustus (*On Clemency* 1.1). But in his later years, the time at
which Seneca was entering public life, Tiberius became paranoid and anti-
social to the point almost of madness. Seneca characterizes the emperor
as horribly unkind and close-fisted, the kind of man who has no notion
of true generosity: even his gifts were always accompanied by reproaches,
leaving such a sour taste that the beneficiaries could never be expected to
feel grateful for them (*On Benefits* 2.7). Seneca tells the story of an old
friend who made the emperor a social visit and was horribly snubbed.

The friend asked Tiberius, "Do you remember...?" and the emperor cut him off, claiming, "I don't remember who I was," and treating his old friend as a spy (*inquisitor*). The emperor wanted to insist that his life before coming to power was entirely forgotten: "He turned away from all his friends ... he wished people to see, think and speak of him only as an emperor" (*On Benefits* 5.25). Seneca's own life in these years would have been deeply affected by the culture of informing, spying, and suspicion—an ancient equivalent of McCarthyism. He describes how there was in the time of Tiberius "an almost universal culture of informing, which was more ruinous for Rome even than the civil wars" (*On Benefits* 3.26). The issue was not only that public forms of speech and writing were controlled; even the most apparently innocent actions, or inadvertent gestures, could be held against one. Seneca tells the terrifying though darkly funny story of a man in the Praetorian Guard who, wearing a ring adorned with the image of the emperor, got drunk and started to lift up a chamber pot, presumably needing to use it rather urgently—and touched the impure object while still wearing his imperial ring (*De Ben.* 3.26). An informant was at the party and called the guests to witness the act of desecration. The man would have been executed had it not been for the quick thinking and loyalty of his slave, who managed to slip the ring onto his own finger just in time, to "prove" his master's innocence. All this helps to explain why Seneca may have extended his years in Egypt rather longer than his illness. It would be understandable if he were reluctant to enter this world of suspicion and fear, as well as for reasons of poor health. But the fact that he did decide to swim in these dirty waters, and that he achieved significant social success under Tiberius, is also revealing of his courage, his curiosity, and his ambition.

Seneca's years under Tiberius gave him a good glimpse of how important it was for an emperor to be able to be generous and merciful to his subjects—topics on which he insisted in his public advice to Nero. They also gave him a clear sense of the dangers involved in an advisor or imperial servant trying to become more powerful than the emperor, as Sejanus had done. The aftermath of the conspiracy only increased the atmosphere of paranoia, in which plots and counter-plots were constantly both created and imagined. The culture of fear among the Roman elite of this period can be seen as a function of the institutional instability of the imperial system: the emperor had to ensure that the aristocracy, the old locus of control in government, remained weak in order to ensure his own hold on the reins of power. But Seneca never suggests that he saw things in these terms. Rather, he presents Tiberius' lack of generosity and cultivation of an atmosphere of terror as merely personal failures. Moreover, his anecdote about the slave and the chamber pot suggests, characteristically, that the best response to this world of constant political danger is constant individual vigilance, the display of personal integrity, and loyalty to one's own social group—not explicit resistance to the regime. These lessons, learned under Tiberius, would follow through Seneca's life under the challenges posed by subsequent emperors.

The culture of fear grew worse six years after Seneca returned to Rome, with the accession in 37 CE of Rome's most notoriously insane emperor: Caligula (Fig. 2.2). Caligula is depicted in all the ancient sources as crazily cruel and perverted: he enjoyed killing for its own sake, he slept with his sisters, and he declared himself to be a god. Of course, all of these sources are written under later emperors, by writers who have a strong ulterior motive for denigrating the current emperor's predecessors;

Figure 2.2 Caligula ("little boot") was emperor from 37 to 41 CE. We are told that he was tempted to execute Seneca but decided not to bother because he was likely to die soon in any case.

modern historians tend to think that Caligula was probably less crazy than the sources suggest.[2]

But Seneca has nothing good to say about Caligula and frequently depicts him as a monster driven mad by rage.[3] He tells a horrible story in his essay *On Anger* of a young man whose elegant clothes and hair aroused Caligula's ire. Caligula threw him into jail, and when the youth's father begged for his son's life, Caligula had the boy executed. He then invited the father to dinner and forced him to sit and drink with him—feeling all the while, as Seneca comments, "as if he were drinking his son's blood" (*On Anger* 2.33). Caligula set slaves to watch the man intently and observe whether he accepted everything he was offered—perfumes, garlands, and drinks. He took it all and showed no sign on his face that he was grieving the murdered boy. Seneca comments chillingly on the reason: "You ask me why he did this? Because he had another son."

The story was clearly in Seneca's mind when, later, he wrote his tragedy *Thyestes*, in which a monstrous tyrant, Atreus, forces his brother Thyestes to eat his own children and drink wine mixed with their blood—and watches him all the while. Caligula, like Seneca's Thyestes, was a kind of dramatic director, who forced those around him into performing roles in his own sadistic theater of cruelty. It has been well observed that the Roman court of this period—under Caligula, Claudius, and later Nero, another great lover of theatrical scenes—created a sense that everybody had to be an actor: not only the emperor himself, but also those in attendance upon him, who were watched to see if their reactions were acceptable or not.[4]

The court of Caligula was a particularly dangerous place for anybody with intellectual talents. Seneca tells the story of one Julius Canus, a Stoic philosopher who aroused the jealousy of Caligula.[5] The emperor told him that he had given orders to have him killed. Julius Canus replied, "Thank you, most excellent ruler" (*On Tranquillity* 14). Seneca comments that the meaning of the utterance is unclear, but "whatever he meant, it was a spirited answer." Canus succeeded in coming across as a man of heart and integrity, but without any outright critique of the emperor. His capacity to use ambiguity was precisely the point. In a world where saying the wrong thing could get you killed, but where abject flattery might turn out to be just as offensive as outright defiance, it was necessary for those near the emperor to cultivate modes of not saying what they meant, or rather, of saying things that could have more than one meaning (*dissimulatio*).[6] But of course, it was quite possible that, with all the good doublespeak in the world, one might still get killed. Julius Canus was executed soon afterward—but at least, so Seneca assures us, he went out with true philosophical dignity.

All this may make one wonder how Seneca himself—also a Stoic philosopher, and also a talented speaker and writer—managed to survive the reign of Caligula, and also, it seems, flourish, gaining money, reputation, and power and moving up the career ladder in this period. Contemporaries asked the same question, and the sources give one story in answer to it. We are told that Seneca,

> who was superior in wisdom to all the Romans of his day and to many others as well, was nearly destroyed, despite having done nothing wrong and not even looking as if he had. It was just because he made a good speech in the senate when the emperor was present. Gaius [Caligula] ordered him to be put to death, but then let him off because he believed what one of his women said, that Seneca had a bad case of consumption and would die soon.
>
> (Dio 59.19.7–8)

It is possible that the story is true: Seneca's health was certainly bad, and he might plausibly have presented himself as deathly ill, even once his chronic condition was under control. Seneca may well have spoken of himself as close to death. Perhaps he really believed it. The nearness of mortality is a constant theme of his writing at all periods of his life. It is also possible that the anecdote was a fabrication invented by people sympathetic to Seneca, who were struggling to explain how he could have flourished under Caligula. In either case, a notable feature of the story is that it is through a woman that Seneca's life is saved: silver-tongued Seneca was clearly appealing to women.

An alternative explanation is given by Seneca himself in a self-justificatory account of his life under both Caligula and Claudius. He insists that his survival of Caligula's reign was the result of his patience and loyalty, which led him to bide his time, not submitting to the allure of suicide but instead waiting things out, for the sake of his devotion to his friends:

> I didn't rush into an extreme course of action to escape the madness of those in power. At the court of Caligula, I saw torture and fire.

I knew that under him, human life had deteriorated to such an extent that those who were killed were held up as examples of his mercy. Still, I did not fall on my sword or leap into the sea with mouth wide open. I wanted to avoid the impression that all I could do for loyalty was die.

(*NQ* pr. 4.17)

The passage suggests that Seneca may have been involved in plots against Caligula's life, or at least was invited to participate. Perhaps this implication is true, or perhaps it merely looked good to imply it, once Caligula was safely dead. In any case, there was no love lost between them. Caligula, speaking in sour grapes at the popularity of Seneca's writing, criticized his style, commenting that his writings were "Just straight-up declamations: sand without lime" (Suetonius 53.2). Sand mixed with lime was used to make bricks in antiquity. The point of the critique is to suggest that Seneca's writing is composed only of the crunchy parts, the neat one-liners that form the sand; it has nothing to glue it together. It is possible that the criticism was leveled at Seneca's father, but probably it is more likely that the emperor was pointing out the ways that the son's style built on that of his father.

During these years, Seneca was becoming increasingly well known as a writer. Probably the earliest of his known works, the *Consolation to Marcia*, dates from around 39 or 40 CE.[7] It tells us a great deal about Seneca's literary, philosophical, and social program. The piece is addressed to a noble lady named Marcia, who was a friend of Livia, the wife of Augustus. Seneca's ostensible purpose is to "console" Marcia for the death of one of her four children: a son, Metilius, who died some three years before. The subject matter allows Seneca to define himself as an adult, one who can offer advice for a grieving mother but not himself be caught up in the emotional turmoil—and at the same time define himself as a writer.

The *Marcia* establishes several key components to Seneca's prose works in philosophy. The first and perhaps most important feature about it is that it is written in Latin. Seneca marks the fact that his ambitions are as much literary as philosophical by using his own language to convey the tropes of Greek philosophy. The text is also important in positioning the author as a well-connected man, one to whom a woman like Marcia could lean on in her grief.

Many readers have found themselves puzzled by the philosopher's distanced stance to a devastating loss; one critic comments that Seneca "notably lacks empathy towards Marcia's individual grief and loss."[8] This response, however, is not entirely fair. After all, the genre of the literary consolation was not supposed to be a display of "empathy." Rather, its purpose—which was well understood by Roman readers—was to allow the writer to display his own ability to rework the clichés that are always used to cheer up mourners, in fresh and vivid ways. The piece does acknowledge (very few) individual features of the dead son, including his beauty. But mostly, Seneca works to redirect Marcia's attention away from the son and toward her other relationships.

The emotional heart of the essay lies in the appeals to Marcia's father at beginning and end. This man was a historian named Cremutius Cordus, who was accused of treason under Tiberius (thanks to the machinations of Tiberius' much-hated henchman, Sejanus) and forced to kill himself in 25 CE. Through his invocation of Cordus, Seneca manages to articulate his own values, implicitly defending a life of intellectual, scientific, and philosophical inquiry, combined with resistance to the worst kinds of political corruption—although he is notably vague about Cordus' defense of the Roman Republic. The lesson of this man's life, for Seneca, is not that one should always fight for political change even if it means paying the ultimate price. Rather, it is that intellectuals can always find a way out of the terrors and limitations of their own age, through writing and through contemplating the vastness of the universe. Whether or not this message was helpful to Marcia (it probably was not), this lesson was one to which Seneca himself was deeply attached; it was to be a primary inspiration for his life and work.

Seneca suggests at the start of the consolation that Marcia should remember how brave a face she put on at that time and recover the same strength to deal with her current loss. At the end of the piece, he builds up an inspiring picture of the life of the dead, both father and son, who wander through "the free and boundless spaces of eternity; no seas shut them out, no height of mountains nor pathless valleys, no quicksands of the shifting Syrtes; there all is level plain, and easily, quick and unencumbered, they mingle with the stars and stars with them in turn" (25.3). Then Seneca imagines Cordus himself speaking. In Seneca's fantasy, Cordus the historian has now moved beyond history and shows how a cosmic, philosophical awareness of the cycles in the universe is both a development of historical knowledge and goes far beyond it:

"I used to enjoy compiling the history of what happened in a single age, in a distant part of the world, among a tiny number of people. Now I can see so many ages, the succession and progression of so many ages; I can see the whole of sum of years."

(26.6)

Cordus had written a history of the Republican period of Rome; the Senate had given orders for the work to be burned at the time of his downfall. But for Seneca, Cordus is able to rise above both his own personal losses and the city that tried to ruin him. Rome itself, in what many still saw as the glory days of the city, is seen as the "distant part of the world"—distant indeed from the viewpoint of Cordus in Heaven. Cordus turns out to be able to see not merely times past but times to come, and he sees the downfall of cities, powers, and empires, and finally, not merely the end of the human race—a small event in the long sweep of cosmic time—but vast geological change, as he predicts the conflagration of the world by fire:

"And when the time comes, that the world will be destroyed to be made new, [all the elements of the earth] will destroy themselves by their own power, stars will clash with stars, and all that now shines in orderly arrangement will burn in a single fire, as the whole matter of the universe catches flame. We too, we happy souls who have achieved immortality, when it seems good to the god to remake the world, we too, when the world falls, will be a tiny fragment of the immense destruction, and will turn again into our old components." Marcia, how happy is your son, who knows these things!

(26.6)

This, the last passage of the dialogue, certainly tells us little or nothing about the mother's grief; Seneca seems to have lost interest in the details of Marcia's particular emotional state. But it is extraordinarily powerful rhetoric, designed to redirect the mind away from any earthly loss. In this early work, Seneca shows that he is already highly effective in a kind of writing that shifts effortlessly from the small-scale view to a cosmic perspective, that reveals the world to be far bigger, far vaster even than we can imagine—and that reaches beyond what any human being can possibly visualize or attain. He also, through his hagiographic praise of Cordus, implies that writing is the way to win lasting fame and recognition.

LEGITIMATE LUST

In returning to Rome from Egypt, Seneca had the opportunity to set up a more stable domestic world for himself, including a wife and child, and close relationships with brothers, mother, nieces, and nephews. He married and had a little boy, who died in infancy in 41 CE (*To Helvia* 2.5). Seneca makes only one brief reference to this. He implies that his baby's death is mostly a source of sorrow for the grandmother, his mother Helvia, who had to suffer the deaths of not one but three grandchildren in quick succession (*To Helvia* 2.4). Presumably the other two dead grandchildren were offspring of one or both of Seneca's brothers. Seneca expresses no emotion, here or elsewhere, about his son. The passage also gives no indication that Seneca himself had spent much time with the child. He emphasizes that the boy was buried by his mother, the child's grandmother; he does not suggest that he himself took an interest in the event. This is the only child Seneca is known to have had in the course of his life.

The ease with which Seneca discusses the death of his infant son, his only child, is likely to strike many modern readers as extraordinarily unfeeling. We should not be too quick, however, to condemn him for callousness: infant mortality was far more common in antiquity than it is in Western Europe and the United States today. That does not mean that people did not grieve intensely for their children, of course, but the death of a little baby was less unexpected, and therefore less shocking, than it would be in a modern Westernized context.

Moreover, our only evidence for the death comes from the *Helvia*, which is, as we have seen, a public and highly polished literary document, not an expression of the author's deepest feelings and emotions, but a rhetorical and philosophical set piece of a virtuosic kind. The point of the exercise is to reduce the intensity of his mother's grief; invoking his own would hardly help achieve that goal. Seneca's pose here is as the Stoic teacher and advisor, who is able to explain to his grieving, all-too-human mother why she must put her grief aside. From a strictly Stoic point of view, the death of a child is an "indifferent thing": it is not preferable, but it is not something that would ever disturb the true wise man's tranquility. Seneca is adopting the persona of a sage; there is no knowing whether the rhetoric matched reality. We may still consider it inhumane even to pretend to see other people—including one's own children—as "indifferent things." But either way, we cannot draw any clear conclusions about how Seneca felt about his baby son's death. All we can say for sure is that he did have an infant son, and that he soon died.

The *Helvia* has two further passages suggestive of Seneca's relationships with children. Seneca urges Helvia,

> Look at your grandchildren! Look at Marcus, such a sweet boy! No sadness could last if you look at him. No crazy grief in anybody's heart is so large or so fresh that it wouldn't be charmed away by him. Whose tears would his cheeriness fail to dry? Whose heart is so squashed by worry that his energetic romping wouldn't set it free? His playfulness would make anybody want to play. Could anybody ever get tired of hearing his chatter, and fail to be charmed by it and get over his bad moods? I pray the gods he may survive us!
>
> (*To Helvia* 18.4–6)

The toddler with the unstoppable cheerful babbling was probably Marcus Lucanus (the future poet Lucan), son of Seneca's brother Mela. It is hard to decide how serious Seneca is being in his account of the little fellow's vociferous charm. But Seneca clearly took the boy under his wing once he was old enough to be taught about literature, rhetoric, politics, and philosophy, and—as we shall see—would introduce him to Nero.

The same passage of the *Helvia* also mentions his niece, the daughter of his older brother, Novatus, in whom Seneca had also apparently taken a strong avuncular interest (*To Helvia* 18.7–8). He suggests that he treated this niece like an adopted daughter, despite having her biological father, Seneca's brother, still alive. Seneca shows an early interest here in how a young person can be given moral teaching by an older role model:

> Now strengthen and form her behavior. The principles which are impressed upon us in early youth are the ones that sink in more deeply. Let her get used to your conversation, let her be shaped by your authority. You'll give her a lot, even if you just give her your example.

The passage suggests a wildly optimistic notion of how easy it is to teach ethics to a teenager, an optimism that perhaps played a part in Seneca's decision to take on the role of Nero's tutor. We have no way of knowing how Novatilla turned out.

We come now to the question of Seneca's wife.[9] Probably he married fairly soon after returning to Rome and beginning his political career.

He must have had a wife by 40 CE at latest, since he had a legitimate son in 41. Seneca mentions a wife in Book Three of *On Anger*, who is, we learn, "long since aware of my habit [of nightly self-examination]" and who therefore tactfully falls silent in order to let her husband go over his day without interruption. Unfortunately, we have almost no evidence about this marriage. We know a little of his wife, Paulina, at the time of his death, and some have argued that Seneca was married only once, to Paulina. But it is most likely that he had an earlier marriage, to a woman whose name and history are unknown. She probably died at some point in the 40s, perhaps in childbirth, leaving Seneca free to remarry. But again, we have no clear evidence for any of this, since neither Seneca himself nor our other sources provide any explicit account of the marriage.

Still, we can learn quite a lot about Seneca's expressed opinions about marriage in general, if not in particular, since he wrote a treatise *On Marriage* of which some quotations survive.[10] Seneca argued against the Epicurean view of marriage, which was that in most cases it is a mistake to marry and to have children, because these things are liable to disrupt one's tranquility.[11] Seneca followed the standard Stoic line instead, which was that love between the sexes was not a source of delusion and frustration but rather a natural and spiritual necessity, which should be founded on reason, not passion. Seneca's treatise may well have been written at or near the time of his own first marriage, perhaps around 38 or 39 CE, or a little later. Marriage was presented in this work as a feature of the ideal life. In accordance with Stoic theory, Seneca admits that marriage is an indifferent thing, not valuable in the same way that virtue is valuable; but it is a preferable indifferent, such that a good wife is definitely better than no wife at all. Seneca insists that the Epicureans were too negative about the institution:

> Epicurus says that the wise man rarely gets married, because marriage is accompanied by many inconveniences. Although riches and honor and physical health are named "indifferent things" by our school, and are neither good nor bad; nevertheless, we can compromise with what you might call a middle position: by how these things are used and how they turn out, they become either good or bad. So too with wives, who are on the cusp of either good or bad things. But a wise man must think hard about whether he's about to marry a good or a bad woman.
>
> (Fragment 5)

Seneca is here, as so often, on the lookout for a compromise between the ideals of old-school Stoicism and the realities of contemporary Roman life. He hopes to reconcile the Stoic notion that only virtue is essential for happiness with the social and psychological reality that most people, including himself, tend to want rather more things in their lives than just virtue, and those things may well include getting married. Moreover, in what could be seen as an entirely un-Stoic spirit, he suggests that what really makes or breaks a marriage is not how "you" (i.e., the husband) behave, but rather, what kind of woman "you" choose to marry. The real issue then is not the husband's behavior, but the wife's. This goes contrary to the hardline Stoic position that what matters is the individual's own behavior, not that of other people. The wife, for Seneca, is the one responsible for making the marriage work.

Seneca strikingly seems to suggest that the greatest moral danger for a married man is not that he might be tempted to have affairs with others and break his marriage vows, but rather that he might love his wife too much. He mocks a "certain man," apparently the source of numerous comic anecdotes, who was joined at the hip with his wife:

> they took no drink unless it was touched by both their lips, and they did other things, no less ridiculous, in which the thoughtless force of their burning passion broke out. Certainly the origin of their love was good, but its magnitude was monstrous. If somebody acts crazily, it doesn't matter how good their intentions are.
>
> (Fragment 26, Haase 1852)

The point is developed: "Lust for another person's wife is base; excessive lust for one's own is just as bad...Nothing is more disgusting than lusting after one's wife as if for a mistress" (fragment 27). Seneca goes on (in fragment 28) to inveigh against marriages that begin with an adulterous affair, and then, after divorce, are legitimated by law. He suggests that such relationships are bound to fizzle out—a wife is not, and never can be, as tempting as a mistress: "the man despises a lust that is legitimate."

The general point Seneca insists upon here is that marriage must be based on something other than lust. That "something else" is not reproduction: as we have seen, children are, for the Stoics, an indifferent thing, although one that many people prefer to have rather than not. The main reason for getting married is rather, for Seneca, to make one's environment more conducive to living a virtuous life, which can happen more readily in the company of a virtuous woman. Marriage could also be helpful in more worldly ways: Seneca presumably did not emphasize the importance of marriage for climbing the social ladder, but this was an essential element of the institution. It is very likely that Seneca's first wife, like his second, was a well-born and well-connected woman, who would have helped him on his ascent to the centers of imperial power.

Seneca's purpose in composing the marriage treatise was not merely to celebrate legitimate forms of marriage, but also to speak out against current Roman legislation that put pressure on people to get married, whether they wanted to or not. "What," he asks, "shall I say of poor men who mostly are led to the name of husband in order to evade the laws passed against the celibate? How can one who weds regulate the habits and advise chastity and maintain the authority of the husband?" (fragment 29). Seneca presents himself as both a political and moral guide, a voice of real ethical strength in a time of uncertainty and social change, especially in relationships between the sexes. As so often, Seneca's writing is unlikely to represent his biographical realities in any transparent fashion: it, too, is an artful piece of rhetoric, calibrated for particular literary, philosophical, and personal reasons. The treatise *On Marriage* may well have been an attempt on Seneca's part to clear his own name, in the wake of his own public sexual scandal—to which we now turn.

Fortune Tested My Loyalty

As we have seen, Seneca seems to have done rather well under Caligula: he had created strong social networks in the court and among the aristocracy, if not with the emperor himself. But in 41 CE, Caligula—who was unpopular, for obvious reasons—was assassinated in a plot that involved several members of the Senate. He had no male heir, and the Praetorian Guard (the group of bodyguard soldiers who protected the imperial palace) insisted that Claudius (Fig. 2.3) should be appointed the next emperor. The Senate reluctantly agreed. Claudius was descended from the Julio-Claudian family, the grandson of Octavia, sister of the emperor Augustus; he thus had a fairly good claim to the throne in terms of birth. But he had a limp and a stutter and was generally considered to be half-witted, so he had rarely been seen as a viable candidate.

Figure 2.3 Claudius, emperor from 41 to 54 CE, exiled Seneca to the island of Corsica on charges of adultery.

However, Claudius turned out to be an active ruler, who produced many public building projects and managed to expand the Roman empire for the first time since Augustus. The most important of these was Britain (Britannia), a Roman province that had been struggling against Roman rule. Seneca later took financial advantage of the opportunities afforded by this new wing of the empire. The ancient historians Suetonius and Tacitus maintain that Claudius was not really qualified for the task of ruling the empire and was therefore the tool of his wives and freedmen.[12] This view has been challenged by more recent historians. One possibility, memorably proposed by the Claudius novels of Robert Graves (and the TV adaptation, *I, Claudius*), is that Claudius was actually far cleverer than anybody around him believed. His pose of weakness and dependency was cultivated in order to stay alive, in a world where any display of ability would guarantee his assassination.

An alternative analysis—not entirely incompatible with the first—is that the real problem for Claudius was the structural or institutional power of the principate, in a culture that was still ideologically loyal to the Republic.[13] The Romans had not always had an emperor, and the

early years of the empire—the time of the Julio-Claudian dynasty—
were precarious in both institutional and political terms. Augustus had
begun a complex balancing act in naming himself Princeps ("first man")
but insisting that he was still a citizen like any other, not a king. It was an
essential feature of elite Roman self-definition that Rome was not a
monarchy, and the kings had been cast out of the Republic back in the
bad old legendary days of Tarquinius Superbus. The emperors were thus
in a difficult position: they had to hold on to power, but without presenting themselves as autocratic. Moreover, there were intense difficulties
in the legal basis for the principate as invented and handed down by
Augustus. The Senate, and the Roman aristocracy more generally, wanted
to see themselves as still living under a republican form of government,
but the empire had moved far away from being a republic, and real
power lay with the military and with the emperor himself. Each successive emperor struggled to govern effectively with a Senate that resisted
his every move. When Claudius became emperor in 41 CE, he rewarded
with cash payment the members of the Praetorian Guard who had
brought him to office, and he was on the lookout against those who
might remain hostile to his rule as emperor; in the course of his reign, he
suppressed at least six plots against his life, and—shockingly for the
Roman elite—executed some thirty-five senators.

It is in this context that we should view one of the earliest actions of
his reign: to banish Seneca to exile on the island of Corsica. Seneca had
developed a powerful literary and political voice and had built up powerful connections, most notably a close friendship with Caligula's sisters,
Agrippina (Fig. 2.4) and Julia Livilla, who were still important figures in
court when Claudius came to power. Claudius had good reason to fear
that Seneca might be a ringleader in a plot against his life. The accusations were apparently brought at the behest of Claudius' wife, Messalina,
although it seems perfectly possible that the emperor deflected responsibility onto his wife—if it had been Claudius' idea to exile Seneca, he
would surely have blamed Messalina. In any case, the story goes that
Messalina accused Seneca of adultery with Julia Livilla, youngest sister of
Caligula and therefore also Claudius' niece. Julia Livilla herself had only
just been recalled by Claudius from a previous relegation, along with
Agrippina; they had been accused of trying to overthrow Caligula.

Was the charge of adultery true? The Greek historian Dio—whose account is often contradictory and untrustworthy—implies in one passage

Figure 2.4 Agrippina the Younger, fourth wife and niece of Claudius and mother of Nero, was Seneca's patron, the main influence in bringing him back from exile.

that Messalina invented the charge of adultery out of jealousy of Julia (60.8.5). But later, Dio implies that the charge of an affair between Julia and Seneca was indeed true, and even adds the charge that Seneca was also sleeping with Agrippina. The notion of the affair with Agrippina is surely a later embellishment, added by gossipmongers to spice up an already salacious story. Historians have taken a range of different views about the facts of the case. Messalina had a political motive for getting rid of Julia Livilla and her most prominent friends and supporters— who included Seneca. Seneca was close friends with the then-husband of Agrippina, Crispus Passienus,[14] and was thus closely associated with the house of Germanicus, the father of Agrippina and Julia Livilla. Messalina was an ambitious young woman who may have been particularly anxious about Julia Livilla's husband, Marcus Vincius, as a threat to her power. He was a friend of Seneca's, had been involved in the assassination of Caligula, and may have had designs on the imperial throne.[15] Perhaps the real reason for the charges was that Julia Livilla and Seneca were believed to be plotting against Claudius. Narcissus, a freedman and close advisor of Claudius, seems to have been important in the prosecution.

Seneca himself gives a vague but suggestive account of his own trial and condemnation:

> I risked my life for loyalty; no word was forced out of me that I couldn't speak in good conscience. I feared everything for my friends, but nothing for myself, except that I might not be a good enough friend. I wept no womanly tears, I did not kneel down low and grasp anybody's hands to beg my life. I did nothing undignified, nothing unbefitting a good person, or a man. I rose above the dangers that faced me, ready to attack those that threatened me, and I thanked fortune that she had wanted to test how highly I valued loyalty.
>
> (NQ 4. preface, 15–16)

The passage is obviously defensive. Seneca wants to present himself as having done entirely the right thing and as having suffered only for the most noble of reasons. He suggests that he resisted speaking in his own defense because doing so would have indicted his "friends," people to whom he owed his loyalty. Probably the main people referred to here are Julia Livilla herself, and perhaps also her husband, both of whom may well have been plotting against Claudius. Seneca insists that he knew he might risk not only exile or death but also torture for his loyalty: and yet he stood firm, unbowed by fear of punishment and unmoved by any hope of gain. But Seneca, looking back on these events at a distance of some twenty years, acknowledges that his own self-justificatory story might not be true: "After telling yourself these things, ask yourself whether what you said was true or false" (NQ 4a18). He admits, in other words, that he might have done something wrong: but he also refuses to tell anybody (except his own secret self) what the wrongdoing was.

There is no reason to rule out the possibility that Seneca was guilty, of political scheming, or adultery, or both. His consolation in exile to his mother (To Helvia) hints that he may be innocent—but then again, a public document addressed to the writer's mother was hardly likely to contain a full confession of the lurid details of an adulterous affair. Seneca had every reason in this piece to present himself as a brave, suffering innocent. By contrast, the essay written in exile to Claudius' freedman, Polybius, seems to suggest at least a possibility of guilt, or rather more.[16] In pleading for his recall from exile, Seneca says nothing to suggest that the charges were a mistake. Rather, he implies that the emperor has shown extraordinary mercy in only exiling him rather than putting him to death. He does not say explicitly that he was guilty as charged and presents himself not as a sinner but as a victim of "Fortune." But the omission of any pleas of innocence tells its own tale. Seneca invites the (supposedly supremely merciful) emperor to treat him as innocent—without actually claiming to be so. "Let him judge my case however he wishes. Either let justice view it as a good cause, or mercy make it so; either one is equally a gift from him to me, whether he should know that I am innocent, or should wish me to be so" (*Polybius* 13.3). The possibility that Claudius might "know" Seneca to be innocent could be taken to imply that his innocence is a fact (and therefore knowable); but the phrasing also allows for the possibility that he was guilty.

Some scholars have argued that Seneca avoids protesting his innocence in order to protect himself from accusing Claudius of injustice. A complaint that the emperor had exiled an innocent man would make the emperor himself look bad—either deliberately unjust, or naively misled.[17] But the cagey usage of subordinate clauses and balanced alternatives makes it difficult to read this as an actual proclamation of innocence, as opposed to a careful avoidance of direct confession. Many of the arguments against the idea of his guilt are notably weak. Scholars cite the fact that Seneca was clearly a moderate person all his life, temperate in alcohol and food, and probably—despite a few slurs in the gossipy history of Dio—not particularly prone to sleeping around.[18] But of course not all adulterers are promiscuous. Seneca may not have made a lifelong habit of sleeping with dozens of married women (or, despite some scurrilous rumors, pretty boys); but that does not prove that he did not have at least one affair.

Political strategy and sexual desire are not incompatible possibilities. Adultery was the standard charge when a woman was involved in any kind of political misdemeanor, because, even within the elite classes of imperial Rome, in which women were increasingly prominent, they were still seen primarily as sexual objects rather than as political and moral agents. But there is likely to have been some truth in the common contemporary perception that political intrigues involving both men and women often also involved sex.[19]

Seneca and Julia Livilla were both charged with adultery in 41 CE and condemned. Julia Livilla was exiled first, to a different location from

Seneca; Claudius ordered her death by starvation in late 41 or early 42
CE. In Seneca's case, there may have been quite a lot of debate about
sentencing before he was finally sent to Corsica, probably sometime in
42, when he would have been about forty-six years old. We are told that
Messalina pressed for the death penalty, but the emperor Claudius miti-
gated the sentence to relegation on the island of Corsica.

Among the Rocks of the Corsican Sea

The choice to punish miscreants by exiling them to islands had become
increasingly common during the reigns of Augustus and Tiberius.[20] One
might think that the reason for choosing this type of punishment would
be that an island, with its water all around, forms a natural high-security
jail. But actually islands were less secure than fortress towns; a coast is
much harder to guard than a hilltop. Emperors favored island exile for its
flexible symbolism. A ruler could modulate the expression of his rage by
his choice of geographical location for the exile. Relegation or exile to
an island sounded worse than being sent to a mainland area. He might
choose a far-distant island, for the worst kind of crime, or a nearby one,
for a less outrageous infraction. By these standards, Seneca's punishment
was relatively mild. He was relegated to a large, well-populated island
that is very near mainland Italy, just a short journey from Rome: the
voyage by sea from Rome to Olbia, the northern city of Corsica, would
have taken just two days.[21]

Relegation was a punishment with significantly different implications
under Roman law from "exile" proper.[22] Exile (*exilium*, or *deportatio*)
implied not merely banishment but also deprivation of civil rights and
often also confiscation of property and money. Relegation, on the other
hand, was usually simply a banishment from a particular place, which
might well prove temporary. It was therefore important for many exiled
Romans—including Ovid as well as Seneca—to insist on the fact that
they were relegated, not exiled. Conceptually and perhaps legally, it was
easier to return from relegation than from exile. But in Seneca's case, relegation may well have included some confiscation of property, and
Seneca likely had half his property confiscated as part of his punishment
for adultery.[23]

In theory, Seneca's attitude toward exile was an entirely positive one.[24]
In his *Consolation to Marcia*, composed before the time of his own exile,
he treats exile as one of the usual list of disasters that may befall a

person—along with other disasters like shipwreck and fire and imprisonment and slavery—which must all be treated with equanimity by the wise person. Similarly, in his works composed after the time of exile, the experience of being made to leave one's homeland is treated as just something one ought to be able to get along with, and indeed, an opportunity to display one's manly virtue.[25] Seneca assures Lucilius in the Epistles that exile is to him, as a good Stoic, of no real importance—it is an indifferent thing, incommensurable with the true value of virtue: "I count as 'indifferent,' that is, neither good nor bad, these things: disease, pain, poverty, exile, death" (82.10). Seneca wrote frequently in praise of the fortitude in exile of Rutilius Rufus, who was banished by political enemies in 92 BCE, during the time of Sulla, and ended up on the island of Mytilene. Rutilius Rufus rejected any suggestion that he ought to be comforted by the possibility of returning home from exile: "'I'd rather have my country blush at my exile than regret my return.' It's not really exile, if nobody is less ashamed of it than the banished man himself" (De Ben. 6.37.2). Rutulius, Seneca says admiringly, "welcomed his exile with open arms" (Epistle 79). He insists, too, that exile can be a small price to pay, to show one's gratitude to friends: "if you want to pay back a favor, you must be willing to go into exile," he insists (Epistle 81)—a line that resonates with his own experience, since his involvement with Julia Livilla and her family had been essential for advancing his career. The reason to have a friend at all, he declares in an earlier letter, is so that one can help them and suffer for them: he makes a friend "in order to have somebody to die for, or in order to have someone for whom to go into exile" (Epistle 9).

One might expect that Seneca in his philosophical role might have been able to see exile as a positively helpful thing—a preferable rather than nonpreferable "indifferent." He could have responded to his own exile as the idealized character "Seneca" does, in the drama *Octavia* that was composed after his death. Lamenting his current constraints under the tyrannical rule of Nero, this "Seneca" cries,

It would have been better to stay hidden, far from the troubles caused by envy,
Far distant, among the rocks of the Corsican sea,
Where my mind was free and under its own control,
And always had the time for my studies.

(*Octavia* 381–384)

Seneca was in exile for eight years. We do not know exactly how he spent these years. Much of his time must have been spent writing and studying philosophy; it is at least possible that some of his tragedies were composed in exile, and probably part of his treatise *On Anger*, to which we shall return later in this chapter. We can be sure of two works he composed in exile, which are designed to appeal against his condition. These are the *Consolation to Polybius* and the *Consolation to Helvia*, his mother. They are very different in tone and content, but both are clearly designed to increase the author's chances of getting back home. Neither of these "consolations" is primarily—or even partly—designed to cheer up the supposed addressee, and indeed, from that point of view they must be regarded as abject failures. But both are highly successful in displaying Seneca's virtuosic command of rhetorical idiom and in making the best possible case for his recall from Corsica.

The *Consolation to Helvia* is a highly original twist on the genre of the consolation essay. The conventional occasion for a consolation was to address a bereaved person on the death of a loved one—who is usually, of course, somebody other than the author himself. But Seneca tries to console his mother for the loss of himself. In doing so, he splits himself in two. On the one hand, he is the strong philosophical comforter, the one who has the power to comfort his grieving mother in her time of need. On the other, he is suffering exile—something, the treatise implies, equivalent to death. He acknowledges that he is creating a new twist on the genre: "although I unrolled all the works that the most famous writers composed for repressing and controlling sorrow, I never found an example of anyone who offered consolation to his family when he himself was the object of their grief" (1.2). The *Consolation to Helvia* displays Seneca's astonishing rhetorical ingenuity.

His double role also allows Seneca to have it both ways: he can present himself as both exceptionally strong in the face of suffering and also suffering in terrible conditions—without coming across as a whiner. He insists on the truth of Stoic truisms, such as the idea that we make our own happiness, and that supposedly "bad" fortune is not bad, for the wise person (4.3–5.1; 6.1). Exile, too, is only a change of place, an indifferent thing; if we look at it the right way, he declares, exile is merely a change of place. But he emphasizes the deprivations he is suffering on the island, while at the same time presenting himself as somebody entirely capable of rising above such merely material forms of suffering. He vividly evokes the pointless luxuries of which an exile is deprived in ways that make clear their pointlessness, and he also makes clear his own strength of mind in his ability to see how little such things matter:

> If [a person] longs for furniture shining with golden vases, silver plate stamped with the names of old master craftsmen, bronze which the insane fashion of a clique has made expensive, enough slaves to make even an enormous house feel cramped, animals whose bodies are deliberately fattened up, and precious stones from all over the world: let him collect those things all he likes—he'll never satisfy his insatiable mind, any more than any amount of drink can quench a desire that does not come from need, but from the heat of one's own burning heart. You see, that's not thirst: it's disease.
>
> (*To Helvia* 11.3)

He goes on to declare that "it is the mind that makes a person rich."

The notion that Seneca's mother needed to be consoled for her son's terrible sufferings suggests that the son was, indeed, suffering, at least in a nonphilosophical sense. He describes the natural environment of Corsica as a "barren and thorny rock" (*To Helvia* 7.9) and juxtaposes it with Sciathus, Seriphus, and Gyarus, all four being "wildernesses, the most rugged of islands" (6.4). He asks, "What other rock is so barren or so precipitous on every side? What place is more infertile for food? Who is more uncultured than the island's inhabitants? What more craggy than the geography of this place? What land has worse weather?" (6.5). The idea that Seneca's time of exile was spent in an extraordinarily harsh environment is echoed by an epigram ascribed to him but probably written by a later author, inspired by various passages from *To Helvia*. The poet inveighs against the island, claiming,

> *Corsica is a barbarian island, enclosed by precipitous cliffs,*
> *awful, enormous, surrounded on all sides by emptiness.*
> *The autumn there brings forth no fruit, the summer brings no harvest,*
> *white winter does not bring the olive, gift of Athena.*
> *No spring is joyful with its birth of rain,*
> *no grasses grow on that unlucky soil.*
> *No bread, no draught of water, no last fire for cremation;*
> *Here there are only two things: an exile and his place of banishment.*[26]

Another similar epigram reads:

> *Corsica is horrible, when summer first grows hot,*
> *And even more brutal when the wild Dogstar shows its face.*
> *Spare those suffering relegation here—that is, the dead.*
> *May your earth lie light upon the ashes of the living![27]*

The poem picks up the implication of the *Helvia* that being exiled to Corsica is more or less the same as being dead. Modern Corsicans tend to resent Seneca, understandably enough, for presenting their pleasant island in this unattractive way: there is a local legend that he had an affair with a native girl, who then scourged him with nettles, and the place on the island where he is said to have lived is still surrounded by nettles (despite being now declared a Historic French Monument) (Fig. 2.5).[28]

But Seneca's negative depiction of his material conditions on the island is largely fictional. In the same passage where he complains of Corsica as a barren rock inhabited only by barbarians, he also notes that many people, including Romans, have come to the place of their own accord. Corsica was actually the location of a vibrant Roman colony,

Figure 2.5 Seneca spent eight years exiled on Corsica, living in this tower. Despite his negative depiction, the island actually had a good climate and a flourishing community of Roman expatriates.

including plenty of elite, well-educated gentlemen. He may even have been able to bring friends and family with him—probably including his older brother, Novatus, and several other friends. It is likely that his wife was also with him.

He certainly had slaves to care for him, even in exile. As he himself acknowledges, an exile like himself is allowed to have more slaves than the great writers and philosophers of old: "It is well known that Homer had one slave, Plato had three, and that Zeno, who first taught the stern and masculine doctrine of the Stoics, had none." Life with friends and family, and at minimum four or five slaves, does not really seem like solitary confinement. Moreover, the material conditions were not nearly as bad as Seneca makes out. Corsica was just across a short strip of sea from Rome and had more or less the same mild climate as the capital; the complaints about the weather are entirely bogus (7.1). Far from being barren, the whole island was overgrown with trees: Pliny ranks Corsica's fir trees as the best in the world, and Diodorus tells us that the whole island had excellent harbors.[29]

There are two main reasons for Seneca's misleading picture of his life on Corsica. The first is that he is modeling his own exile on the most famous earlier Roman writer to suffer exile and to write home to Rome describing his situation: the poet Ovid.[30] Ovid was exiled by the emperor Augustus in 8 CE for what he himself terms "a poem and a mistake." He had apparently been involved in the adulterous affair of the emperor's daughter, Julia (he says he saw something he should not have seen), and he also shocked the emperor with his poem giving advice on the best seduction techniques (the *Ars Amatoria*). Ovid was exiled to a much more distant and genuinely barren and harsh place than Corsica: to Tomis, on the Black Sea. The ways that Seneca describes Corsica are clearly modeled on Ovid's depictions of Tomis; they fit the latter but not the former. Tomis really was cold, bleak, barren, and distant from Rome and had almost no inhabitants who could speak Latin other than Ovid himself. Corsica was very near Rome, was full of Roman colonists speaking Latin, and had a nice climate and a lush, fertile landscape; but Seneca writes about it as if it were exactly the same as Ovid's Tomis. Seneca is careful never to mention Ovid by name, and he avoids associating himself too closely with the bad-boy poet, who was never recalled from exile despite his many pleas. But Seneca is also keen to align himself subliminally with a poet whose work he knew well and much admired.

The second reason for the literary deception is that Seneca is keen to emphasize his suffering. If he presented himself as perfectly happy in exile, his chances of ever being recalled back to Rome would not be improved. Seneca presents himself as bravely rising above the assaults of Fortune, thanks to his common sense and his philosophical mind. He does not suggest that he actually has little to complain about at all—which would have been a much more truthful claim. The rhetorical device of putting the grief for his own exile into the mouth of his addressee, his mother, makes it possible for him to avoid explicit complaining, while also constantly implying that his own pain is an established fact. "I tell you clearly that I am not miserable: I will add, to comfort you even more, that it is not possible for me to be made miserable" (*To Helvia* 5). The insistence that he is not miserable, which Seneca makes again and again in the *Helvia*, is a way of implying, again and again, that he is experiencing troubles that would break a weaker man—a very useful fiction.

The second of the consolations from exile, the *Consolation to Polybius*, is addressed to a favorite in the court of Claudius, his beloved freedman advisor who worked as his private secretary. It was composed after Seneca had been in exile for about two years, around 43 or 44 CE. This text has often been seen as one of the major embarrassments of Seneca's corpus in that it includes some abject flattery both of Claudius himself and of Polybius.[31] Dio mentions a letter sent from Corsica, cringing to Messalina and the freedmen of Claudius. He reports that, "Seneca was latterly so ashamed of it that he suppressed it."[32] There has been a lot of scholarly ink spilled over whether this "letter" is identical with our text of the *Consolation to Polybius*; it seems most likely that it is. If so, Seneca clearly did not suppress it effectively, although it is not hard to see why he might have tried.

Polybius' brother had died, and Seneca responds with an essay invoking the usual tropes of consolation literature. But he intersperses them with complaints about his own situation, stuck in exile on Corsica, and with some fairly revolting flattery to the emperor. In ways that will by now be familiar, he exaggerates the grimness and loneliness of his life on the island. He ends the letter by claiming that he (like Ovid…) is barely able to write Latin any more, since he is surrounded by a community of barbarians:

> I have written this letter as best I could, with a mind made weak and
> dull by long rusting. If you think it does not properly address your

intelligence or is unsuitable for curing your grief, think about how a person who is gripped by his own troubles cannot have time to comfort others, and how difficult it is to gather Latin words fluently, when one is surrounded by the wild noise of barbarian yelling—which is annoying even to the more human of the barbarians themselves.

(18.9)

Seneca mixes up the flattery with the consolation by suggesting that Polybius will surely recover from his grief immediately if only he turns his attention to the wonderful emperor whom he has the good fortune to serve. He prays that Claudius may rid the sick world of troubles caused by his mad predecessor, Caligula (12.4–5), and insists that Claudius has already shown mercy to himself by remitting his sentence to exile rather than death. He thanks his stars that he lives under an emperor who makes the lives even of exiles more peaceable than princes under Caligula—a claim that rather undercuts his description of the awfulness of life on Corsica.

It is difficult to decide how harshly we should judge Seneca for the more unfortunate passages in the *Polybius*. There are moments where Seneca seems to allow a subversive interpretation of his most abject flattery of the emperor. He urges Polybius not to begrudge his brother the opportunity to be, in death, at last free, peaceful, safe, and tranquil (9.7). The obvious implication is that everybody else—all elite Roman men living under the one-man rule of an emperor, however benevolent he may been—are never at rest, free, safe, or without terror. Moreover, the genre of the begging letter is always a difficult one to manage: too little distortion of the truth, and the document will not do its work in buttering up the recipient, but too much, and the recipient may feel mistrustful. The *Consolation to Polybius* obviously did not work; Seneca was to remain on Corsica for another six years after writing it.

The difficult question is not why Seneca stooped to flatter the emperor in order to try to be recalled from Corsica but rather why he wanted to leave the island at all. As we have seen, life on Corsica was probably not at all bad; Seneca could have lived out his life there in quasi-solitude, writing and studying, accompanied by just a small household and a few friends. The *Consolation to Polybius* can be seen in retrospect as a plea by an antelope, begging the lion to let him back inside his den. The fact that Seneca was so very eager to rejoin the social center of Rome can be seen as a mark of his unstoppable ambition—or, to put it another way, of his need to be at the center of things, his desire to exert benign influence on those in power, and his yearning to participate in a large social circle of friends, admirers, colleagues, students, patrons, and dependents.

If political appeals failed, he had philosophy to fall back on: a philosophy that always offered the promise of autonomy, masculinity, and total control over life, despite any of the assaults of fortune. The thought of the constancy of the wise man must have comforted Seneca in these years of exile. It is possible that it was during this period (though it may have been later) that he composed two of his most influential prose works on the topic of tranquility in adversity: *On Providence* and *On the Constancy of the Wise Man*. The first is addressed to his friend Lucilius (later the addressee of the Moral Letters) and is concerned with the classic question: "Why, if Providence rules the world, it still happens that many bad things happen to good men?" (*Providence* 1.1). Seneca's answer is that God is like a good, strict father (similar to Seneca's own father) rather than like an indulgent mother. God makes us stronger by testing us. For this reason, no bad thing can ever happen to a good man. Every apparent misfortune is an opportunity to be tested, to become stronger, and to know oneself the better: "Nobody learns what he can do, except by trying" (3.4.4). A good man may be exiled, reduced to poverty, and have his wife or children die—all events that Seneca suffered; but that good man "can be called miserable, but can never be so" (*Providence* 3.1). The real danger to a person's happiness comes not from danger and adversity but from excesses of luxury: "A man who has always had glazed windows to protect him from the draught, whose feet have been kept warm by hot compresses which are regularly changed, whose dining halls are warmed by hot air under the floors and moving round the walls: that man will be in danger if he's brushed by a gentle breeze" (*Providence* 4.10). The person who suffers the assaults of fortune (including exile and loneliness) can comfort himself with the thought that he is never really away from the center, and never really alone, while he can conform his will with that of the universe: "it is a great comfort, to be swept away along with the whole world" (5.8).

The essay *On the Constancy of the Wise Man* deals with a comparable subject and is addressed to another great friend of Seneca's, Serenus Annaeus (possibly a relative, who later became a powerful man in Rome—probably thanks to Seneca's intervention). The name "Serenus" means "Calm," and his name may be partly why Seneca chose this friend as his addressee: the piece focuses on the way that a wise man can remain both calm and steadfast in the midst of any misfortune. He will be unchanging, "constant," regardless of what happens all around him. Seneca insists particularly on the idea that Stoicism is the most masculine response to misfortune: the Stoics, unlike other philosophers, set us on the "manly" path to virtue, or rather, to *virtus*, which literally means "manliness." He also insists—borrowing from Cynicism as well as Stoicism— that the wise man can lose nothing, even in the worst apparent misfortune: "his only possession is virtue, and he can never be robbed of that" (5.5). The man who pays no heed either to hope or fear will never be disappointed and will never suffer loss (9.3). Moreover, such a man is, even if he finds himself in exile, serving the good of the whole political realm of which he is a part: if you maintain the place of virtue, you are always in "the place of a man," regardless of your apparent social position. And this in itself is political service: "it belongs to the Republic of Humanity, that there should be something unconquered, somebody against Fortune can do nothing" (19.4).

Seneca rebuffs all possible insults to his own status in the *On Constancy* by insisting that the truly wise person cannot be harmed by any such thing. Offering a rare glimpse of his actual physical appearance, he insists that he cannot be hurt even by mockery of the "baldness of my head, the weakness of my eyes, the thinness of my legs, and my height. Where's the insult, in hearing what is obvious?" (16.4). Seneca was obviously not a physically impressive specimen, but he manages to turn even that to his own (rhetorical, literary, and philosophical) advantage.

Where Anger Leads

The various writings Seneca composed during his time on Corsica may not have had the immediate effect of securing his recall, but they did have some effect, collectively, on the opinions of the elite public, back in Rome. They allowed him to continue to accrue honor and admiration for his rhetorical skills and learning, thus laying the groundwork for his appointment as the tutor of Nero. Just as importantly, Seneca's writing during his time of exile allowed him to work through the feelings of grief, boredom, powerlessness, and—perhaps especially—rage that must have felt at times overwhelming in his forced exclusion from the world of the capital.

Anger is a topic about which Seneca writes particularly well. His treatise *On Anger* cannot be dated with certainty.[33] It is possible that *On
Anger* was composed immediately before Seneca's exile, but far more
probable that he wrote it after he was sentenced. Most likely the first two
books were composed in exile on Corsica and the third soon after his
return to Rome, since this last book seems to be later and was clearly
written in the city.[34]

Presumably the topic of anger had a particular personal resonance for
Seneca. It was a useful subject for him to meditate on during his time of
relegation. He was surely conscious of an impulse to feel incandescent
anger at being accused, condemned, having his property taken, and being
sent away from Rome. Perhaps he was enraged at being punished for a
crime he did not commit. Even if he was guilty of plotting or adultery
or both, such public punishment, humiliation, and deprivation must
have been deeply irritating. But in his written discussion of anger, Seneca
deals with his emotions in an entirely sidelong, displaced fashion. The
essay has nothing that deals in any specific way with the author's own
experiences of anger and its cures.

Whose anger, then, is at stake in the treatise? The addressee is Seneca's
older brother, Novatus, who has supposedly urged Seneca to write about
how anger may be calmed. Perhaps Novatus saw Seneca himself as a particularly grumpy person, or perhaps Novatus himself was prone to fits of
rage that disrupted his general peace of mind. More likely, one of Seneca's aims was to persuade the emperor to stop being angry with him
and bring him back to Rome. The essay focuses on the anger of those in
positions of power over others. The piece begins with the hyperbolic
claim that "no plague has been more costly to the human race." Anger,
we are assured, is the root cause of bloodshed, poison, arson, slavery, cities
cast down from their foundations, violent death and assassination, and
war in which "whole peoples have been condemned to death in common
ruin" (1.2.3). This analysis gives huge weight to the causal power of
human emotions and little to economics or political ideology. Seneca
sidesteps the big political picture in favor of a limited focus on the individual. We can associate this with the position of the Roman elite of the
time, deprived of real political power, but we can also trace it fairly directly to Seneca's own position, as the victim of a single man's anger.

But it would be reductive to see *On Anger* as solely designed to persuade the emperor for pardon, or to impress the general public and

increase the author's popularity at Rome. A more satisfying approach is to see it as an address to all those who are tempted to submit to their excessive emotions—that is, to all of us. Seneca here, as very often in his writing, is able to transcend the details of his specific situation (exiled on Corsica) and take a view from above, addressing the human condition. The topic of the "passions," or negative, excessive kinds of emotions, was important for all the various schools of Roman philosophy, as for their earlier models in Hellenistic philosophy; the Stoics were not the only ones interested in emotional disturbance. After Alexander the Great's annexation of Greece and the demise of the old Greek polis in the fourth century BCE—in which all elite male citizens had an active role to play in government—intellectual life became increasingly focused on the individual, and the ethical philosophy often became closely allied to what we would call psychology. Philosophers in the Hellenistic period had become interested in working out how a person might be able to achieve a consistently calm state of mind—the Greek word is *ataraxia,* or "untroubledness." The Stoics were distinctive in this context in the depth with which they investigated and catalogued the various ways in which a person might become troubled by false thoughts, which lead, according to the theory, to negative emotions, or "passions."[35]

The Stoics categorized the bad kinds of emotion into four general types: pleasure, pain, desire, and fear. Excessive emotions of these types are, they thought, the most important reason why people may fail to achieve appropriate spiritual tranquility. It is important to remember here that the Stoics did not believe that all feelings of every kind are bad: feelings that line up perfectly with reality, defined in Stoic terms, are a positive good. For example, the truly wise person will feel "joy" at her awareness of her own goodness.[36] But these feelings are sharply distinguished from the "passions," which are emotions based on false ideas about reality and are characterized by their capacity to overwhelm right thinking. So, for example, a person who is anxious through fear of death has a belief that death really is a bad thing rather than merely indifferent (albeit sometimes nonpreferable).

Seneca suggests that anger is the worst of all such passions because it is so utterly aggressive and destructive: "All other emotions have an element of peace and quiet. Anger is entirely violent, and exists in a rush of pain, raging in an almost inhuman desire for weapons, blood and punishment. Anger does not care about itself, as long as it harms somebody

else" (1.1). Seneca defines anger, following an older philosophical tradition, as "the desire to avenge an injury," including injuries which the
person believes has been, or will be, imposed: "anger is aroused by the
direct impression of an injury" (2.1.3). He argues, in classic Stoic fashion,
that all anger is wrong, an enemy to inner peace, and useless for any good
political or social purpose, even government or war. There may be times
when a soldier has to fight and kill, or when a ruler has to pass sentence
on a criminal, but these things should always be done according to the
dictates of reason, never at the whims of hot passion. Law, not anger,
should be the primary weapon of the state.

Seneca's focus on the leader's responsibility to control his emotion has
a clear political resonance at this period of the early Roman empire.
Rome had, after all, only recently made the transition from a republic—
a constitution in which power was shared between multiple people in
particular ruling groups, including the tribunate, the military, and the
Senate—to a principate, in which ultimate power lay with the emperor.
Political and cultural habits of mind had not caught up with the new
reality.[37] The members of the Roman elite were still, culturally and ideologically, attuned to thinking of themselves as members of a truly governing class, even though, in terms of real political power, they were
subject to the emperor. Moreover, the power of the emperor himself, to
a frightening degree, actually depended on maintaining the goodwill of
the army. Law was no longer the final call of appeal, as it had been under
the republic; the emperor, with the backing of the army, had the final
word. This made it more important than ever that the emperor should
be able to negotiate between the twin poles of anger and clemency.
Seneca cites with horror and condemnation Caligula's dreadful words:
"Let them hate, as long as they fear": *oderint, dum timeant*.[38] His central
point is that this degree of aggression goes beyond appropriate expression of authority into the merely monstrous.

But it is not only emperors who need to beware of being angry. The
essay deals with that central concern of Seneca's writings: how to achieve
a position of safety in an uncertain world and how to get genuine power,
not merely false promises of control that prove, in the end, illusory. Anger
is, for Seneca, tempting to everybody because it may seem akin to genuine goods, such as justice and a safe position. But like all the other passions that tempt one to go against Virtue, anger is a false friend: "Only
Virtue is lofty and sublime; nothing is great that is not also calm" (1.20.4).

One of Seneca's most original contributions to the Stoic study of the emotions is his emphasis on involuntary feelings.[39] This allows him to give a much more nuanced, and more plausible, account both of anger and of the other "passions." Seneca insists that there is a distinction to be made between "impulses" (*motus*), which are preconscious responses and do not require the assent of the mind, and real "passions" (*affectus*), which necessarily imply a particular set of beliefs.[40] If somebody pours a bucket of cold water on your head, you will shiver; if somebody says bad words, you may blush; if you watch a play, you may feel anger, pity, and grief for the characters, despite the fact that you know they are not real. But for Seneca, none of these are real "passions," unless you then give your consent to a (false) belief about them.

Seneca's metaphors in his discussion of anger constantly come back to medicine. Being angry is incompatible with human happiness and is therefore like a sickness, to be cured by philosophy. If we are healthy, in moral and psychological ways, we will be happy: "being joyful is the distinctive and natural characteristic of virtue" (2.6.2). Conversely, the wise person will not be enraged when he sees other people behaving idiotically. If he started being angry every time he saw other people behaving badly, it would never end (2.7–8), so the wise person sees himself as a doctor, surrounded by the sick (2.10.7). He feels pity and a desire to cure their disease, but he is never angry, because he knows he is never injured by their behavior.

The treatise is particularly interesting in its depiction of the formation, development, and training of behavior. Seneca acknowledges that some people will think that it is too difficult to eliminate anger altogether rather than simply control its expression. But he insists that in fact, the Stoic way is easier and more practical than the alternatives, since it is "easier to exclude dangerous things altogether, than to moderate them" (1.7.2). Other critics may suggest that in some circumstances, it is right to be angry—in order, for instance, to exact righteous punishment against somebody who really has done wrong. But the best thing, Seneca suggests, is to pretend to be angry rather than really feel angry: a theatrical performance can be controlled; real anger cannot (2.16.ff).

Seneca discusses the proper way to educate not only oneself but also children and young men into the correct approach to anger. Presumably Agrippina, mother to Nero, read these early books of *On Anger;* perhaps they were part of her reason for appointing Seneca as the tutor to the

young prince. *On Anger* is suggestive about Seneca's own commitment
to education, especially education of the young. He argues that "education calls for the greatest attentiveness, and attention in this time will also
prove most useful; it is easy to train minds that are still young, but difficult to curb faults which have grown up with us" (2.18.2).

Seneca is largely very pessimistic about the overwhelming, corrupting, debilitating, and brutalizing effects of anger (and other negative
emotions) on human life. But he is also highly optimistic about the possibility that one can, with the appropriate kinds of training, make progress toward eliminating the passions altogether. We have only to look at
ourselves when angry to see that rage is a hideous disease, which any
person who wants to be healthy and happy must expunge entirely.

The largely optimistic depiction of the passions as something readily
curable, in Seneca's prose philosophical works, contrasts sharply with how
he represents violent emotion in the tragedies. We do not know when
Seneca composed the eight tragedies that have come down to us under
his name: *Oedipus, Agamemnon, Phaedra, Medea, Hercules Furens, Trojan
Women, Thyestes,* and the unfinished *Phoenissae.*[41] But it is likely that they
were written over many years; internal stylistic considerations suggest
that some are relatively early and may have been composed under Caligula or during the years of exile, while others (*Thyestes* and probably
Phoenissae) could be Neronian. The relationship of the tragedies to the
philosophical works has long been controversial. One possible approach
is to argue that the tragedies show us what happens to people who fail to
control their passions: they are Stoic morality plays depicting the downfall
of non-Stoics who become overwhelmed by anger, lust, and fear.

But this seems unfaithful to the experience of reading or watching
the plays, since the depiction of passion seems so vigorous, so vivid, and
indeed, so pleasurable. This is not to say that the tragedies have nothing
to do with Seneca's philosophical meditations on passion and its negative
effects, but rather, that they are more like dark mirror-images of the
prose than illustrations of it. Writing tragedy allowed Seneca to imagine
himself into the minds and voices of characters who are mad with un-
satisfiable desire, and to relish their bombastic rhetoric.

Seneca probably spent some of his time in exile composing the first
books of *On Anger,* but he may well also have spent time composing
such plays as the *Medea.* Based on the same myth as Euripides' play by
the same name, the drama shows us a Jason who has already retrieved the

Golden Fleece, with the help of the native princess of Colchis, Medea. They have been married for several years and have children together; now they are living in Corinth, and Jason plans to marry again, to the Corinthian princess Creusa, in an attempt to consolidate his position in Greece. Medea is, understandably enough, enraged by this plan, and, like the angry person of the treatise, longs to take revenge. She devises a plan to kill first the princess, with a poisoned dress and crown, and then her own children by Jason. After committing the murders, she flies off in a chariot drawn by dragons, conveniently provided by her grandfather, the Sun God Helios.

Medea's position, as an infuriated exile from her homeland, committed both to revenge on her enemy and to maintaining her own dignity and autonomy, is like a dark echo of Seneca's own life in exile. Her rage is brilliantly imagined, and at times she seems almost to be quoting from Seneca's own treatise on anger, as when she declares how difficult it is for Creon, king of Corinth, to cure his anger:

> *I learnt in my own royal house how hard*
> *it is to turn a mind from rage when it is roused,*
> *and how a person who has touched proud scepters*
> *believes a king should go where anger leads.*

(Medea 203–206)

Medea is highly conscious of how rage can delude a person's mind and of how particularly corrupting anger can be for those in positions of authority. Other lines anticipate Seneca's prose meditations on the obligation of those in power to be merciful (*De Clementia*):

> *This is the great and glorious right of kings,*
> *the thing that time can never snatch away—*
> *to help the helpless and protect the suppliant,*
> *sheltered in a loyal hearth.*

(222–225)

Medea is parallel to the emperors whom Seneca advised, but also to Seneca himself. She accuses Jason of making her an exile, not once but twice over: "We are fleeing, Jason, fleeing! Changing place is nothing new; / Only the cause is different" (447–448).

The real appeal of the play, like many of these tragedies, lies in the astounding vigor with which Seneca's Medea articulates her own autonomy, her selfhood, and her power to continue as herself, regardless of any external circumstances. Declaring her intention to surpass all her earlier crimes (such as killing her brother) in her new plan to kill her own children, she presents herself as having matured into her own (mythic and heroic) identity, such that now, at last, she is worthy of the name "Medea":

> *my pain was only practicing*
> *in those earlier things I did. What deed of daring*
> *could young hands do, or rage from just a girl?*
> *Now I am Medea.*

(907–910)

Seneca's Medea is matured by suffering into the capacity for actions that are truly worthy of her adult self. She has eliminated her own family and old friends, and in doing so has cast off her past, weaker self: now she can live up to her full potential, as granddaughter of the Sun—a figure whose ubiquity and power are reminiscent of the emperor. There are some striking resonances here with Seneca's own experiences in this period.

Seneca's tragic heroes, including Medea, have a desperate need for an audience. Medea, having killed one of the children, tries to repress her grief for the boy's death, but then notes the fact that she has wasted the opportunity, because Jason was not there to watch:

> *Poor me! What have I done?—Even if I regret it,*
> *I've done it, and I feel a creeping joy, against my will.*
> *And look! It's growing! This is all I needed:*
> *that Jason should be watching. Till now, I think I've achieved nothing;*
> *the crimes I did without him were a waste.*

(986–990)

Perhaps an intense need to have people watching him was one of the author's strongest motivations for leaving Corsica—however dangerous it might be to ascend into the dragon chariot.

We, have, frustratingly, no evidence about the actual audiences for these plays, nor for their performance conditions. Some have argued that they were never meant for the theater at all, but recently the scholarly pendulum has swung the other way, and it is now fairly generally agreed that Seneca probably did write for the stage. Perhaps there were performances of these dramas at Rome while their author was still in exile; if so, this might help explain how his name remained so well known in the big city. In fact Seneca seems to have become increasingly famous during the eight years in which he was absent from Rome.

THE RECALL FROM EXILE

I despised death and came back.[42]

In 48 AD, Messalina, the wife of Claudius who had engineered Seneca's exile, went too far: she got married, to consul-elect, Gaius Silius, while Claudius was away.[43] Claudius, we are told, colluded with this by giving her papers annulling the marriage before he went away. The ancient sources predictably present Messalina as a nymphomaniac, but modern historians tend to see her as a canny and ambitious political schemer, who hoped, with the help of her male friends, to exploit Claudius' absence to stage a coup and get total control of the city, and perhaps the empire. Unfortunately for her, Claudius turned out to be smarter than he looked and got wind of the plot: on his return, he put Silius to death. The death of Messalina was engineered by Narcissus, the favorite freedman of the emperor, without his having to sign consent forms. Apparently Narcissus feared that Claudius might not go through with it. Messalina left behind her a son, Britannicus, who was only seven at the time of his mother's death.

In the absence of Messalina, Claudius was in need of a new wife—a necessity for any emperor, since it was the way to secure the succession and also allowed him to shore up his dynastic credentials by consolidating with another branch of the Julio-Claudian family. He chose the ambitious Agrippina ("Agrippina the Younger"), his own niece and sister of Seneca's dead friend, Julia Livilla. Tacitus reports that they were sleeping together before marriage and that Agrippina's seductive ways, along with the ancestry of her son, were the deciding factors in Claudius' choice of her over the other candidates, but they put off the wedding, fearing the public reaction at the marriage of an uncle and his niece (*Annals* 12.5.1). Agrippina made good use of the time to secure another power marriage: she engaged her teenage son to Octavia, daughter of Claudius. Claudius and Agrippina married in 49 CE.

This turned out to be good news for Seneca, although of course he could not have predicted the turn of events. Tacitus tells us that

> Agrippina, so that she might not only be known for her wicked crimes, begged for Seneca's banishment to be pardoned, and at the same time for him to get the praetorship. She thought it would be popular with the public because his intellectual accomplishments were famous, and she wanted to have her son Domitius [the future Nero] trained in his childhood under that kind of tutor. She also hoped that both she and Nero could make use of his advice for the purpose of gaining power. The reason for the choice was that Seneca was believed to be loyal to Agrippina because he remembered how she had benefited him, and hostile to Claudius, bearing a grudge against him.
>
> (*Ann.* 12.8)

Tacitus shows a characteristic sense of irony in this passage. He presumably knew Seneca's own work fairly well and hints at hypocrisy: Seneca, who defined anger as the desire for vengeance at an injury (*iniuria*) and argued that it must be eliminated, was himself motivated by rage against Claudius when he fell in with Agrippina's plans. There is another veiled gibe implied by the use of the word "benefit" or "favor," *beneficium*, since as we shall see, Seneca was to write a treatise on "favors," dwelling at length on the importance of gratitude—while himself, at least in Tacitus' narrative, showing absolutely no loyalty to his benefactress, Agrippina. He was "believed" to be loyal, Tacitus tells us, but he turned out not to be so.

We can only speculate about what Seneca's feelings might have been when he got the news that his long years of exile were over. Did he hesitate about the decision to return to Rome? Did he consider turning Agrippina's offer down? One ancient suggests that Seneca's real hope was not to go back to Rome but to be allowed to move to Athens, to live out his life among the philosophical schools there, studying and teaching—a choice that was no longer possible, ever, once he accepted Agrippina's generosity.[44] The trap closed in. Seneca—who had, after all, lived through the reign of Caligula and been exiled by Claudius already—could have had few illusions about how free or how safe his environment would be as a member of the imperial court. The recall must have seemed, from the start, fraught with terrible danger. Perhaps part of the reason Seneca went along was that Agrippina had made him an offer he could not refuse, or at least not without incurring even more imperial disfavor. If things were not that bad on Corsica, they could always become much worse. He could have been exiled to an island that was actually, rather than fictionally, barren and deserted. Or the emperor could have been goaded by his wife to order the philosopher's death. The choice to return was perhaps hardly a choice at all. In the year 50 CE, when Nero was twelve, he was adopted as son by Claudius, and at the same time (so Suetonius tells us) Seneca became his official tutor.

But presumably Seneca felt hope as well as dread in returning to Rome. Like his own Medea, he needed an audience, a set of address-ees if not friends. He needed the praise, love, admiration, and sense of achievement that could only come with a position in the big city of Rome, not in the backwater of Corsica. He needed a new challenge, new labors to take on. Perhaps, too, his fear and his ambition were less in tension than one might imagine: only once you reach the end can you be sure nothing else can happen. The final motive that must have played some part in his decision to return was a genuine desire to do good, by influencing for the better the person who might well become leader of the whole Roman empire. Like his own hero Hercules (the favorite mythical hero of the Stoics), he needed to have a sense of being useful, of benefiting humanity by engaging in society and destroying the mon-sters that threaten civilization. Seneca's old tutor, Attalus, had claimed to be a king because he was a Stoic Sage: Seneca could now hope to outdo his old teacher by converting to Stoic sage-hood a boy who would also become, in the real political world, an emperor. After spending much of his adult life abroad, first in Egypt, then Corsica, this man from the prov-inces was finally back in Rome, where he would remain for the rest of his life—for good or ill.

"VICES TEMPT YOU BY THE REWARDS THEY OFFER"*

Exile is better for you than a return like this.[1]

S eneca's play about the downfall of a victorious warrior king, the *Agamemnon*—in which, as in Aeschylus' version of the same myth, the title character is murdered in his bath—begins with the Ghost of Thyestes, who has been dragged back from the underworld to portend doom for his descendants. He declares,

> *On this throne sit*
> *those who bear in their hands the royal scepters.*
> *Here is their council-chamber, here is where they feast.*
> *I wish I could turn back! Would it not be better*
> *to live by the grim, sad waters [of the underworld] . . . ?*

> (*Agamemnon* 9–13)[2]

The Ghost is reminded of the horrors he experienced in his own day, when he was forced to eat his own children. But he predicts that there is even worse to come: being back in Hell—a place of frustration rather than monstrosity—would surely be better. And yet he is compelled to glimpse this place of horror. Seneca himself likely had some of this sinking feeling when he returned from Corsica to the Rome from which he had been expelled and took up his position in the household

---

* Mercede te vitia sollicitant (Epistle 69.4)

of the emperor who had exiled him, along with his new wife Agrippina (sister of his now-dead, perhaps-erstwhile-lover, Julia Livilla) and Agrippina's son by the dead Tiberius: Nero. Suetonius reports a rumor that the night after Seneca began tutoring Nero, he had a terrible dream: he imagined that he was the tutor of Caligula (Suetonius, *Nero*, 7). An unreliable ancient source tells us, "Seneca quickly realized that Nero was born savage and cruel and tamed him, often saying to his close associates that that savage lion had only to taste human blood once for his inborn savagery to return."[3]

Perhaps Seneca hoped, in those early years, that he could turn things around. He also took over Nero's education, serving as his main tutor from the time the young prince was twelve years old, to the time of his accession at the age of seventeen (Fig. 3.1). We know little about the details of his pedagogical methods; perhaps he soon abandoned hope of improving his charge, but perhaps not. At the same time, as a praetor, he had administrative duties in government; he would have had opportunities to intervene in the active running of the court and probably also played a role in judging criminal prosecutions.

Figure 3.1 Seneca was hired by Agrippina to teach rhetoric to her young son Nero. The teenager may well have been a resistant student, as this depiction suggests.

Seneca was hired by Agrippina to teach Nero rhetoric, not philosophy: she considered philosophy a drawback for a future leader (Suetonius, *Nero,* 52). The notion that philosophy in general, and Stoicism in particular, was incompatible with practical politics was a major target of Seneca's writing during the next decade or two. But Agrippina clearly hoped that he would be able to take on a much more extensive advising role—not tutoring in the Stoic mode of expelling negative emotions and becoming a sage, but rather, political strategy and speechwriting, through which she could advance her own interests and those of her son, allowing Seneca himself some payback along the way.

Seneca trained the boy in the methods he had learned from his father and from his tutors of rhetoric at Rome, teaching him to give pretend legal speeches, as if in a court of law. The young student enjoyed the theatrical elements of rhetorical training: Nero thought of himself as a magnificent actor. But we are also told that Seneca limited Nero's reading in early oratory "to perpetuate his admiration for his teacher" (Suetonius, *Nero,* 52). This may or may not be true; it seems quite likely that Nero himself wished to focus on poetry rather than rhetoric. We get conflicting accounts of how good or bad Nero actually was as a poet. Seneca quotes one rather overwritten line of his, claiming it is "so cleverly written": "The moving necks of the Cytherean doves are shimmering" (*NQ* 1.5.6). Perhaps, as well as promoting his ward's creative writing, Seneca also acted out scenes from his own tragedies with the boy. Whether the fault lay with the teacher or the student, or both, the results were not promising: Nero did not make much progress in rhetoric. Seneca acted as Nero's speechwriter in later years, although all earlier emperors had been capable of composing their own speeches. Nero was resistant to teaching rather than lacking in all natural talent: he was an intelligent but willful boy, uninterested in buckling down to the rigors of either rhetoric or philosophy. We cannot tell how hard Seneca tried to counter these tendencies. Tacitus tells us that Nero focused on other pursuits, and Seneca could do little to keep his curriculum focused: he was a keen painter, actor, engraver, poet, singer, horseback rider, and charioteer (*Annals* 13.3.3).

Perhaps Seneca did not even wish to restrict these cultural pursuits. One clue to Seneca's attitudes toward moral training, for himself as well as for Nero, is suggested by the third book of *On Anger,* which was written during these years. Seneca insists on the importance of self-knowledge before any undertaking (3.7.2), an important message to send to the young Nero, and advises his readers to seek out the company of those with whom they can be their best selves (3.8). Hot-tempered people—and Seneca's ward would have fit the category—are advised to soothe themselves with poetry, history, and music (Fig. 3.2).

The most famous passage of this third book of *On Anger* is Seneca's fascinating account of his own practice of self-improvement, through daily, or rather nightly, sessions of self-examination. Seneca's discussions of the process of self-questioning have been seen as an essential step in the development of modern conceptions of selfhood and the will (or the "I") in that he is, far more—or at least more explicitly—than most previous ancient thinkers, preoccupied with self-fashioning. This passage is also, as we have seen, one of Seneca's few references to the existence of his wife—who is presented as remarkable only for her ability to fall silent in order for the husband to pursue his thoughts. There is no way to tell which wife this is.

> When the light has been taken away, and my wife, who has long been aware of my habit, is quiet, I examine my whole day, and I retrace my actions and my words. I hide nothing from myself; I skip nothing. Indeed, why should I be frightened of my mistakes, when I can tell myself, "See that you don't do that any more. I forgive you this time. In that argument you spoke too grumpily; in future, don't spend time with uneducated people. They've never learnt, so they don't want to learn. You scolded that man more freely than you should have, and as a result, you didn't fix him, you just made him annoyed. Next time, watch out not just for whether you're speaking the truth, but whether the person you're talking to is able to handle the truth. A good man likes being reproached; the worse a person is, the more irritable he is with one who corrects him."
>
> (*On Anger* 3.36.3–4)[4]

Seneca continues with more vivid evocations of the trials of daily life for the elite Roman man, such as rude conversation at a drunken dinner party or being awarded a less-than-honorable position in the seating arrangement: "Silly man! What difference does it make what part of the couch you lie on?"

From one point of view, Seneca's practice of daily self-examination can be seen as a precursor to meditative practices and the literature of self-scrutiny: Augustine's *Confessions,* or the monastic exercises of Ignatius

Figure 3.2 Seneca must have known he was doing something very dangerous in returning to Rome and putting his literary talents at the service of Agrippina and Nero. This medieval bust suggests the connection between Seneca's writing and his eventual death by showing his pen as the scalpel that cuts into his wrist.

Loyola, or in more modern times, diaries, memoirs, and the psychoanalytic couch. It is an attempt to recall times past in the present—that central concern of the work of Woolf, Proust, and Joyce. We may see his attention paid to the interior self as a prototype for the self-examinations of Montaigne or Descartes (both deeply influenced by Seneca). But Seneca's account of "self" examination is very different from any of these, because it is not really focused on an individual self at all. His account of his day slips from the self who is supposedly the subject of the analysis to gaze around at all the other people he has encountered in the course of his waking hours. In discussing, for instance, how he snapped at an "uneducated person," he does not then try to work out what made him snap; instead, he shifts to analyze why this kind of person might not be teachable, and therefore, why one ought to avoid such people. If this is the kind of moral training Seneca gave Nero, it is easy to see why the boy did not become strikingly self-aware or self-critical. For the teacher himself, this kind of nightly self-examination would have been a very useful tool for psychological resilience in the court of Nero, because it gave him a space in which he could meditate on his own strength, self-mastery and constant improvement, while also contemplating the hateful behavior and incurably bad character of everybody else around him.

Seneca clearly built up close alliances and friendships in court during these years. His most important ally was Sextus Afranius Burrus, the man chosen by Agrippina in 51 CE as head of the Praetorian Guard (the emperor's personal bodyguard). It was normal for the Guard to be led by two men, so the appointment of Burrus in sole command was a sign of Agrippina's trust in him and of her desire to keep all important posts in the hands of her own people. Seneca provided the intellectual and rhetorical structure for Agrippina's power base, while Burrus was in control of this crucial military position. Burrus was experienced both in military spheres (he had served in the army) and in the world of court intrigue, having served Augustus' widow Livia, then Tiberius and probably Caligula, before receiving his promotion under Claudius and Agrippina. Both Seneca and Burrus were clearly close to Agrippina herself during these years; she depended on them as advisors and agents of her growing power and that of her son.

When Nero was fourteen years old, in 41 CE, he took up the "toga of manhood" in a highly public ceremony (Tacitus, *Annals,* 12.41.1–3). Agrippina seized on the opportunity to increase her son's celebrity over that of Claudius' natural son, Britannicus. We are told that Nero rode through the town in triumphal clothing, Britannicus in the plain white toga of a young boy. Some expressed pity at this treatment of Britannicus, and Agrippina, claiming to be outraged at the implied insult to her own son, used the occasion as an excuse to get rid of all Britannicus' most loyal attendants. She persuaded Claudius (according to Tacitus) to exile or execute his best tutors and instead install guards chosen by herself. Britannicus had no supporters left, at least not close at hand.

A couple of years later, in 53 CE, when Nero was sixteen, the engagement to Octavia was fulfilled, and they got married. At this period, too, the young Nero began to show off the skills he had learned from Seneca in public speaking, developing fantastical speeches on behalf of particular communities, such as a colony that had been afflicted by fire and another that had had an earthquake (*Annals* 12.58.1–2).

As Britannicus approached his age of maturity, around fourteen, Claudius may well have begun to reconsider his favor to Nero at the expense of his natural son. Agrippina's grip on power was threatened. She had strong reason to ensure the death of her husband and the speedy accession to the throne of her son. Moreover, if Agrippina's power fell, so too would that of her circle, including Seneca and Burrus, both of whom were too closely associated with the Empress to be welcome members of a new regime. As good luck or quick action had it, in 54 CE Claudius died after eating a dish of his favorite mushrooms; rumor had it that Agrippina had had him poisoned.[5] It is possible, even likely, that Seneca and Burrus were complicit in the plan; but there is no way to be certain.

Whether or not she did actually kill her husband, Agrippina immediately seized the opportunities for advancing her son that were afforded by his stepfather's death. Nero later joked that mushrooms were indeed the "food of the gods," since they were the vehicle by which Claudius was deified (Suetonius, *Life of Nero*). Burrus and Seneca were essential agents in establishing the young heir on the throne as quickly as possible, precluding any possible challenge from the friends of Britannicus. Claudius' condition was unclear for a few desperate hours in the night of October 12, 54 CE. He vomited the dish of fatal mushrooms, and it was hoped by some, feared by others, that he might recover. But eventually—some said after Agrippina's personal doctor smeared his throat with poison, pretending to give him an emetic—he passed away.

It is possible, as Tacitus hints, that Seneca played an essential role in advising Agrippina over the course of the night's events. She acted carefully to make sure that there was no muddle over who should inherit the throne, making sure that Britannicus was detained in her arms: Tacitus tells us that she cuddled him, as if needing the comfort in her time of grief, and assured him that he looked just like his father—anything to keep him from leaving his room and seizing power. As soon as it was clear that Claudius was definitively dead, Burrus, accompanied by his full military guard of soldiers, flung open the palace gates and brought out Nero in triumph as the new emperor. "Some, it is said, hesitated, and looked round and asked where Britannicus was; then, when there was no one to lead a resistance, they yielded to what was offered them" (*Annals* 12.69.1–2). It was hard to argue with a government that had the army on its side.

Seneca and Burrus played key roles in advising Agrippina and Nero through the transition of power.[6] Burrus backed the new emperor with the sword, while Seneca did so with words. Immediately after Nero's accession, Seneca wrote a speech for the teenager to deliver to the Praetorian Guard, promising the soldiers that he would continue to support them with all the perks they had received from Claudius (Dio 61.3.1). Seneca also wrote a speech for the boy to deliver on the occasion of his adopted father's death. In Tacitus' account of the speech, it began with a fine, dignified tone: "As long as [Nero] went over the antiquity of [Claudius'] family, the consulates, and the triumphs of his ancestors, he was taken seriously by himself and others" (*Annals* 13.3). But then the speaker turned to discuss the subject of the famously foolish emperor's "prudence and wisdom," and things fell apart: "Nobody could restrain themselves from laughing—though the speech, being by Seneca, was just as elegantly-written as one would expect from that celebrity" (Tacitus, *Annals* 13.3) (Fig. 3.3). One may wonder whether Seneca really expected the audience to take this seriously: was the laughter a mark of how badly he had judged the probable mood of the meeting? Given Seneca's highly advanced social skills, it seems much more likely that he deliberately praised Claudius for virtues he was not thought to possess, so that the occasion for mourning the old, dead emperor could

Figure 3.3 Seneca, depicted here in a toga as a Roman orator, was Nero's speechwriter.

also slip into mockery, underlining the supposed superiority of the new inhabitant of the post.

Seneca composed for Nero an important speech to the Senate that defined the new principles of the future regime. He declared, we are told,

> that he would not be the judge of every case, and wouldn't shut the accusers and defendants up together to allow a minority to gain ever greater power. Nothing in his own household (he said) would be open to bribes or canvassing; home and state were separate. The Senate would keep its old responsibilities, and Italy and the provinces would be responsible to the tribunes of the consuls. They would give access to the senators, while he himself (he said) would focus on the armies under his care.
>
> (Tacitus 13.4, cf. Dio 61.3.1)

Tacitus says that Nero put these principles into practice by restoring the Senate in many respects, and won approbation from his respectful demeanor as consul in 55.[7] The new regime, then, began in a spirit of hopefulness that things would be far better for the Senate and for the Roman government in general than they had been under Claudius.

In December of the same year, Seneca composed another piece of writing that suggested the superiority of Neronian rule over the regime of Claudius: the *Apocolycyntosis, or Pumpkinification of Claudius.*[8] This text was probably produced for the Saturnalia, a festival celebrated in late December, from December 17 to 23 (one of the precursors to the modern Christmas), in which there was a tradition of partying, feasting, and gift-giving, and in which masters were supposed to trade places, temporarily, with their slaves. The *Pumpkinification* was a good fit for the topsy-turvy world of the Saturnalia. It begins with an appeal to be allowed to speak freely—a common trope for the satirist, but an essential element in the Saturnalian festivals. The feast was associated mythologically with the temporary return of Saturn as king of the gods, before Jupiter was restored again to his rightful place—a suggestive background for the political context.

The *Apocolycyntosis* is an extraordinary work, unlike anything else in ancient literature. The premise is the journey of the dead and deified Claudius up to Olympus to take his place with the other Olympian gods. The word, "apocolycyntosis," is a term invented by analogy with the word for becoming a deity—*apotheosis*. Claudius is shown as having become a god, but he also becomes an empty-headed gourd—or rather, he is revealed as always having been one. The attitude toward the dead emperor includes some aggressive personal gibes: it mocks Claudius' limp by commenting that he is hobbling with uneven steps up to heaven, and his speech defect by having Mercury announce the arrival of a sub-human specimen who speaks incomprehensibly. The tone also hovers between playful irony and more serious political commentary.[9]

Seneca's critical attitude toward Claudius in this text is obviously in stark tension with his brownnosing to the same emperor in the *Consolation to Polybius* (12.3–14.2), and some have therefore questioned whether Seneca was really the author of the satire. But clearly Seneca had a strong reason for being flattering to Claudius when he was still alive and had the power to release him from Corsica; he had no motive to be kind about him once he was dead and Nero had taken over.

Seneca is shockingly irreverent in his mockery of the whole institution of deifying an emperor. But it is possible that the *Apocolocyntosis* was not intended for a wide circulation among the general public, but simply for a private audience at court. For Nero and his cronies, the irreverence would have been delightful.

The skit also had a more serious purpose: it advised Nero himself about how to govern, by showing him where Claudius went wrong. Seneca's Claudius, once he reaches Olympus, is criticized sharply by the dead Augustus for his practice of killing people without trial, including Julia Livilla and a number of senators and knights. The institution of Heaven turns out to be closely modeled on the Roman Senate, whose norms Claudius is said to have violated. "Tell me, deified Claudius," asks Augustus, "why did you convict these men and women whom you killed, before you could examine the case, before you could hear the evidence? Where is this customary practice? It isn't so in Heaven." Claudius is eventually punished, sent down from Olympus to Hades, without trial, to be the slave of Caligula—the worst imaginable fate.

However much one may sympathize with the critique of injustice in the *Apocolocyntosis*, there are elements in its satire that are hard to like. Some of the satire against Claudius is very mean: he is mocked for his physical disabilities, and his final words in the text are, "Oh no! I've shat myself." The humiliating treatment afforded to poor Claudius is justified only partly by the claims that he failed to respect the Senate and the rule of law. There is also the rather less attractive complaint that under Claudius, too many upstarts began to wear the Roman toga: Claudius extended citizenship for any number of Greeks, Gauls, Spaniards, and Britons (presented by Seneca as upstarts who ought to have remained excluded). It is surprising, and indeed revolting, to read such complaints from a man who was himself Hispanic and had done rather well under the regime of Claudius. But there's no class more snobbish than the nouveau riche. Probably Seneca was particularly eager to defend the pure blood of the Roman aristocracy, since his own claim to belong to the club was so dubious—a version of the Uncle Tom syndrome. Seneca assiduously flatters the new emperor Nero, presenting those spinning sisters, the three Fates, as breaking off the thread of the "lumpy life" of Claudius to weave an amazingly long, golden thread for Nero. Apollo, god of the sun, comments that Nero is like his twin in good looks and musical talent and prophesies that this golden boy will bring in a new age of prosperity, as he rises like a morning star: "Such a Caesar is here, such a Nero Rome now shall see. His radiant face blazes with gentle brilliance; his shapely neck blazes with flowing hair..."

In fact, Nero was no Apollo, and his claim to the throne was questionable, since he became emperor only through his right as adoptive son of Claudius—over the head of the legitimate blood son, Britannicus. At this stage, the young emperor was impressionable, and there was a struggle between two different sets of influence upon him. On one side, his mother, Agrippina, was trying to increase her own power over the new imperial regime, drawing the powerful allies she had already cultivated under Claudius' rule, including the freedman Pallas, who had been her husband's favorite advisor. On the other side, we are told, were Burrus and Seneca.[10]

THE FIRST FIVE YEARS

Seneca's speech for Nero on his accession to the principate had involved a vow that the new emperor would be different from Claudius. Claudius had won enmity through a reputation for cruelty and a failure to keep distinct the affairs of the palace from those of the empire. Nero promised that he would do neither of these things. In what Tacitus tells us of his promises at the time of his accession, he insisted that he came to power with no sense of enmity or desire for vengeance against the friends of his predecessor. He vowed to be guided by his good counselors (meaning, primarily, Seneca and Burrus) and to allow the Senate and the army to retain all their old powers. He also swore to make sure that "his private establishment and the State should be kept entirely distinct" (Tacitus 13). Tacitus suggests that for a while, the influence of Burrus and Seneca was strong enough to restrain Nero's worst impulses; it was only once he began to assert his own autonomy, against the moral guidance of his early tutors, that he began to turn into the monstrous Nero of legend (Fig. 3.4).

Figure 3.4 Nero became emperor at the young age of seventeen in 54 CE.

Many historians have insisted that the first five years of Nero's reign, in which Burrus and Seneca supposedly guided the young emperor, were much better than the subsequent period, in which Nero freed himself from their guidance and got out of control. The good five years have been dubbed the *Quinquennium Neronis*, the Five Years of Nero. But (as Miriam Griffin has shown) we should not exaggerate the impact of these advisors or the difference between these five years and the time that followed: there is no reason to believe that there were any institutional or legal changes initiated by the new regime. Moreover, the notion that the emperor's private establishment and the state should be kept entirely distinct was simply not possible given the structure of the Roman principate in this period.[11]

One real change created by the accession of Nero was in the social class of the main advisors to the emperor. Claudius had notoriously relied heavily on a group of freedmen as his main advisors, whom he endowed with enormous wealth and, supposedly, treated as the most important influences on his political decisions. These included Polybius, to whom Seneca had written to try to plead for his reprieve. Polybius was put to death by Messalina for crimes against the state (or, some said, because she was bored of sleeping with him). But other powerful freedmen, such as Pallas and Narcissus, retained their hold on power. The Senate particularly hated the presence of the freedmen, which drove home all too obviously the fact that the emperor relied heavily on advisors who had no official position. With the accession of Nero, Seneca and Burrus took on many of the functions of the freedman advisor under Claudius: they advised the emperor, massaged his public image, and received large sums of money and other wealth in return. Seneca and Burrus were both from the *equites* ("knightly") class, not the senatorial class, and they seem to have been always at a certain distance from the world of the senators. Most of Seneca's close friends, even during his years in power, came from the knight's class. But these knights were far more able than the freedman had been to communicate with the Senate in ways that the latter found relatively congenial. The aristocratic, senatorial-class historian Tacitus treats the early years of Nero's realm as relatively successful, because they marked a period of relatively good communication between emperor and Senate. The secret of the perceived success in these years lay in Seneca's skills in public relations.

There was a fairly long tradition in Greco-Roman antiquity of philosophers advising monarchs or tyrants. Plato acted as temporary advisor to Dionysius of Syracuse, trying unsuccessfully to persuade the tyrant to turn into a Platonic philosopher-king. In the Hellenistic period, there was a series of treatises and counter-treatises, discussing the proper relationship of kings and philosophical advisors; Stoics and other intellectual schools were keen to combat the Epicurean notion that the philosopher ought really to have nothing to do with a monarchy.[12] These treatises made the case that kingship was actually a natural form of government, and that kings could avoid tyranny by learning virtue from the lips of the philosopher in residence. Seneca was deeply aware of this tradition and helped to reshape it for a Roman context.

Seneca served for part of a year as consul, in 56, the highest official political office in Rome. He took over partway through the year for someone else who dropped out. Serving just a partial term was known as being "suffect consul." Seneca's tenure as consul lasted only a few months, but even a short stint as consul was hugely important in symbolic terms: it meant that Seneca had—like Cicero before him—reached the highest official rank in Roman government. After service as consul, a Roman man, and all his male descendants after him, had attained the rank of the aristocracy: he now counted as a "nobleman," *nobilis*, on a level with the oldest Roman families.[13]

It was probably in this period that Seneca married a woman called Pompeia Paulina, daughter of a man from the equestrian class named Pompeius Paulinus (his daughter being named for him, as was the Roman custom). We know frustratingly little about this relationship, although there is every reason to believe that Seneca loved his wife: he calls her "my Paulina" (Epistle 104.1.2.5) and Tacitus describes her as "especially beloved by Seneca" (*Annals* 15.63.2). They seem to have had no children, but there is no evidence that this was a source of grief or anxiety to Seneca. As well as providing love and companionship, the marriage solidified Seneca's relationships with his wife's male relations.

Seneca's appointment under Nero was largely unofficial: he was termed the emperor's "friend" or "teacher" or "advisor," with no specific legal or administrative title attached. Seneca seems to have succeeded in pulling strings to make sure his friends and family advanced within the social ladder and his enemies fell. Lucan, Seneca's nephew, the son of his brother Mela, was brought back from his studies in Athens and, although he was five years younger than the usual age and had not done the usual prerequisite of military service, he was given a quaestorship, an official rank on the career ladder or *cursus honorum*, which brought social credit and involved working as a financial overseer. Mela himself became a respectably ranking financial officer (a procurator). Seneca's new wife's brother, Pompeius Paulinus, became an imperial legate in Germany. And Seneca's dear friend Annaeus Serenus was given command of the night watch. All this suggests that Seneca had plenty of influence behind the scenes to choose who did well or poorly under the Neronian regime, and that he used it to promote the people he knew.

Roman elite male society in this period depended on a complex set of networks, favors, and obligations exchanged between men of the equestrian and senatorial classes. One important social practice that tends to seem alien from a modern perspective is the adoption of adult young men by a new father.[14] The practice was not unusual: it has been estimated that some four percent of men in the equestrian class in the Julio-Claudian period were adopted into another family. This happened in Seneca's family when an old friend of Seneca the Elder, a senator named Junius Gallio, adopted our Seneca's older brother, Novatus. Novatus then, as was standard practice, took on the name of his adoptive father, becoming Lucius Junius Gallio Annaeus. In modern Western society, childless couples usually adopt children very young, with the purpose of nurturing them to adulthood. In Roman society, however, the main purpose of adoption was not nurture but social networking and securing one's estate: elite men wanted to increase their bonds with their peers and to have an heir to whom they could pass on their wealth and name and social status. Gallio had been widowed at a fairly young age, had no sons, and apparently was unwilling to get married, despite being urged to do so by Ovid.[15] Seneca the Elder, who had three male heirs, was in a good position to pass one of them off to a friend, thereby increasing his own social credit within his circle as well as increasing the son's opportunities and the whole family's position within the Roman aristocracy. In purely financial terms, too, the practice allowed elite men to share their wealth in ways that were mutually beneficial: through being adopted, Novatus could expect to inherit his adoptive father's wealth. The adoptive father, Gallio, was a well-known orator, poet, and declaimer of Seneca the Elder's generation, who had been a friend of the poet Ovid and who had been exiled to the island of Lesbos under Tiberius, though soon recalled. Perhaps the adoption improved the status of the Annaeus family in literary circles as well as their finances.

Our Seneca was, as we have seen, close to his elder brother and seems to have worked hard to promote his career, although Novatus was managing well in any case by his own diligence. Novatus had been appointed as the Roman magistrate ("proconsul") in charge of Achaea and is most famous for having dismissed charges brought by the Jews against the apostle Paul: "and Gallio cared for none of these things" (Acts 18.12–16). Gallio thus seems to have followed the usual Roman practice in the provinces of refusing to intervene in local quarrels whenever possible. Novatus, like his brother, suffered from a medical condition in his lungs, involving coughing up blood; perhaps he terminated his post in Achaea for medical reasons, although the condition cannot have been so debilitating as to prevent him from further life in office.[16] After he returned to Rome, Novatus was appointed in 55 as a suffect consul—perhaps through the help of his powerful younger brother. After his appointment, Novatus seems to have traveled to Egypt for his health's sake, as his brother had done before him.[17]

Seneca was less close to his younger brother, Mela, but he was certainly attached to Mela's son, his nephew Lucan. Lucan may well have seemed like a surrogate son to Seneca, who had no surviving children. The boy was almost the same age as Nero (just two years his senior), and they seem to have gotten along very well, at least in the early years. Lucan shared with Nero a keen interest in poetry and the arts; Seneca helped both of them develop their rhetorical and literary skills. Lucan wrote an extempore "Praise of Nero" for the celebration of the realm in 60 CE, as well as an extempore poem on Orpheus for the same occasion.

Seneca's quick thinking and social tact were instrumental in reducing the power of Agrippina—who hoped to manage things behind the scenes during her son's principate. Agrippina used to lurk behind a curtain for official meetings with ambassadors so she could hear the proceedings, hoping to be able to intervene in the affairs of state. Early on in Nero's reign, she tried to claim a more public role and emerged from hiding—potentially creating a state scandal, since women were not supposed to participate in politics at this level. We are told that on one occasion, when Armenian ambassadors were pleading with Nero on behalf of their country, she was actually getting ready to climb up the emperor's tribunal and preside with him; everybody else was paralyzed by fear, but Seneca gestured to Nero to go and meet his mother. Appearances were maintained, by a show of filial affection (Tacitus, *Annals,* 13).

Burrus and Seneca helped restrict Agrippina's tendencies toward killing as many of her enemies as possible. They maintained their influence on Nero by allowing him to indulge his pleasures (*Annals* 13.2). Seneca's service to Nero was not as a policy advisor beyond the palace, but rather as chief speechwriter and public relations officer, as an advisor both in the selection and dismissal of other government officials and in helping Nero consolidate his position in the palace—for instance, by working with him against his mother.

Nero's arranged marriage to Claudius' daughter Octavia was one of the building blocks by which Agrippina had ensured her son's claim to the imperial throne, but Nero was not interested in his wife and treated her badly. He embarked on a public affair with a freedwoman called Acte. Agrippina regarded this as scandalous and tried to put a stop to it—which only encouraged Nero in the relationship (Tacitus 13.12). Seneca intervened on the side of Nero and Acte, arguing the ruler had a right to his own decisions about his personal life—and thereby increasing his own intimacy with the boy.[18] Seneca even helped out in the practicalities of the affair, persuading his friend Annaeus Serenus to pretend to conduct an affair with Acte and give her the presents that actually came from Nero.

This story is a useful indicator of the kind of influence Seneca exerted over the young emperor. It was mostly not "moral" influence; rather, Seneca was interested in extracting Nero from the control of his mother and increasing his own power with the boy and on the wider social scene. Seneca was a pragmatist: it was unrealistic to expect the young emperor to be faithful to a wife he had not even chosen, when all Rome was available; the philosopher saw no harm in gaining some political capital for himself out of something that was bound to happen anyway.

Distinguishing himself from Agrippina was particularly important for Seneca, since it would have been easy for Nero to perceive him as her tool—which would have meant that, once Agrippina fell from favor, Seneca would have fallen also. Seneca owed his recall from exile to Agrippina, and there were (predictably) rumors that he had at some point been having an affair with her. It was therefore important for Seneca to prove, both to Nero and to the public, that he was on a different side from that of Agrippina: his political and literal survival depended on it.

There was a delicate balance of power among Nero, Agrippina, and their various advisors in the early years of Nero's reign. Agrippina was aware that her own influence over her son was slipping and complained bitterly over his relationship with Acte, and (implicitly) his lack of obedience toward her, and the growing power of these new advisors, Seneca and Burrus—who were proving less malleable than she had hoped. Agrippina made a series of attempts to win Nero back. One strand in the ancient gossip suggests that Agrippina tried to seduce him back to her side by sleeping with him; others suggested that he himself initiated sex with her. Either or both or neither may be true.

Things went from bad to worse when Nero sent his mother the gift of an elaborate dress complete with jewelry. Agrippina protested that it was not a proper gift: her son was presenting her with only a small piece of property while keeping the whole treasure for himself. If true, the anecdote is revealing both about Agrippina's assumptions (that she ought to have an equal share in the wealth and power of the imperial house) and the tensions at stake in the relationship, which focused on gifts and gratitude. Agrippina presumably felt that she herself had won the throne for Nero (and he ought therefore to pay her an undying debt of gratitude by sharing it); Nero himself wanted to be sole emperor, and his mother was beginning to get in his way.

He began to reduce Agrippina's power, beginning by stripping her of her most important advisor: the freedman Pallas, who was the last vestige of the regime of Claudius, in which the most powerful imperial advisors had been freedmen. Pallas was certainly a person Agrippina had relied heavily upon for moral support and strategic advice, and some said they were lovers; certainly Pallas, who served as treasurer, acquired great wealth while in office, perhaps even more than Seneca (Dio puts the figure at 400,000,000 sesterces: 62.14). Nero granted Pallas the concession that the books would not be audited, so that he was allowed to keep the riches he had acquired in office, but in political terms, he was gone.[19] Pallas was later put on trial, along with Burrus, for conspiracy; he was acquitted, but his name was further blackened (Tacitus 13.23). Agrippina retaliated at the loss of her favorite by threatening to switch sides and support Britannicus over her son. Nero expelled Agrippina from the palace, stripped her of her honors and powers, and took away her personal bodyguards (Suetonius, *Nero,* 34). He even, supposedly, threatened to follow the example of Tiberius and abdicate, to live out his life on the island of Rhodes—which would have left Agrippina entirely powerless.

As Nero began to slip out of the control of his mother, Agrippina took things badly. She spoke out against both Seneca and Burrus, dubbing them "the cripple and the exile"—one, Burrus, having a maimed arm, and the other, Seneca, a "rhetoric-teacher's tongue" (*Annals* 13.14.3). But she also fought back against Nero and his new supporters, beginning to favor Britannicus as the true heir to the throne. Britannicus was about to reach the age of maturity or manhood, at fifteen.

All of a sudden, unsurprisingly, Britannicus dropped dead. It was February 12, 55 CE, immediately before his fifteenth birthday, when he would have become the obvious heir to the throne. The official story was that he died of an epileptic fit, but the universal opinion of the ancient sources is that Nero had him poisoned. He hired a woman called Locusta, a poison specialist, who put some toxic substance in a pitcher of water. Britannicus, being wary of poison, had his wine tasted, but it had been made too hot. He then added water to cool the mix, drank it without having the taster check it again, and immediately had a fatal seizure.

Soon after the murder, Nero ousted his mother from the palace, claiming that she had been plotting against his wife, Octavia. Now the young prince had dispensed of his only real competitor and had also freed himself from the clutches of his mother. In the future, he could act as badly as he wished.

A State Unstained by Blood

In late December of this same year, 55 CE, or early in 56, Seneca composed an essay addressed to the eighteen-year-old Nero on the topic of *clementia*—mercifulness. Seneca declares that the young emperor's most striking quality is his innocence, his restraint from bloodshed:

> You, Caesar, have given us the gift of a state unstained by blood. This proud boast of yours, that you have spilt not a drop of human blood in the whole world, is all the more remarkable and amazing, because nobody ever had the sword entrusted to him at an earlier age.
>
> (*On Clemency* 1.11.3)

It was quite true that Nero was the youngest person to become heir to the whole Roman empire, but the other element in this fulsome praise—Nero's gentleness—is harder to reconcile with reality, since this Caesar had, only a few months earlier, had his own stepbrother murdered. The dating of the treatise has sometimes been questioned for this reason: scholars have shrunk from believing that Seneca could have had the *chutzpah* to praise Nero for his astonishing mildness, innocence, and lack of cruelty at such a time. But the evidence that Seneca did indeed compose this work right after the death of Britannicus is incontrovertible.[20] The question, then, is how exactly the *De Clementia* responds to Nero as murderer.

One can read the treatise as a gesture of abject flattery, a sign that Seneca was willing to praise this violent, dangerous, and terrifyingly powerful young ruler even to the extent of absolutely denying the reality of his behavior. This is certainly a reading that seems tempting at the start of the essay. Seneca declares early on that "All your citizens are compelled to acknowledge that they are happy, and that nothing more can be added to these blessings, except for them to last forever" (1.1.7). Certainly there was quite a lot of optimism among the Roman elite in the early years of Nero's rule, so this may not have seemed laughably false. It is also possible that aristocrats would have been less troubled by the murder of Britannicus than we might think.[21] After all, their real fears would surely have been for their own safety; whether or not the emperor was prone to kill his own family members might be less important to them than whether or not he would kill the powerful men who were outside the imperial household.

But there is still a real ambiguity about whether the Seneca of *De Clementia* is telling Nero that he already has all possible virtues, or that he needs to acquire them. The text begins with Seneca announcing that he wants to write about mercy in order to act as Nero's "mirror," reflecting the emperor as somebody who will attain the greatest possible pleasure:

> I have undertaken to write about clemency, Nero Caesar, in order that I may in some way fulfil the function of a mirror, and in order that I may show you to yourself as you are about to arrive at the greatest of all pleasures.

The notion of mirroring between the book and its addressee is handled here with great delicacy. On the one hand, the metaphor suggests that Nero is already in possession of all possible virtue, including amazing degrees of mercifulness; all the writer has to do is reflect back to him the things that he is already doing. But on the other, Seneca qualifies his use of the metaphor (he is not like a mirror, but "sort of" like a mirror); and he promises to reflect not simply what Nero is now, but Nero in the state that he will attain in the future. It is possible to read that state of maximal pleasure as the attainment of the maximum amount of power, in the position of being emperor. This interpretation seems to be confirmed by the speech Seneca puts into the mouth of Nero at the start of the treatise, in which the boy-emperor boasts and luxuriates in the enormous control he has over the whole world. But it is also possible to see the "maximum pleasure" in a more Stoic light, and imagine that Seneca is showing Nero a self that he has not yet attained but that he may grow into through reading the treatise. The mirror is not only an instrument of reflection but also an inspiration for change.

The *De Clementia* is a kind of debriefing, done in full consciousness of the truth about Britannicus. Seneca is telling Nero not to make a habit of such actions. He warns the emperor that the good hopes that people have about him would be based on nothing if his fine moral character were not innate: "No one, after all, can wear a mask for long. Pretence quickly lapses into its true nature." Seneca carefully leaves it ambiguous which category Nero belongs to: is he a truly good person or a hypocrite wearing the mask of goodness? Paradoxically (and implausibly) it is only by maintaining the mask of reasonably good behavior that Nero will be able to "prove" that it matches his face. The teacher wants the student to feel inspired by the benign image he holds up to him. He hopes that showing him a reflection in an idealizing mirror will make the student want to become what the teacher tells him he already is, or soon will become.

But *De Clementia* was not written only to be read by Nero himself: the wider public must have been eager for any possible information about the future directions of the new regime. Seneca's work both in the *Apocolycyntosis* and in the *De Clementia* combined to form a clear image of the ideology of Nero's realm, insisting that this emperor would be a vast improvement on those who had gone before, thanks to the strong influence upon the young man of his Stoic teacher.[22] The *De Clementia* works to reassure the elite Roman public that this act of bloodshed, the murder of Britannicus, would not be characteristic of the future behavior of the Neronian rule, and that the right-hand man of the new emperor, his old tutor Seneca, was strongly opposed to any kind of cruelty and was in full control of his moral education. Seneca insists that he is no flatterer to the emperor: "I would rather offend you with the truth than please you with flattery" (2.2.1). Readers could feel reassured that the young leader was in strong, moral hands.

Many might reasonably doubt whether philosophical teaching works quite so effectively as a cure for autocracy. The real ideological problem for many senators lay with imperial government itself, and Seneca's treatise does nothing to allay the concerns of those who missed the days of the Republic. Rather, it presents the emperor as possessing absolute power, whose source is never explained or justified.[23] Seneca addresses this problem by invoking the moral Roman values of mercy and of Stoicism, which will, he insists, enable the emperor to rule with something even better than justice: with virtue.

Clementia was in some ways a surprising topic for a self-confessedly Stoic piece of writing. Leniency was considered a bad thing among the Greek Stoic philosophers because the true wise man is just, so he always imposes precisely the right punishment on a wrongdoer. To punish with a milder sentence than the crime deserved would show a ruler's injustice and would likely be a sign that he had been misled by emotional impulse rather than reason—not something a wise Stoic ought to do.

The fact that Seneca chooses to focus on clemency is thus a mark of his originality in the field of Stoicism, and also of his interest not in abstract philosophy but in the specifics of Roman politics. From the days of Julius Caesar, as one-man rule had taken hold in Rome, successive emperors had seized on the notion of personal mercifulness as a way of dealing with the people's fear of, and hostility toward, the idea of tyranny. Seneca reconciles Stoic philosophy with the realities of Roman politics by redefining *clementia,* "mercifulness," as something entirely different from *misericordia,* "pity." The latter, in Seneca's presentation, involves being misled by emotional impulse to pardon those who really ought not to be pardoned. It may lead one to excessive kinds of forgiveness, which may be bad even for those pardoned, as well as for society as a whole. But *clementia* is always rooted in reason. It is, we are told, "mental moderation in the power of revenge or leniency of a superior to an inferior in deciding on punishments" (2.3.1). It is thus not the opposite of justice, but the opposite of cruelty, and an essential component of the Stoic principle of *humanitas.*

Seneca's treatise reassures those who might be worried about Nero's regime that the new leader will act gently toward his inferiors. The emphasis on avoiding cruelty is a way of insisting that Nero will not resemble Caligula or Claudius, who killed multiple members of the Senate and other citizens. But from the perspective of those who still regretted the loss of the Republic, Seneca's treatise is not reassuring at all. *Clementia* is presented as a virtue that can only be achieved by a person in a superior position of power. It only makes sense for the Princeps, who was the ultimate legal authority in the Roman state. Seneca's work thus provides a theoretical framework for what was already true in practice, that the emperor was above the law—and therefore had need not of justice (which would imply obedience to a nonexistent higher law than himself) but of mercifulness toward his inferiors. These inferiors have no rights in relation to him and can only hope that he will treat them kindly.

Seneca's treatise is a strong statement that Stoicism did not necessarily imply hostility to one-man rule. The point needed making, since some of the most famous Stoics of earlier generations had also been defenders of the Republic: the best known is Cato the Younger (95–46 BCE), who committed suicide by disemboweling himself rather than submit to the rule of Julius Caesar. Seneca often writes admiringly of Cato but obviously did not share his strict opposition to the principate. In Seneca's own generation there were other Stoics in the Roman government who stood up strongly against Nero and in favor of Republican principles: the most important of these was Thrasea, to whom we shall return. Seneca's nephew Lucan, too, seems to have been a Stoic or at least Stoic fellow-traveler and was eventually an adamant opponent of one-man rule. Stoicism was increasingly seen as a politically resistant movement, and a generation after Seneca's death, in 95 CE, the emperor Domitian expelled philosophers from Italy—a move probably targeted primarily at the Stoics. Seneca was doing important public relations work on his position within the court as well as with the elite general public, assuring the emperor that his philosophy is morally credible enough to give a patina of legitimacy to the new regime, but without posing any political threat to the principate.

Seneca's tragedies include many scenes that parallel the discussion of *clementia* in this prose work. There are many Senecan tragic tyrants who describe themselves as above all laws. Our author uses the tragic stage to play out the other side of the story, to imagine exactly what happens, in gory detail, when all-powerful rulers operate without any thought for mercy toward their inferiors. A common sentiment is that the ruler's power inevitably comes at the cost of being hated: "A man who fears to be hated doesn't really want to rule," declares Eteocles in the *Phoenissae*—a line that echoes the quote from Caligula that Seneca cites with disgust in the *On Mercy and On Anger:* "Let them hate, as long as they fear." One of the most shocking examples of lack of *clementia* in the tragedies comes in the *Trojan Women*, set after the fall of the city, where Andromache, wife of the dead warrior Hector, is clutching their baby son in her arms and seeking sanctuary at her dead husband's tomb. She begs the triumphant general, Ulysses (Odysseus), to show mercy toward herself, or if not that, then at least to spare her child. She suggests that a true hero and a true king ought to follow the example of Hercules, who showed mercy to a little boy—to Priam in his childhood. But after a series of heart-wrenching pleas from Andromache, Ulysses refuses: "I wish I could be merciful. I cannot" (763), he says. He gives brutally short orders to the men, who will lead Andromache to slavery and throw her baby from the city walls: "Seize her: she is holding up the Argive fleet" (812). The city has fallen, and the most innocent members of Trojan society—the little boy, Astyanax, and the little girl, Polyxena—are slaughtered without mercy.

We do not know exactly when Seneca composed the *Trojan Women*: it may have been written before Nero came to power, or it may not. In either case, one can see the play as again a dark twin of *On Clemency*. In the prose treatise, we are shown how one-man rule can function well, if only the single ruler can act with mercy toward his inferiors. In the play, we see a transition from one government to another that is entirely violent, entirely lacking in either mercy or justice, and in which the innocent are slaughtered. Perhaps Seneca's devastating depiction of children's deaths in tragedy was a way of dealing with some of the guilt he felt at having helped to cover up the murder of young Britannicus. The slaughter of children was certainly on his mind and played out in an even more horrible way in the *Thyestes*.

Nero was apparently pleased with Seneca's work as major spokesman for the ideology of his regime. He rewarded him lavishly, with gifts of money, villas, and other kinds of wealth. Tacitus comments that, after the elimination of Britannicus, Nero "loaded his best friends with gifts" (13.18), presumably referring primarily to Seneca, especially since he goes on to remark that there were "accusers" who objected to the fact that "men who claimed to be so self-restrained" were actually, "at such a time," profiting by dividing up "town-houses and country-houses, like loot." Ulysses in the *Trojan Women*—the clever strategist who is willing to say or do anything to please the king, win the war, and go home loaded with trophies and wealth—begins to look rather like his creator, Seneca.

SENECA'S WEALTH

Poison is drunk from gold.[24]

We turn now to one of the most fraught questions about Seneca's life story: his vast accumulation of wealth under Nero.[25] For our purposes, there are three central questions. First, how rich was he? Second, how exactly did he get his money? And third, how can we reconcile his accumulation of wealth and property with the overwhelmingly negative depiction of riches in his writings? The first is relatively easy to answer; the second is harder; the third is by far the most difficult.

It is clear that Seneca was extremely rich. Cassius Dio tells us that under Nero, he accumulated over three hundred million sestertii, a very large sum, as well as a great deal of property, including several houses in Rome and elsewhere, and apparently large areas of land in the prime real estate area of central Rome as well as in other parts of Italy. He may well also have owned land in Egypt (Epistle 77), an important source of revenue, since Egypt was the primary grain supplier to the Empire. It is impossible to translate Roman money with any accuracy into modern currency, since the relative values of different types of object, and the value of labor, was radically different: property values were proportionately less, and, as in any preindustrialized economy, manufactured goods cost more. The ubiquity of slave labor also made the service economy very different. But we can get some idea of the scale of Seneca's wealth by knowing that a single sestertius could buy two loaves of bread or a jug of wine, and that a legionary in the Roman army, in Seneca's lifetime, earned 900 sestertii per annum. By today's standards, then, Seneca was at least a multimillionaire.

Roman society in this period had an enormous wealth and power gap: the elite class was, in general, vastly richer than the mass of the general population. It has been suggested that there was not really anything equivalent to a middle class in Rome in this period; there was nothing in-between the super-rich and the working classes or peasants.[26] More recent studies suggest that there were middle-income Romans, but those constituted no more than ten percent of the population: the vast majority of people in the Empire lived at subsistence level or close to it, while the top one and a half percent controlled about a fifth of the total GDP (a proportion that is actually lower than in the contemporary United States but one that still represents a vast socioeconomic gap between rich and poor).[27] But Seneca's wealth went beyond the norms even for the elite. By the latest estimates, the average yearly income for a man in the senatorial class was around three hundred thousand sestertii, and for one in the equestrian class it was less than a tenth of that figure. In this context, Seneca's wealth was far above the average even in his disproportionately rich social class. Only a tiny handful of people in this period would have had anywhere near this much money and property.[28] Seneca's assets were comparable not to the normal run of wealth enjoyed by the aristocracy, but to those acquired by the freedmen who were the favorite advisors under Claudius, Narcissus, and Pallas.

A detail that is mentioned by Dio, as a mark of his extraordinary conspicuous consumption, is that he ordered five hundred tables made of citrus wood, with legs of ivory, all exactly identical, and he served dinner parties on them. In a world where mechanical reproduction was impossible and everything had to be manufactured by hand, the ability to have matching furniture was a mark of extraordinary wealth. Seneca's tables were also made of the most luxurious possible materials, ivory from elephant trunks and expensive citrus wood. Moreover, they were an item that only somebody who could afford to throw regular banquets would actually need. Seneca, as this detail suggests, spent much of his money on entertaining. He spent lavishly in order to acquire and maintain his social capital.

Some of the money may have been inherited, since Seneca's family was already wealthy before his exile; Seneca the Elder, as we have seen, was a successful businessman. Moreover, Seneca's estates were themselves a source of further revenue, since he would have rented them out while not in residence, and grew produce, especially grapes, on the land (or rather, had his slaves grow it, under his supervision). But a great deal of the wealth seems to have come fairly directly from Nero, who paid Seneca very generously for the work he did for him, as strategist, speechwriter, and spokesman for his regime.

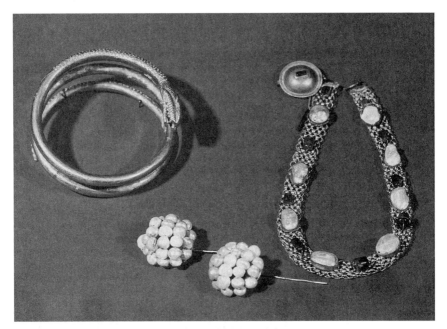

Figure 3.5 The Roman elite enjoyed conspicuous displays of wealth, such as this jewelry and this silver cup. One of Seneca's favorite topics is the emptiness of this kind of consumerism.

How do we reconcile "Super-Rich Seneca" (*Seneca Praedives*), as Martial calls him, with Seneca the philosopher, the austere Stoic who sees riches as merely an indifferent thing, albeit a preferable one? Wealth is a common topic in Seneca's writing, and he never has a good word to say about it; yet he enjoyed, or at least acquired, all its trappings (Fig. 3.5).

The question was certainly posed at the time by Seneca's contemporaries, including a man called Publius Suillius, an informant who developed a personal enmity against Seneca. One of the major ways in which financial corruption was exposed was by quasi-professional informants, who brought legal accusations against people they believed to be indulging in corrupt business practices—for instance, governors who stole funds from the provinces they were supposed to be regulating, a common form of malpractice.[29] It is easy to imagine these people as tattletales or worse, but in a system where the gap between rich and poor was so vast, and where there were increasing opportunities for financial corruption, the informants played an essential role in acting as a check on abuse.

Publius Suillius had been brought low by a revival of an old law against judicial corruption; the law was revived as a deliberate, *ad hominem* attack on Suillius by his enemies, who apparently included Seneca. In bitterness at this, Suillius turned on Seneca in 58 CE and accused him of financial and moral abuses that went far beyond his own.[30] He criticized Seneca of having acquired a vast personal fortune, three hundred million sestertii, in a mere four years of service to Nero. He claimed that Seneca had a personal grudge against anybody—presumably including himself—who spoke in defense of his fellow citizens, and against anybody who had been a friend to Claudius, under whom, he said, "Seneca endured a well-deserved exile" (Tacitus 13.42.4). Suillius' attack interwove claims of sexual corruption (beginning with adultery with Julia Livilla, and also suggesting that Seneca slept with Agrippina and seduced Nero himself) with attacks on his wealth: "In Rome, he spread his nets to catch the wills of childless men; Italy and the provinces were sucked dry by his insatiable usury" (Tacitus 13.42.4).

The implications of Suillius' attack were that Seneca was not only very wealthy, but wealthy despite an entirely false claim to be "philosophical," and wealthy at the expense of other citizens. Legacy-hunting was a common corrupt practice in Rome at the time, memorably depicted in literary texts such as Petronius' *Satyricon,* in which the central character, Eumolpus, poses as a childless, sickly, rich old man in order to trap the legacy-hunters into pretending to befriend him. The charge of preying on the wills of the childless elderly was such a common trope of Roman moralists that it would have appeared in Suillius' list of accusations regardless of truth. But there is no reason to doubt that Seneca was indeed very much interested in cultivating social relationships in the city, and it seems at least possible that some of those whom he wined and dined, on those ivory tables, were also old, childless, and rich.

The charge of "sucking the provinces dry" is morally the most serious, and it is also hard to rule out. It was common for rich elite Romans to lend money at interest to the provinces, and it seems perfectly likely that Seneca did this. Cassius Dio tells us that his usury helped precipitate the British rebellion of 61 CE, since Seneca suddenly called in a loan of forty million sestertii. The figure may be exaggerated, and the relationship between the rebellion and Seneca's loan is not likely to have been so direct; but still, there is no reason to doubt that Seneca did profit by moneylending, and also no reason to think that he felt particularly ashamed about it.

Seneca, Tacitus tells us, was soon told about Suillius' accusations and quickly retaliated. A series of prosecutions against Suillius for corruption began and were successfully executed: half his estate was confiscated, and he was sent into exile. Seneca thus succeeded in taking savage revenge on one of his most outspoken personal enemies. Suillius, however, made the best of his situation: he remained "uncowed" during the condemnation and lived out his life in exile at ease and surrounded by luxury—never making the mistake of trying to return to Rome. It is possible that Seneca, enraged by his enemy's spirit, tried to push his hatred even further: we are told that the son of Suillius was also prosecuted, but the emperor himself put a stop to it, arguing that vengeance had gone far enough (Tacitus 13.43). Here the pupil showed far more *clementia* than his philosophical teacher was able to muster.

But the charges obviously stung Seneca. Moreover, Suillius was presumably not the only person to make these charges, so ousting one enemy was not enough to silence the irritating attacks. Seneca wrote an extensive self-justification, probably the year after the accusations by Suillius, in 59 CE: *On the Happy Life*.[31] This is a philosophical essay addressed to Seneca's older brother, Novatus, which provides an important window into Seneca's response to the critics who accused him of hypocrisy as well as excessive and unphilosophical profiteering. The value of worldly goods is addressed directly. Seneca approaches the issue by first discussing the relationship of happiness to pleasure (*voluptas*). He adamantly rejects the idea that pleasure is an inherent component of happiness. The popular but thoughtless version of this view is quickly dismissed with scorn: the supposed goods of wealth, eloquence, and power are not guarantees of real, lasting happiness; they are delusions, which "are shining on the outside, but miserable within" (2.4).

A more sustained and complex attack has to be made against the defenders of the philosophical school that was the most prominent rival of Stoicism in Rome of the period: Epicureanism. Seneca, far more than some opponents of Epicureanism, acknowledges quite fairly that the Epicureans were by no means hedonists, and he expresses some real respect for the true teachings of Epicurus: "[Hedonists] do not think about how restrained and moderate that Epicurean 'pleasure' really is—and indeed, I think it really is pleasure; instead, they rush to the name to find some justification and veil for their own cravings" (12.4). The problem, then, is not so much with Epicurus himself as with his false followers, those who call themselves Epicureans but fail to follow the austerity of the master. But Seneca also insists that the Epicureans are wrong to equate pleasure with virtue. The point is not that pleasure is to be despised by the truly wise person, but rather that it must always be secondary to the main aim of virtue. Physical pleasures have a place in the ideal life, but only if they are in a place "like the auxiliaries and light-armed troops in the camp: let them be slaves, not masters" (*On the Happy Life* 8.2). Virtue does bring pleasure, but it is chosen for itself, not for any pleasure it may bring. The problem with equating pleasure and virtue, as the Epicureans do, is that it risks making one too vulnerable to Fortune. Any physical pleasure, even the most moderate joy an Epicurean takes in his crust of bread and swig of water, seasoned only with hunger and thirst and eaten with a single good friend—even this can be taken away.

We can hear a resonance with Seneca's own life choices in his adamant insistence that one must never be seduced by the desire for physical comfort into making choices that might be contrary not only to virtue, but also—and this comes to the same thing—to his own freedom. The insistence suggests an attempt to address the author's discomfort with the choice he himself has made in serving the emperor—and thereby compromising his own freedom. Political language recurs when Seneca discusses the Stoic ideal of following god and Nature at all times: "We are born under a king's rule; to obey god is freedom" (15.7). Clearly the service of Nero was not freedom, and Seneca knew it. He arranges his philosophical thinking to present himself as actually in service to a higher power than the earthly power of the emperor, and thereby he suggests the paradox that his higher kind of service allows for a higher kind of freedom—regardless of the constraints of his merely physical existence.

The treatise makes an explicit answer to the charges of hypocrisy. Seneca imagines an unnamed, typical accuser approaching him and asking "the usual thing." This "usual thing" turns out to be a very long list of usual things, accusations about his wealth and his interest in things that, to a Stoic sage, ought to be merely indifferent:

> Then why do you talk so much more bravely than you live? Why do you repress your words in front of a high-up person, why do you think of money as a personal necessity, why do you get upset when you lose things, why do you cry when you hear about the death of your wife or your friend, why do you think about reputation, and why are you affected by gossip? Why do you have more land in your estate than the needs of nature require? Why do your dinners not correspond to your teaching? Why do you have polished furniture? Why do you drink wine older than you are? Why this pretentious bird-house? Why do you plant trees that give nothing but shade? Why does your wife wear earrings that cost as much as a fancy house? Why is your retinue of slave footmen adorned in such expensive outfits? Why is it an art-form to be a waiter at your table, and the silver isn't just put down any old way—there's enormous skill involved in laying it out and serving the meal, and there has to be a special professional carver for the meat?
>
> (17.2)

The list goes on, with more and more examples of absurd luxury: it is almost comically too long. If the list stopped after three or four instances, one would have got the point; since he continues, the reader comes to wonder whether he is only indicting wealth, or whether he actually might be enjoying contemplating his wonderful heap of possessions.

But as the passage continues, the focus on excessive quantities of material possessions gives way to even more pointed questions about why one who teaches temperate Stoic philosophy should want not only riches beyond what other people have, but even riches beyond what the possessor himself can keep track of—riches that make no possible sense, that entirely violate reason:

> Why do you have property over-seas? Why more things than you've even seen or known? Are you so horribly spoilt that you don't even

know your few slaves, or such a fat-cat that you own more slaves than you can possibly remember?

The voicing of these reproaches suggests an attempt by Seneca to address his critics, but the confrontation is still far from direct. For instance, the critic first complains that the hypocrite-philosopher shows unbecoming grief at the death of a wife, and then objects that his wife—presumably a living woman—wears inappropriately expensive jewelry. It is quite possible that Seneca had, in fact, suffered the loss of his first wife and remarried by the time of this essay. We are told, in fact (by Dio), that he made a "brilliant marriage" in "this period," and it is likely, as we have seen, that this was when he married Paulina. But even if the dead wife and the wife with expensive earrings are both biographical facts, it seems equally possible to take the contradiction as an attempt to keep things properly vague: this is about any philosopher who fails to live up to his ideals, whether or not his name is Lucius Annaeus Seneca.

The confusing slippage from the particular to the general, and back again, allows him to have it both ways: this both is, and is not, a confession. The unnamed critic, too, slips from accusations directed to a single person to general complaints about the hypocrisy of all philosophers. *Aliter loqueris, aliter vivis*, he says: "You talk one way, and live another" (18.1). But the accused are also multiple, a general category as well as an individual: "Philosophers don't practice what they preach" (20.1).

There is another kind of slipperiness at play in the accusations Seneca's unnamed critic levels against a person who both is and is not himself. There is little discussion of where all this wealth comes from: questions like "Why do you suck the provinces dry?" and "Why do you hunt for legacies?" are not included on the list. Nor does any imagined interlocutor ask, "Why do you, a so-called philosopher, serve and promote and grow rich in service of a ruler who murdered his brother?" The questions focus almost entirely on material possessions, of which slaves are only an expensive subcategory. When more difficult and important problems are mentioned at all, Seneca moves extremely fast away from them: "Why do you repress your tongue in front of a superior?" The implied answer is presumably that the "philosopher" risks exile or death if he talks back to the superior.

Different again is the question, "Why do you weep when you hear of the death of a wife or a friend?" The implied answer here is that the philosopher, who claims to have such detachment that he can bear any loss calmly, is actually subject to human affection. Seneca here acknowledges the would-be philosopher's dependence on other people. But the gulf between these two weaknesses, avarice and love, is for Seneca less large than it might appear. The allure of material possessions, as he presents it, is precisely that they allow the owner to maintain and increase his social status. The rich man in this text does not want rich food or fancy wine or a well-dressed wife for reasons of physical greed or lust, or for purely aesthetic reasons, or even because he likes them. Nothing, in fact, is said about the actual flavor of the vintage drinks, or the beauty of the earrings. The temptation of consumerism, for Seneca, is that impressive possessions allow one to impress other people. We have an insatiable desire for more wealth, not because these objects are desirable in themselves, but because we want to seem admirable in the eyes of others. Avarice is therefore a function of false consciousness: the person who does not know how to become truly good (and therefore truly admirable), by becoming wise and virtuous in the proper Stoic mode, will grasp at these false goods, which can never nourish true self-respect.

Looked at one way, these consumerist desires seem utterly absurd: why would one want things that one never even sees and never gets to use? But Seneca's way of framing the supposedly unanswerable question also implies an answer. These are not things that are wanted for the sake of use; we want them because they are a symbol of social power. The idea that gaining more wealth helps one up the social ladder was a particularly concrete one for any Roman, since social rank was based on a combination of political assets, inherited nobility, and wealth. There was often a tension, very visible in the case of Seneca, between the systems: a man's rank based on his birth might be lower or higher than his financial census ranking. Seneca gained assets that put him well above the equestrian class into which he had been born.

In tragedies such as *Thyestes*, Seneca presents us with characters like Atreus, whose desire for dominance and outdoing others is so insatiable that even making his hated brother eat his own children is not novel or horrific enough: "Crime should have a limit when you do it for the first time, / Not when you're taking revenge. Even this is too little for me" (1052–1053). In the prose work, Seneca reverses the tragic trope of limitless, insatiable lust for power by suggesting that he can have a limitless aspiration toward virtue, even if he never achieves the goal. His first line of defense against the accusations of hypocrisy is to acknowledge their partial truth: he admits that he does not fully practice what he preaches. But he also insists that he is, at the very least, attempting to get closer to the ideal every day. Then he tries to turn the accusation back on the accuser:

> I am not a wise man, and—here's food for your spite!—I never will be. Don't ask me to equal the best people. I just want to be better than the worst. It's enough for me, to reduce a bit from my faults every day, and to blame my mistakes. I haven't reached health, and I never will get there. I'm alleviating my gout not curing it. I'm satisfied if it comes more infrequently, and causes less agony. I'm weak, but look at you; compared to your legs, I'm a racer!

It is striking that, despite the gestures toward generalization in the portrayal of the hypocrite-philosopher, the counter-attack becomes addressed to a single, utterly flawed individual. This allows the conversation to shift from point of principle to the specific behaviors of an individual. One might think that the accusation of hypocrisy ought to be addressed in itself, regardless of who brings it, but Seneca presents the problem in much more personal terms. He also shifts again away from identifying himself entirely with the voice of the philosopher, even the imperfect philosopher: "What I say is not spoken on behalf of myself—for I am in the depths of every vice—but on behalf of the man who has really done something" (17.4). He shimmies quickly from self-accusation, to self-defense, to self-accusation again.

Another prong of the defense lies in turning away from Seneca himself toward the famous philosophers and moral exemplary figures of the past: Plato, Epicurus, Zeno, and the famous Cynic philosophers all suffered accusations of failing to practice what they preached (18.1–19.3). He reminds us that even these great heroes may not have always matched their actions to their words; but the real point about them is not how they failed, but what they achieved. "The practice of trying to become healthy is worth praising, regardless of whether it works. Surely it isn't surprising if people who set off on the steep path don't reach the very top. If you're a man, look up to those who are attempting great things, even if they fall" (20.2). In an inspiring crescendo, Seneca celebrates the attempt to live up to Stoic ideals, even if one fails ever to fully achieve them. But there remains a certain sense of anxiety, a suspicion that ambition, even philosophical ambition, can be dangerous. Seneca ends his call to philosophical aspiration with a quotation from Ovid: even if one fails, "still he fails from mighty acts of daring" (20.5). As Seneca knew, the context in Ovid is the moment when Phaethon, son of the Sun-God, begs to take his father's chariot across the sky: he fails to control the divine horses and falls to his death, scorching the entire earth.

Seneca returns, then, to the topic of whether a philosopher should possess wealth and other material benefits and avoid the "indifferent" problems of death, sickness, or exile. He suggests that the real issue is not whether one has wealth, health, or life; it is how one feels about the possessions. The philosopher will not object if such things fall in his lap and will, in fact, be glad of them; he will be equally calm if they happen to depart: "He does not love riches, but he would rather have them" (*On the Happy Life* 21.4). The justification for this position is that the philosopher is particularly glad of the extra opportunities wealth gives for the practice of virtue: "In poverty, there is only one kind of virtue—not to be oppressed or crushed by it. But in wealth, there is a wide field of opportunity for being moderate, for being generous, for being hard-working, for being orderly, and for greatness." He continues: "The wise man would not despise himself, even if he were a midget; but he would rather be tall" (*On the Happy Life* 22.1).

He goes on to discuss explicitly the Stoic doctrine of the "indifferent things" and to emphasize that even indifferent things, like wealth, may have some value, and some are more desirable than others ("they are worth something, and some are more important than others"). As the orthodox Stoic position held, Seneca withholds words like "good" from the indifferent things: they are valuable, but not good, and the distinction is important. Valuable items are worth choosing over others, if all things are equal; but they are not, in themselves, sufficient for human happiness, and hence, not truly good. Only the life of virtue is truly good. But Seneca does, again in accordance with normal Stoic belief, suggest that some indifferents are better than others. The real question is whether one can enjoy wealth without feeling in the least bit upset if it should ever go away: "If my wealth goes away, it takes with it nothing but itself" (22.5). "To sum up: my wealth is mine; you belong to yours."

Seneca insists, then, that there is a right and a wrong way for a philosopher to be rich. There are three central elements in being rich in the right way. One key factor, as we have seen, is that the wise man will not be dependent on his wealth for happiness; he should be able, like the addressee of Kipling's poem "If," to meet both fortune and disaster "and treat those two imposters just the same." The second major criterion is that the philosophical rich person must acquire his wealth honestly, without taking it illegitimately from anybody else; wealth must not be "stained with somebody else's blood." It is not at all clear that Seneca's own wealth would pass this test. He clearly became wealthy in the service of Nero, as well as through usury that caused suffering in the provinces; and he was at least complicit, if not actually actively responsible, for some of the bloodshed of the regime, including the murder of Britannicus. It is noteworthy that Seneca writes only in the third person about the importance of acquiring wealth honestly. He does not say, "My wealth is taken from nobody else nor tainted with blood," but rather, "The philosopher's wealth will not be stained with another person's blood" (23.1). Moreover, there is some obvious evasiveness about Seneca's treatment of how the "philosopher," that nonexistent abstraction, might actually manage to achieve the vast wealth that, Seneca assures us, he will enjoy but never abuse. It comes, we learn, from "the generosity of Fortune" (23.2); the implication is that it would be rude to reject the gifts of such a goddess. There is no acknowledgment that Fortune might operate through rather unsavory human agents, such as Agrippina and Nero. Indeed, there is no discussion of how, exactly, Fortune might go about depositing wealth into the lap of the philosopher without his doing anything dubious, or indeed anything whatsoever, to acquire it. Like Byron's Don Juan, who finds beautiful women constantly throwing themselves at him without his ever lifting a seductive finger, Seneca's version of the rich philosopher acquires his wealth by a kind of divine accident.

The third essential feature of the Philosopher's behavior around wealth is his generosity. He will show exactly the right degree of beneficence and munificence to those less fortunate than himself—giving constant and ungrudging gifts, not carelessly but with judgment. After all, one of the primary reasons why wealth is beneficial is that it allows an opportunity for giving: *Ubicumque homo est, ibi benefici locus est*: "where there's a human, there's a chance to give" (24.3). But rich people have a chance to give more than poor people and are, in that sense, better off. There is no suggestion here that the best kind of things one could give another person might be immaterial: no suggestion that a *beneficium*, a benefit, might include love or time or labor or thoughtfulness or kind words.

Seneca argues that there are two types of the philosophical rich man. The first type is an imperfect sinner, a philosopher only in the sense that he aspires to become better. He cannot fit his life to his words, but at least he is trying: "You've got no right to push me to live up to my own standards. I'm fashioning myself, I'm molding myself, I'm living myself up to my ideal; if I achieve the goals I've set, then push me to answer words to deeds" (24.4). The other type is stronger and more self-assured. He prefers being rich to being a beggar under the Sublician Bridge (*Pons Sublicius*), a famous haunt of the homeless in Seneca's Rome. He prefers wearing a toga and sandals to "showing naked shoulders and cut feet" (25.2). But he can be happy either way. The tiny acknowledgment of the life of the poorest of the poor in contemporary Rome is striking, not least because the ideal type of philosopher obviously has no impulse whatsoever to help them in their plight. They are an image of what he could be; they are not people whom he might have a responsibility to help.[32]

Seneca does not present himself as one who has achieved the ideal relationship to wealth. The ideal philosophical character is not himself but Socrates, who takes over the essay and declares his support for the Stoic point of view. Socrates—famous for not charging for his teaching, and for owning only a single cloak that he wore both summer and winter—is not an obvious supporter for the idea that the philosopher would like to be very rich, if possible. But Seneca insists that Socrates is, when it comes down to it, on his side: those who criticize philosophers for being rich are no different from those who attacked, imprisoned, and executed that long-suffering Athenian: "Go on, jump on me, attack me: I'll conquer by enduring" (27.3). The charges of hypocrisy against philosophers are, it turns out, leveled by people who are themselves hypocrites, and who fail even to listen carefully to the philosophers' words: "So I don't live one way and talk another," says the wise man; "I talk one way and you hear another. You don't even ask what my words mean" (25.8).

Other moral issues raised by the philosopher's wealth are given short shrift. Seneca barely touches on whether the acquisition and possession and use of wealth by an individual represents and causes significant social injustice. He mentions, briefly, that wealth should be acquired legitimately, but that is all. Perhaps unsurprisingly, there is no mention in his extant work of his own activities as a moneylender or real estate agent. Nor, again unsurprisingly, is there any explicit discussion of his acquisitions from Nero and from the imperial house in general.

Seneca says far more about where wealth should go than about where it comes from. He does place a significant amount of attention on the issue of what a rich person ought to do with his (always *his*) money. But the focus in his most extensive treatment of this issue—*On Benefits*—is far more on the motivation of the giver than on any benefit accrued to the recipient, and far more focused on the horizontal relationships between peers than on the vertical relationships between people at different levels of society.[33] He is not interested in whether the poor have a right to receive some of the money accrued by the rich; the idea of redistribution of wealth, for Seneca, as indeed for almost everybody in antiquity, does not arise. Seneca has little or no interest in wealth as an issue of political justice. His major concern, rather, is with the kinds of debts and social obligations that are incurred for the rich man by giving and receiving wealth.

In terms of Seneca's everyday life, being wealthy and influential created a whole set of daily social interactions. Seneca was a patron to many lesser people and felt the thrill that came from seeing so many others dependent on him and eager to solicit his favor: a man's dignity (*dignitas*) was directly correlated to the number of clients he accrued. His day began with a great crowd of morning callers, men who would show up at his house and compete for his attention, petitioning for favors, gifts, money, and recognition. Even once he left the house, he would be followed by a trail of his clients. Later in the day, he was expected to entertain them at lavish dinner parties; those five hundred ivory-legged tables had a lot of use. Clients were people who were officially and legally under the rich man's patronage. He took care of them financially and politically, and in return, they would show deference to him, visit him and follow him around, promote him if he tried for any public office, and generally contribute to his popularity, honor, and safety. One important member of Seneca's clientele was Fabius Rusticus, a writer who composed either a history of the period or a biography of Seneca, now lost. His favorable account of Seneca's life and character helped shape his reputation among subsequent Roman historians who used his work as a source. The patron, in this instance as in others, benefited from the client. Seneca was a generous patron: Juvenal laments the fact that in his own generation—at the end of the first century CE—patrons are not as beneficent as Seneca was in days of yore. He tells his contemporary benefactor, "No one asks you for the kind of noble presents that Seneca, kind Piso or Cotta, used to send to their lowly friends: in the old days, the glory of giving was considered grander than titles or fasces" (Juvenal, *Satire*, 5).[34] Seneca used his enormous wealth to maintain his social circle, creating for himself a position at the center of an alternative, parallel world to Nero's court.[35]

KINDNESS AND GRATITUDE

Seneca did not stand entirely aloof from the hedonistic and theatrical antics of Nero and his court. One ancient rumor, preserved in Dio, reports that he had many affairs with "boys past their prime"—in ancient thinking, sleeping with grown men was a far more disgusting practice than sex with a young adolescent—and taught Nero to do the same (Dio 61). But this is likely to be the kind of gossip that would have accrued to any prominent intellectual; philosophers were assumed to have unpleasant Greek-style patterns of behavior. The same source also suggests that early on in Nero's reign, Seneca tried to avoid going to the emperor's dinner parties, giving the "excuse" that he wanted to be able to philosophize in peace. It is likely that Seneca sometimes longed for some time alone or away from the absurdities and excesses of court life, but he must also have known that too much rejection would make the emperor angry. Rather than withdraw, in fact, he took an active part in the emperor's decisions, both personal and political, throughout the 50s.

As we have seen, Seneca had been helpful in enabling Nero's love affair with the freedwoman Acte. But the emperor's romantic life became even more complicated when he fell in love with a noblewoman called Poppaea Sabina and wanted not only to seduce her but to marry her. Poppaea was the wife of Nero's party-loving friend, Otho (who would later, briefly, seize control of the empire). Various versions of the story circulate in the ancient sources; Dio tells us that Nero arranged the marriage of Otho and Poppaea in order to have ready access to her. In any case, Nero hoped to divorce Octavia and marry Poppaea.

All that stood in his way was Agrippina's disapproval: she did not want her son to divorce the wife she had chosen for him. Nero was presumably motivated not only by desire for Poppaea but also (a theme that emerges even more strongly in the ancient sources) by desire to be rid of his mother's power and influence once and for all. He had ejected her from the palace and made her move to a villa in the south of Rome, but he was still haunted by the possibility of her exerting control over him or, as Tacitus puts it, the thought that "wherever she might be, she would be a heavy burden upon him" (14.3.1). So Nero decided to kill his mother.

Even by the unscrupulous standards of the Julio-Claudian dynasty, this was a radical move and one that would be difficult to pull off. The Roman public, if they discovered the truth, were not likely to treat matricide as an acceptable type of behavior. There were hardly any precedents, and those few were not such as to inspire confidence in the would-be killer. In Egypt some hundred twenty years previously (80 CE), the new ruler, Ptolemy XI, had been instructed in his uncle's will to marry his stepmother; he obeyed but then killed her (for reasons unknown). He was immediately lynched by the citizens. Nero must have believed that his hold on power, and on public opinion, was firm enough that he could take the risk and not suffer the same fate. The decision displays not only his extraordinary lack of moral scruple or family feeling but also his implicit faith in his advisors: without the help of Seneca, Burrus, and his other aides, Nero could never have pulled it off.

On the recommendation of a freedman called Anicetus—his childhood tutor in the days before Seneca took over—Nero decided on the elaborate scheme of putting Agrippina in a boat out at sea that would be prefabricated to fall apart in the water. He invited her for a pleasure trip in this doomed boat. Agrippina was not stupid and was quite well aware that she was not in her son's good graces, but she may have found it hard to believe at first that her own child wanted to kill her. Moreover, to betray her suspicions would have given Nero further ammunition against her. So, despite being wary of a trick, she came and embarked in the boat. But the plot failed; the boat did not disintegrate as planned, and Agrippina escaped with only slight injuries (Tacitus 14.6).

However, after this fiasco, Agrippina was all too well aware that her son was trying to kill her. At that stage, Nero knew that he needed more help in following through his plan. He turned, of course, to his closest and most reliable advisors, Seneca and Burrus—who may already have known about the plot. He summoned them and told them what he hoped to do. We are told that they were at first silent. As Tacitus notes, it was not clear whether they were shocked or just taking time to strategize—as if they might already have known his intentions all along. Then, we are told, "Seneca took the initiative. He looked at Burrus and asked if the military should be ordered to carry out the killing" (14.7). They did so, and Agrippina, in her bedroom, was pounced upon by a mob of soldiers. She knew, of course, that they came from her son. She told them, as they began to club and cut her to death, "Strike here!"—pointing to the womb from whence Nero came (Tacitus, *Annals*, 14.8). In Dio's account, Agrippina had always suspected it might come to this: in scheming for her son's rise to power, she declared, "Let him kill me, as long as he rules" (Dio, *Roman History* 61.1.2).

What are we to make of Seneca's role in this appalling story? Agrippina was Seneca's most important benefactor. She was the woman who had secured his recall from exile and had made him an essential member of court by appointing him as the tutor, and then primary advisor, of her son. And yet he not only colluded in her murder but took the lead in strategizing on how it should be done, and in the aftermath, it was Seneca who wrote a letter to the Senate—supposedly from Nero, who was hiding out in Naples—justifying what had happened. It suggested that Agrippina had been plotting to assassinate Nero, and that, when a concealed weapon was discovered on the person of her freedman, Agrippina had had to die. She deserved death anyway—the letter claimed—for having hoped for "partnership in the empire" and for the degrading prospect that the Guard, the Senate, and the people should all submit to the rule of a woman. All evils of the Claudian period were ascribed to Agrippina; now, the letter suggested, the nation would live under luckier stars (Tacitus 14.11–12). Nero was made to present himself as having been under threat for his life from Agrippina: the letter included the line, "Even now, I neither believe in my safety, nor am happy about it" (Quintilian, *Institutes* 8.18). Even in a world where dissimulation was the norm and where imperial households were commonly stained with blood, Seneca had gone too far, and the public was disgusted. People were more outraged, we are told, by Seneca than by the barbarous Nero, at whom there was no longer any point in being shocked: "Seneca wrote a confession in that letter," they believed (Tacitus 14.11). Despite private mutterings, most people, including the Senate, went along with the official position. Celebrations were held and yearly thanksgivings established for the salvation of the emperor from danger.

Seneca's complex, guilty, apologetic. and defensive response to what he had done can be glimpsed through one of his longest and most challenging works of prose: the treatise *On Benefits,* a seven-book account of social obligation.[36] This work was probably composed over a fairly long period, with the earlier books being written perhaps very soon after Agrippina's death and the last books closer in time to Seneca's attempt at retirement. The book gives a glimpse into Seneca's mind, in his attempt to untangle the obvious questions raised by his relationships both with Nero and with Agrippina. For instance: What, if anything, did he owe them? In bringing Seneca back from exile, in supporting his career and employing him and elevating him to the top advisory position in the land, had she put him in her debt? Had Nero himself put Seneca in his debt, by giving him money, villas, friendship, and social status? What exactly is a gift, and what kind of return does it demand from the receiver of that gift—if any? And conversely, had Seneca himself given anything to Agrippina and her son, through his intellectual and political service? How could material gifts be weighed against intellectual gifts? Or might they be incommensurable? It is unsurprising that such questions were on Seneca's mind, although it is fascinating to see how thoroughly, indeed obsessively, he deals with them in *On Benefits,* which many have seen as an oddly repetitive book. He circles round the key questions over and over, as if constantly unsatisfied with the answers he insists on giving.

Seneca's essay is very abstract, applicable to any human being in a position of giving or receiving something from another. But it is very obviously the product of long and deep meditations on Seneca's own situation in particular. As a public document—which it certainly was—*On Benefits* serves as a response to those who might suspect Seneca of ingratitude towards poor murdered Agrippina. It also provides a platform for Seneca to defend himself against any suspicion that he might be serving Nero only for material advantages. And it also acts to defend Seneca against the possibility that he might never be able to pay back these benefactors for their gifts. This is, then, a subtle and effective mechanism for dealing both with the author's own guilt and anxiety about his position and with the public suspicions of a philosopher in such a position of power.

As Emerson wrote in his famous essay "Gifts," the "law of benefits is a dangerous channel." On the one hand, gifts are socially obligatory; they are supposed to cement our ties to one another. On the other, the idea of sealing a relationship with a material object is inherently problematic. Either the recipient will be delighted with the object (in which case there is a risk that he or she likes the commodity more than the giver) or else the recipient does not care for the gift (in which case the process is pointless). Or it is worse than pointless: the practice that seems designed to bind us to each other may actually create hostility and reinforce our sense of inequality. We do not quite forgive a giver, because accepting gifts inevitably puts us in a position of dependence. Emerson suggests that, for precisely this reason, good gifts are those that have no obvious utility value but represent ideals of beauty (like fruits or flowers). The best gifts of all involve the gift of oneself. "There is no commensurability between a man and any gift," and thus, the exchange of material objects has no real correlation to the element of gift-giving that actually matters, which is our relationships with one another. Emerson's piece ends by suggesting that what really matters is not whether we give each other things, but whether we love each other. Without love, all gifts are an insult and cannot buy the one thing needful ("they eat your services like apples, and leave you out"). With love, the god of gifts, the material value of any gift is irrelevant; kingdoms and flower-leaves count for just the same.

Emerson's approach to the complex social network created by gift exchange is not identical with Seneca's. But Seneca, like Emerson, is interested in exploring the dilemmas involved in power, generosity, and dependence and in searching for an alternative to the kind of relationship that is always concerned with profit and status. Seneca begins by declaring that "among all the many different mistakes of those who live thoughtlessly and foolishly, almost none is as disgraceful, excellent Liberalis, as the fact that we don't know either how to give or receive benefits." The exaggeration is familiar from other essays (as, for instance, we were told in *On Anger* that anger is the most destructive of all forces in human life). The addressee, Aebutius Liberalis, is a man from a fairly old and respectable family, about whom very little is known. One may suspect that one reason Seneca chose him as addressee was for his name: "Liberalis" connotes freedom and also the behavior of a free person, as opposed to a slave. The treatise is concerned with how we might be able to deal with each other without being trapped in social obligations and exploitation.

A benefit—*beneficium* in Latin—is literally a good deed. Seneca defines it in the first book as "a well-intentioned act that both gives joy, and takes joy in giving it, and is ready and voluntarily prepared for the gift." The giving and receiving of benefits (in Greek, *euergeteia*) was a practice that had first become prominent in Hellenistic culture, with the development of large urban centers, in which the wealthiest members of society displayed and increased their status by donating part of their wealth to the community rather than to particular members of their family or close friends. In Rome, benefits became associated with the patron–client relationships, in which a rich and powerful man would have a group of men, usually of somewhat lesser social and economic status, whom he protected and enriched, in return for political support and other kinds of social help. The crucial fact about "benefits" in both Hellenistic and Roman societies was that they were favors distributed to people outside the donor's kinship circle or close friends. Giving favors was thus an important tool for social cohesion in big urban societies.

Seneca draws on lost Hellenistic Stoic sources in his discussion of the topic,[37] but he seems to have modified their approach to generosity and gratitude, in characteristic fashion. He focuses less on the theoretical ethical ideal of the wise man (who alone, so the Greek Stoics insisted, can give a true benefit, or be grateful for one received) and more on the practicalities of social behavior for real people in the contemporary city, who are not yet perfectly wise. He criticizes Chrysippus, the third Greek leader of the Stoic school and the most important thinker in creating Stoic doctrine, for being too abstruse in his account of gift-giving and generosity and for relying on Greek myth rather than practical examples: Chrysippus, he declares, was "a great man, no doubt, but a Greek" (1.4.1). Seneca's Roman focus is more practical and more focused on the sociopolitical: "We must set down the method that most binds human society together." For this purpose, fancy interpretations of Greek myth are of no use at all. The figure of the perfect Stoic sage is of interest to Seneca not as an abstraction but as a tool to enable his readers to behave better toward one another. The paradoxical theories of Stoicism are, he insists, entirely reconcilable with the normal intuitions of common sense. The word "benefit" has two meanings. We associate "doing right" by somebody with actually causing some kind of material improvement in his or her situation, and we associate repayment with making a material gift back, in kind. But on the other, we think of a "good deed" as involving an intention, on the part of the benefactor, to act benevolently—whether or not the recipient actually receives a material advantage, and a grateful attitude from the recipient is, in itself, a form of repayment. Seneca insists, in keeping with the standard Stoic view, that the second, internal and immaterial kinds of "benefit" and "repayment" are the really important ones. But he also insists that if one has the right attitude, the right gifts and the right social relationships will usually follow; the abstractions of Stoicism are thus entirely reconcilable with the needs of contemporary society.

But there are still tensions in Seneca's account between ideal and reality, and between the needs of the donor and the needs of the recipient. These are, as Seneca acknowledges, significantly different. The recipient—especially if he is receiving a gift or a favor from a richer or more powerful person—wants to avoid feeling humiliated by his position of dependence. From this point of view, it is important for Seneca to insist that social relationships can rise above the merely material: intentions matter more than base profit, such that the recipient, in feeling grateful, has already discharged his obligation. But in addressing the donor's point of view, it is also important for Seneca to insist that one should continue to give in material ways, even to those who have no hope of paying one back materially, since one's own virtuous action is its own kind of profit. One should think of these acts of generosity "not as investments, but gifts" (1.9). "A person who thinks of repayment when he gives, deserves to be deceived" (1.10).

Seneca's essay insists that a wise man can go beyond the hierarchical relationships of power and patronage and exchange to an ideal social relationship in which neither party wants to profit by the other.[38] But the language of debt, exchange, and profit keeps coming back: for example, Seneca compares the rich male patron to a high-class prostitute (a *meretrix* or courtesan, whose clients hope for intimacy as well as sex) who has to parcel out her favors in such a way that every client gets something and can "believe he is preferred to the rest" (*De Ben.* 1.14.4).[39]

Like Seneca's other treatises, then, the *De Beneficiis* has many passages that are deeply resonant with the conditions of Seneca's own life. Seneca's arguments in the essay allow him to suggest positive interpretations of his own service to the Neronian court, even though he never actually draws the connection directly. For instance, his insistence that the most important benefits are not material at all allows him to offer an implicit answer to those, like Suillius, who complained at how rich he had become in the course of a few short years' service at court. This might seem, as Suillius suggested, unfair and corrupt, but the unfairness dissipates if one accepts Seneca's argument that tangible benefits are unimportant: "A benefit cannot be touched by the hand: it concerns the mind." This is a wonderful way of having his cake and eating it too. Nobody need be jealous or critical of his own huge material benefits under Nero, because wealth and status are not real benefits; the real gift Nero has given him, if any, comes from the mind.

The treatise deals extensively with the issue of whether a person of lesser status or wealth must necessarily feel humiliated by gifts from a patron. Seneca must inevitably have been seen by others as dependent on the emperor, as in a material sense he certainly was, and he himself struggled with the problem of whether that put him in a degrading position or compromised his freedom. The notion that a real benefit is an immaterial thing, a function of the mind's intentions, is some help in this psychological dilemma. From this point of view, Nero—and Claudius and Agrippina before him—gave Seneca no more than he gave to them, or perhaps rather less.

But there are several passages that suggest that Seneca is struggling with the question of whether he really ought to have put himself in the position of accepting the gifts of the court, and the related question of whether he even had a choice about it at all. He tells the story of Socrates' encounter with Archelaus, ruler of Macedon, who invited him to come and visit and receive "benefits" from him. Socrates replied that he would not go, because he could not pay back the favors, since he was a poor man (*De Ben.* 5.6.2–5.6.7). On Seneca's reading, Socrates was being disingenuous, or characteristically ironic. Of course he was able to give the king far more than the king could give him, but he wanted to avoid putting himself in a situation where "he might be forced to accept gifts that he didn't want: forced to accept something unworthy of Socrates" (5.6.6). He was declining a position of "voluntary servitude" (*voluntaria servitudo*). This story about Socrates is paired with another, early on in the essay, in which we are reminded of Aeschines, who could offer Socrates nothing for his teaching—except himself, which was (of course) the most valuable thing of all: "By this gift Aeschines surpassed Alcibiades." Seneca suggests, in this pair of anecdotes, a yearning for the freedom of Socrates. He works hard to dispel any suggestion (by, again, the likes of Suillius) that he might be serving Nero for mercenary reasons. But he was clearly anxious that he might be trapped, having made the choice to work not with a poor Aeschines, but a rich Archilaus, as his student and patron.

Seneca several times seems to fantasize about the possibility of rejecting the patronage of the emperor. He evokes the possibility that one might want to reject a benefit: "Take it back! I don't want it! I am happy with what I have!"... "Sometimes it is a pleasure not just to give back what you've received, but hurl it away!"

But he also gives an implicit defense of his own choices in accepting the favors of Claudius, Agrippina, and Nero in the first place. For instance, he discusses the possibility that one might be offered favors from somebody one did not entirely respect. He notes that Crispus Passienus—a powerful and intellectual man who was briefly married to Agrippina but then was poisoned, possibly by her—used to say that one ought to gain the respect of people one respects (rather than their material favors) but take material favors from people one does not respect. The examples he gave of the two categories were the admirable Augustus and the despicable Claudius. Seneca challenges this view, suggesting that "one should never seek a favor from one whose respect you despise" (1.15.6).

How, then, could Seneca justify accepting a favor from the despised Claudius—such as recall from exile? He has an ingenious answer: one can accept a benefit "as if from Fortune, whom you realize might next minute become unkind." This is a clever psychological move: whenever you are in the shameful position of being under an obligation to a person you do not admire, simply imagine that the gift comes from Fortune, not the human donor. Conveniently enough, it also implies that Seneca need feel no particular obligation to those—like Agrippina—who might seem to have been his benefactors, if they should turn out to be less-than-admirable people. "The gift of a huge sum of money is no more a benefit than a treasure trove, unless it was given with reason and proper intention. There are many gifts that should be accepted, but impose no obligation" (1.15.6). From this point of view, far from being trapped by the duty to be grateful to his despicable benefactors, Seneca was entirely free from any obligation toward them. There was no need, therefore, to feel even the slightest twinge of guilt over his benefactress' death.

The question still arises of whether one might be in a humiliating position through being too dependent on somebody else's material and social support. Seneca repeatedly returns to this question: he is highly conscious of the ways that receiving favors can make the recipient feel vulnerable and hurt: "The repeated reminder of our services wounds and crushes the spirit" (2.1.11). Some gifts harm the recipient (2.1.14): one may say, "That man killed me by love" (2.14.5). At times, he suggests that one is always free to say no. He discusses the philosophical hypocrisy of a Cynic who had a "declared hatred of money" and yet asked a king for a handout (2.14.2). But he also suggests that sometimes one can be made an offer one can't refuse. Seneca imagines an interlocutor asking, "But I'm not always allowed to say, `I don't want it'; sometimes I have to accept a benefit, even if I don't want to" (2.18.6). In that case, he suggests, we can reimagine what is happening: you are not accepting, but obeying. In cases where one is unable to refuse a gift one does not want, one must either imagine that the favor comes from Fortune, not the despicable donor, or else define it as something other than a favor: "The benefit is none at all, if it is coerced." He still acknowledges that "it is absolute torture to be obliged to somebody you don't like" (2.18.3). But the mental torture can be reduced if you can deny that you are really so obliged.

Milton's Satan memorably articulates the rage and horror aroused by the obligation of gratitude for one who wants to feel fully autonomous. Satan hates "the debt immense of endless gratitude, / So burdensome: still paying, still to owe" (*Paradise Lost* 4.52–53). This is in many ways a very Senecan sentiment (and Satan a very Stoic kind of hero). But Seneca, in his philosophical rather than tragic mode, finds a solution: one need not feel trapped by gifts that seem too munificent, because gratitude itself is repayment of the debt of gratitude. In itself, it fulfills the spiritual debt: "you may pay with what you have" (2.35.5).

What of the problem with which the treatise begins: ingratitude? We are told that it has three causes: pride, greed, and jealousy (2.26.1). Seneca's discussion of these vices is highly reminiscent of his depiction of various tragic figures who are overwhelmed by their overweening ambitions and desires, such as Atreus in *Thyestes*. "Desire goes beyond itself and does not understand its own happiness, because it looks not to where it came from but to where it goes." By contrast, true gratitude begins with an awareness of nature and the gods, from whom we come. In taking seriously the issue of ingratitude, Seneca implicitly defends himself against it; he defines himself not as one who has covered up the murder of his benefactress, but rather as a man who understands how to be truly grateful—although only where gratitude is genuinely appropriate. Plato in the first book of the *Republic* had raised a philosophical problem that recurs in later ancient discussions of justice, namely whether one must always pay back what one owes—even if the lender changes. Plato's example is of a man who lends you a knife: should you give it back if he goes mad? Seneca turns to this problem in Book 7 of the *Benefits* and gives it a political twist, imagining that the lender might turn "as savage and dangerous as Apollodorus or Phalaris"—notorious tyrants (7.19.5). The problem thus takes on an obvious relevance for Seneca's own relationships with Claudius, Agrippina, and Nero. If one of these supposed benefactors turned bad, would Seneca still be under an obligation to pay him or her back? Seneca's response is startlingly optimistic: he argues that such a thing could never happen. "Nobody who has ever adhered to wisdom could fall into the utmost evil; he is too deeply-dyed for the color to wash out entirely and take on a wicked shade" (7.19.6). Seneca is here reassuring himself as much as the reading public that his training of the young emperor has been so effective that it can never be erased.

But the issue of whether he has been ungrateful to Agrippina seems still to lurk in the background. He tells the story of a Pythagorean philosopher who bought some shoes without paying for them and came back later to give the money. In the meantime, the shoemaker died. The philosopher was at first happy to get away without paying, but in the end, overwhelmed by conscience, he returned to the store and dropped the money into the locked door of the dead man's house, as a lesson to himself to avoid being in debt (7. 21.1–2). Seneca tells the story with sympathy and suggests that it makes no difference whether the donor is alive or dead, nor whether the donor is good or bad: one still has a duty to remember the act of generosity and to repay it. "First pay, then accuse."

The attempt in *De Beneficiis* to create an ideal picture of social relationships, in the always-generous donor and the ever-grateful but never-humiliated recipient, constantly comes up against the issue of profit—both metaphorical and literal profit. Seneca inveighs against the notion that one should aim only for profit, or even at all for profit; yet he also suggests that gratitude is, at least metaphorically, the profit reaped by the donor from the recipient, and the fulfillment of a debt. Benefits should not be loans and should not be associated with "shameful usury" (1.2.4).

Theory and practice did not entirely match up. Soon after Seneca composed *De Beneficiis*, trouble arose in the provinces that may have been partly exacerbated by his profiteering. In 60–61 in Britain the king of a native tribe, the Iceni, named Prasutagus, had died and had specified in his will that he wanted half his estate to go to his daughters. The

Roman overseer ignored the request and seized the whole estate; the daughters were raped. Dio tells us that at this same delicate time, a group of Roman financiers, including Seneca, suddenly called in large loans that they had forced on the British natives in the hope of making a quick profit. This was an economic disaster, which reinforced the British people's discomfort with being under the thumb of Rome. The story might be false: it does not appear in Tacitus, perhaps because he had reason to disbelieve it. But it is at least possible that Seneca may have been at least partly responsible for increasing the suffering and rage in this particular distant Roman province.

The British rebellion makes a fascinating counterpoint to Seneca's discussion of gratitude and generosity, in particular to the issue of whether "benefits" from a despised patron must necessarily compromise the recipient's freedom. The native king's widow, Queen Boudica (Fig. 3.6), led her people in rebellion against Rome and gave brilliant and rousing speeches against the foreign overlords, who taxed them and threatened to take away their liberty and their identity: "But let us do our duty

Figure 3.6 Queen Boudica led her people (the British Iceni) in a failed attempt at rebellion against Roman rule—an uprising that apparently took place when rich moneylenders, including Seneca, suddenly called in their loans from Britain.

while we still remember what freedom is, to leave our children not just its name, but the reality. . . . Let's go against them boldly, trusting fortune. Let's show them that they are hares and foxes trying to rule over wolves!" (Dio 61). The rebellion was put down, and Boudica died (perhaps by suicide), but her insistence on autonomy and freedom from the external power of the Romans stands in marked and shaming contrast to Seneca's pandering to Nero's wishes.

SPECTACLES OF POWER

"Like a Theater" (theatric more)[40]

It is tempting to defend Seneca's compromised position in the court by arguing that he had no choice; after all, if he had spoken against any of Nero's actions—including the murders of Britannicus and Agrippina— or been reluctant to defend them to the public, he would not have lasted long. Certainly, it would have taken enormous courage to back out of the hole. But it would surely have been possible, if Seneca had been able to live by his more defiant words about the ever-present availability of death. Megara, wife of Hercules in Seneca's play of that name, stands up to the tyrant Lycus and declares, "If you can be forced, you don't know how to die" (Hercules Furens 426). It took Seneca a long time to teach himself this lesson.

There was a strong contrast between Seneca's position in Nero's court and that of the most prominent other Stoic in government at the time: Thrasea Paetus. Thrasea was not a philosopher or writer but a politician and an aristocrat, a member of the Senate, who is presented, in both Tacitus and Dio, as a man of absolute integrity. He was the only one who expressed disapproval of the speech Seneca delivered to the Senate in defense of Nero's killing of his mother: when it was delivered, Thrasea walked out (Tacitus 14.12). In Dio's telling, Thrasea gave a very practical reason for not bowing to Nero's will, namely that even those who flattered the emperor were likely to be killed anyway; why compromise oneself if safety is never guaranteed? "Why should one humiliate oneself for no reason, and then die like a slave, when it's possible to pay the debt to nature like a free man? As for me, men will talk about me in the future; but those flatterers will never be spoken of, except to record the fact that they were put to death" (Dio 61.15.4). He would also declare, "Nero can kill me, but he cannot harm me." The existence of Thrasea suggests at least the possibility of refusing to compromise under Nero—a possibility that Seneca manifestly did not take up. This is not the only time that Seneca looks rather shabby in comparison to Thrasea.

Thrasea's integrity is associated particularly with his adamant opposition to the culture of falsehood and theatricality that Nero cultivated in his court. Seneca and Burrus tried in vain to restrain Nero's more extravagant passions for sport and theater but realized it was impossible to stop him, so they tried to reduce the damage. For instance, when he was keen to try chariot racing, and also interested in singing the lyre on stage, they urged him to focus on the chariot racing and to do so in a quiet, private spot where he would not be seen (Tacitus 14.14). In fact, Seneca and Burrus had quite a good motive for promoting the chariot racing as much as possible, since it was an extremely dangerous activity. But the emperor survived.

Nero was not to be restrained from his desire to sing and act on stage, and it seems very unlikely that Seneca ever hoped he could be. It has been well noted that Nero not only acted himself but forced all those around him (with the notable exception of Thrasea) to become "actors in the audience," playing the part of the good, appreciative spectator. Theatricality was the dominant mode of the age. The spectacular entertainments available to the Roman public included not only chariot racing, theater, and athletic displays but also, of course, gladiator fights in the Colosseum, in which men—usually prisoners of war or condemned criminals—were forced to fight to the death either against each other or against exotic wild animals (lions, elephants, bulls, tigers)—or both. The Games were hugely popular and had their own theatrical conventions, costumes, and props: the man with the net was known as the *reticulator* and the man with the sword was the *gladiator*.

Seneca has often been celebrated as one of the most humane voices from this most inhumane of historical periods in his hostility to gladiator fighting. He certainly does provide vivid and articulate accounts of how brutally cruel the practice was. In the mornings, Roman gladiatorial shows were usually carefully scripted theatrical performances, involving elaborate costumes, props, and weapons for the fighters and expensive wild animals to attack the humans. But during the lunch break, spectators were treated to a show that involved far less trouble for the organizers: condemned criminals were simply pushed into the arena and forced to kill one another. It is against this practice that Seneca's greatest ire is aroused:

> In the morning they throw the men to the lions and bears; at lunchtime, to the spectators. The audience demands that each person who has killed should face the one who will kill him in his turn; they keep the victor for another slaughter. The end of every fight is death; it's enacted by sword and by fire. This happens when the arena is empty! You may say, "He's a robber! He killed somebody!" And so, what follows? He deserves to suffer this punishment for his crime. But you, poor man, what did you do that you deserve to watch it?
>
> (Epistle 7.5)

The passage is certainly a denunciation of the practice of having these criminals kill one another in public. But the central complaint Seneca raises against it is not that it is unfair on those killed; he suggests that they deserve all they get. Rather, it is damaging to those who watch and are brutalized by watching.

We might feel disappointed that Seneca does not take a broader political stance against an institution that will strike most modern people as brutal and cruel. Why did Seneca not call for an end to gladiatorial combat rather than watch it and then complain about it? Why does he show so little empathy for the non-elite people who suffered and died in the arena—as opposed to his deep attentiveness to the psychological needs of the elite who watched the torments with pleasure? But it is asking too much for any person, however philosophical, to rise far above the culture of his or her own time. As Miriam Griffin has emphasized, Seneca was very much a man of his own era, shaped by the culture in which he was born and raised. His views on gladiator fighting were not all that different from those of other philosophers and intellectuals of the period. The distinctive feature of Seneca's writings about this practice, and the feature we ought to continue to admire and praise, is the unforgettable vigor with which he evokes the bloodlust of the audience at the games and the psychological truth of his central insight that watching acts of pain and cruelty does real harm to our souls. Seneca complains that he returns home worse from every trip to the arena (Epistle 7.3). Seneca was entangled in a world of cruelty and theatricality, but he was also willing to acknowledge that we can do ourselves real harm by our habits of cultural consumption.

Nero did not share his old tutor's doubts about the value of the Colosseum, but he wanted to be the performer, not the spectator. He responded to the tensions and pressures of his position as emperor by transforming power into a kind of performance art. When Nero performed, either on his lyre, or reciting poetry, or as an actor on stage, everybody was forced to applaud, and everybody fell into line. Only Thrasea refused; everyone else gathered eagerly to watch and pretended to love the show (Dio 62.19). Moreover, Seneca and Burrus, we are told, would coach Nero on his performances on stage: "Beside him stood Burrus and Seneca, like teachers, prompting him; they would wave their arms and togas at everything he said, and lead others to do the same."[41]

We can contrast Seneca's willingness to engage with Nero's theatrical performances with the strong opposition of another, somewhat younger Stoic contemporary: Epictetus. Epictetus, a Greek from the city of Hieropolis in Phrygia (modern Turkey), was from an entirely different social and economic class from Seneca or Thrasea: he was an ex-slave, who was poor all his life. He was a man with no claims to literary or rhetorical education and no political ambition, who spent the whole of the first half of his life as a slave. He was a lifelong cripple, probably the result of having his leg broken by a cruel owner in early life. But he was brought to Rome in his youth and owned by Nero's secretary, the freedman Epaphroditus. During that time, he studied Stoic philosophy with the great Stoic teacher, Musonius Rufus. Epictetus himself became a great and influential philosophical teacher, whose lectures and teachings were recorded by a devoted pupil, Arrian, as the *Discourses*. Unlike Seneca—in this respect as in many others—Epictetus was not interested in crafting beautiful prose that would live through the ages.

In 1.2 of the *Discourses*, Epictetus raises the wonderful question—essential too for thinking about Seneca—of how a person can preserve his own proper role or "face" or "mask" in every possible circumstance, even when threatened with death, torture, slavery, amputation, or any other of the "nonpreferable" indifferents. Epictetus deals explicitly with the question of what one should do when asked to compromise with Nero—for instance, when asked to contribute to a festival by the emperor. The language is deeply theatrical and deeply concerned with a conflict between multiple different dramatic events: the drama of Nero's literal festival; the drama of political life in general; and the more individual drama of a person's own life, in which he or she has a responsibility to act out the proper part assigned by nature. Epictetus writes,

> When a person once stoops to the consideration of such questions [as whether to contribute to a festival of Nero's], he comes close to those who have forgotten their proper character. Come, what is this you ask me? "Is death or life preferable?" I answer, life. "Pain or pleasure?" I answer, pleasure. "But unless I take part in the tragedy I shall be beheaded." Go, then, and take a part, but I shall not take a part."

Epictetus thus provides a model for how it might have been possible, for Seneca or anybody, to opt out of the dissimulations and dramas of Nero's court. His account also presumes, as in standard Stoicism, that a man's true nature is incompatible with playing a part. He picks up the hostility to theater that is a common trope in Roman literature of this period. As Cornelius Nepos notes, "Almost everywhere in Greece, it was thought a high honor to be proclaimed victor at Olympia. Even to appear on the stage and exhibit oneself to the people was never regarded by those nations as something to be ashamed of. Among us, however, all those acts are regarded either as disgraceful or as base and inconsistent with respectability" (Nepos pr. 5).[42] Epictetus often suggests a certain distance, and even hostility, toward the life of the imperial court, insisting that becoming "Caesar's friend" is not actually the path to happiness.[43]

By contrast, it is quite possible that Seneca not only participated in Nero's theatrical displays but also enjoyed them. Nero "forced" Roman noblemen on stage to "pollute themselves" by performing speeches or poems in this degrading public environment (Tacitus 14.20); one of those so polluted was Seneca's nephew, Lucan, the poet. We do not know if Seneca himself performed on stage, although it is very likely that he did. We also do not know if Seneca's own dramas were used in Nero's shows. But it is easy to see that Seneca's tragedies are dramatic meditations on cruelty, pollution, and disgust, on horrific extremes of behavior, on power, on failed attempts at teaching restraint or moderation, and on spectacle—all themes to resonate very suggestively with the world of Neronian Rome.

In writing plays, Seneca was providing Nero with his favorite art form, catering to his cultural needs, and showing himself as a kindred spirit to the great man. He was simultaneously rivaling the emperor's art with his own and holding up an unflattering mirror to Nero's Rome as a world of violence, naked ambition, and excess. But the mirror reflects the author as much as his student: through tragedy, Seneca was able to contemplate his own ambitions. The tragedies show how acutely aware Seneca was of emotional complexity, including the emotional toll borne by those who, through their own bad choices, destroy their own lives. One recurrent trope of these dramas is the long list of far-flung place names, tracing out the limits of the Roman Empire: even in so vast and rich a world, Seneca's tragic characters constantly find themselves trapped inside their minds. Another repeated trope is the listing of the punishments of the underworld—Sisyphus pushing the rock uphill, Tantalus always hungry and thirsty, Ixion on his wheel. Even death, in these dramas, provides no relief from the endless sense of being trapped and frustrated.

At least one of Seneca's tragedies, the brilliant and terrifying *Thyestes*, was probably written under Nero and can be read as an extensive, deeply pessimistic meditation on Seneca's service to the emperor. It suggests his awareness of his own ambition, weakness, and fear and of how badly his attempts at educating and advising Nero had gone. The central motif of the tragedy is eating—of the most horrible, cannibalistic kind (a father eats his own children). More generally and abstractly, this is a drama about appetite and its discontents. Desire is utterly destructive and utterly inescapable. The play tells the story of two brothers, Thyestes and Atreus, the grandsons of Tantalus. Tantalus had stolen up to heaven, discovered and revealed the secrets of the gods, and topped off his blasphemies by serving up his own son, Pelops, the famous charioteer, as a sacrifice to the gods—who refused to eat it, except for Demeter, who was too distraught by grief for her abducted daughter to notice what she was eating, and nibbled a little of his shoulder. The sons of Pelops struggled for control of the throne of Olympia; Thyestes seduced Atreus' wife and was exiled, while Atreus seized power. Seneca's play begins with the Ghost of Tantalus, who—like the Ghost of Thyestes in *Agamemnon*— wishes he could return to the safety of the underworld. But this is an even darker interpretation of the motif than in the earlier play. This Ghost is driven on by a Fury and forced to become the curse to his own household. The encounter between the Ghost and the Fury is one of a series of scenes of instruction in wickedness, in which one character initially resists another's attempts at moral perversion but then acquiesces: staying strong against evil seems to be beyond anybody in this play.

The scene that is most obviously reminiscent of the relationship between Seneca and Nero is that in which the scarily tyrannical Atreus
discusses his wicked plans to take revenge on his brother with a Servant
or Attendant (a *Satelles*). The Attendant seems at first to adopt a position
of moral strength, advising Atreus of the best practices and responsibili-
ties of an ideal ruler. He tells him that one should seek genuine praise,
not admiration forced by fear. Atreus responds that false praise is exactly
what he wants—a mark of his success, since only the most powerful
people get flattery. *Quod nolunt velint!* ("Let them want what they don't
want!") (212). This is a strong vote of confidence in a culture of dissimulation. But the Attendant still holds out the notion that a king ought to
set a moral example for his people: "Let a king want what's right; everyone will want the same" (213). Eventually, after Atreus declares his adamant hatred of his brother, the Attendant's scruples all seem to fall by the
wayside, and he begins to give advice on the practicalities of how exactly
his master can kill his brother. "Let him die by the sword," he suggests
(245), and when Atreus rejects that possibility as too mild a punishment,
the Attendant is prepared to go through a list of other possible killing
methods.

We can read the scene as a reflection of Seneca's own experience. Like
the Attendant, he attempted temporarily to advise a tyrant toward ethical
philosophy. Also like the Attendant, he ended up becoming a sounding-
board and assistant in that same tyrant's plans to kill members of his own
family (in Nero's case, Britannicus and Agrippina). The scene implies an
entirely pessimistic notion of whether moral teaching is possible. The Attendant fails to teach the tyrant anything, but the tyrant teaches the Attendant how to fall in with crime, how to dissimulate, and how to betray
his values. The Attendant takes the line that teaching can be dangerously
effective: Atreus may simply teach his victims to take revenge upon him.
"Crimes often return to their teacher" (311). But Atreus responds that it
is pointless to worry about corrupting influences, since power in itself
teaches vice: *regnum docebit* ("Kingship will teach it") (313). From this
point of view, Seneca's whole project of trying to influence Nero for the
better was doomed from the start. Moreover, the theme of the vicious
cycle of revenge allows Seneca to explore a dark counterpart to his discussion of the virtuous cycle of favors, benefits, and kindness. The villain-
ous Atreus seems to echo Seneca's discussions of gratitude in the prose
treatise, but with a perverted twist, when he declares that "Crime should

have some limit when you're doing it—not when you're paying it back"
(1052–1053).

We encounter yet another scene reminiscent of Seneca's own life, and
resonant with the problems inherent in moral teaching, when Atreus'
brother Thyestes returns from his long exile. At first, Thyestes is ready
with conventional, quasi-philosophical wisdom about the relative unim-
portance of indifferent things, like power and wealth. He declares to his
young son—named Tantalus for his ancestor—that the real blessing is a
life of simplicity and stability, untainted by wealth or danger:

> While I stood high,
> my fear was endless; I was even frightened
> of my own sword. How good it is, to stand
> in no-one's way, to eat your dinner safely,
> lying on the ground.

(447–451)

But Thyestes' sentiments fall away almost comically quickly once he
learns that his brother claims to have forgiven him and to welcome him
back to the palace. Through repeated puns, Seneca suggests that Thyestes
is motivated not only by filial love but by a residual desire to regain
power: for instance, he declares, "Brother, all that's yours I count as mine"
(535)—suggesting not only that he will share everything with Atreus, but
that Atreus must share everything with him. His last utterance before entering the palace is a declaration that the "laws and army will serve you—
and me too" (543), with an implication not only that Thyestes will share
power with Atreus, but also that Atreus will have control over Thyestes
along with everything else. Thyestes submits half-knowing he is making
a horrible mistake but also apparently unable to resist temptation.

If the weak-willed, greedy, pompous Thyestes is one side of an unflattering self-portrait by Seneca, then Atreus, the monstrous artist, driven by
ambition and an insatiable lust for power, is another. One can see both
Nero and Seneca himself in this insane character who is one of Seneca's
finest creations. The drama traces, with loving detail, how desperate Atreus
is to achieve something new, something unprecedented, beyond common
revenge. Killing his nephews is not enough. Even feeding them to their
own father is not enough; Atreus complains that he really ought to have
planned better and made sure Thyestes knew what he was eating (1053–
1068). The ultimate audience for the pedophagy is Thyestes himself. The

play brilliantly evokes a world in which vice and greed know no limit, and in which the desire to see and be seen is unlimited and insatiable. Atreus is much more vivid and interesting than his pallid, hypocritical brother. The desperate, overreaching desire of Seneca's most horrible tragic heroes (like Atreus, like Medea) is uncannily reminiscent of Seneca's philosophical ideal, the Stoic Sage (Fig. 3.7). The ideal of virtue, as of vice, is for absolute autonomy, absolute power over circumstance and

Figure 3.7 Seneca in his last years tried to retire from Nero's court and devote himself only to his books.

fortune—a desire that the tragic heroes try to achieve not by a life in conformity with nature, but by actions and passions that run counter to every natural law. One can also read the *Thyestes* as a gesture of admiration (as well as disgust) at the excesses of Nero: beside the emperor's Atreus-like cruelties, Seneca sees himself as nothing but a Thyestes, or an Attendant.

The play could not go on forever. In 62 BCE, Burrus, who had shared with Seneca the task of advising the young emperor and trying to restrain his behavior, suddenly died. The story went that he was poisoned by an unknown hand. Some said that the poison had been sent by Nero himself, in the guise of medicine for a sore throat (Suetonius, *Nero,* 35). Many—including the new head of the Guard—were delighted to see him gone. Without the backing of Burrus and the Praetorian Guard, Seneca's position in Nero's court became very weak and very dangerous. It was time to try harder to get out.

"THERE'S NO EASY PATH FROM EARTH TO THE STARS"*

"What are you doing, Seneca? Are you abandoning your party?"[1]

We turn now to the last years of Seneca's life—years in which the man himself felt he was living on borrowed time, practicing daily for death. It was in this period that Seneca produced some of his greatest prose work, including the *Letters to Lucilius*, a series of highly literary but also highly engaging epistles to a slightly younger friend, dealing with many different aspects of the philosophical life, and the *Natural Questions,* his most extensive discussion of natural, scientific phenomena.

After serving as Nero's speechwriter and political advisor for some time, Seneca became alienated from the emperor, whose behavior had become increasingly autocratic and histrionic. Seneca engaged in an ongoing struggle to withdraw from a public life that he himself had freely embarked upon but that had become impossible to maintain except at the cost both of his integrity and personal safety.

When returning from exile, Seneca may have considered going to Athens, to be a teacher and student of philosophy, rather than coming back to Rome to teach rhetoric to the young Nero. Now again, at this

* Non est ad astra mollis e terries via (Hercules Furens, 437)

much later stage of his life, he must have looked around him at the other philosophers and teachers of his time and wondered if his life in politics and as a famous writer had been a mistake. Should he, rather, have devoted himself solely to study and teaching of Stoic philosophy, as others were doing even at Rome? The most prominent of these was Musonius Rufus, a slightly younger contemporary whose life and works stand in fascinating contrast to those of Seneca. Musonius was, like Seneca, from an equestrian background, from Etruria, and he devoted himself to lecturing and writing about Stoic ethics. His most famous student was Epictetus. Musonius' main, indeed more or less exclusive, focus was on behavior rather than the more theoretical fields of Stoicism (physics and logic). He treated philosophy as the central means by which people can liberate themselves from false beliefs and corrupt desires. Musonius' version of Stoicism is more exclusively practical, less self-centered, and more focused on human kindness than that of Seneca. His central concerns are with recommending that people live together with affection and without cruelty and make simple, ascetic lifestyle choices (he gives instructions, for instance, on how to keep one's hair and beard neat without wasting too much time on such frivolities). His work survives only in records of his opinions taken by a student; Musonius, like Epictetus but unlike Seneca, was not much interested in literary production or political power, and instead focused on getting across the content of his ideas in order to change his students' behavior.

Musonius' priorities on social issues were clearly very different from Seneca's. He takes a genuinely original line in combatting what he presents as social abuses, such as the exposure of unwanted babies, and in arguing that women, as well as men, ought to study philosophy; their minds are no different, no worse. He seems to have taken an interest in politics and been willing to take risks for his beliefs: he supported a rival of Nero, Rubellius Plautus, who was exiled in 60 CE. Musonius followed him into exile in Asia. He came back in 62, when Plautus was dead, but Nero continued to dislike him. Musonius was thus a parallel figure to Seneca, one who showed far less willingness to make social and political compromises.

But Stoicism in itself did not imply political dissidence. In the sixties there were certainly some—like Seneca's own nephew, Lucan—who were Stoic-sympathizers and also sympathetic to republicanism. But there were also plenty of others, like Seneca himself, whose philosophy was not necessarily identifiable with political dissidence. Stoicism was not the problem with Seneca, from Nero's perspective; rather, the old man had outstayed his welcome and had gone from being a useful aide in Nero's schemes to promote himself and his own pleasures, against the obstacles of public opinion, to being a killjoy and a hindrance.

Seneca's dilemma after the death of Burrus was how to extricate himself from an untenable position as minister to an emperor who no longer trusted him and whose behavior was increasingly erratic, without arousing further suspicion or being killed. Seneca had been thinking about retirement for a long time; the dilemma was starker now, but it was by no means new. For many years, Seneca must have been wondering about his exit strategy. One way to avoid any suspicion that retirement meant treason was to adopt "philosophy" as a mask and to suggest that any person might have purely psychological, not political, reasons for wanting to be away from the rat race. In an essay *On Leisure,* probably composed quite a long time before he actually withdrew from Nero's court,[2] Seneca vividly evokes the benefits that come from retirement from public life—and in doing so, also evokes the psychological and moral pressure involved in being in the public eye. He tells his addressee (who may be again his old friend Serenus) that only alone, in retirement, is it possible to maintain a consistent purpose in life. The problem with contemporary society is that it creates a life that is not only immoral but, worse, fickle: people constantly change their minds and their actions, based on fashion and the influence of those around them. Only in retirement, and in solitude, can one stick consistently to whatever it is that one really wants to do with one's time.

In another piece, *On the Shortness of Life*, Seneca writes to another friend, Paulinus, urging him to withdraw from the hustle of public life. Paulinus did give up one of the top administrative positions in Rome, the prefecture of the grain supply (*praefectus annonae*), in 55, which was probably when Seneca's essay was composed. One could surmise that Paulinus simply took Seneca's advice. But it is much more likely the other way round: Paulinus was forced by Agrippina to retire in order to leave room for the appointment of one of her own favorites (Faenius Rufus).[3] Seneca's essay was thus designed to save face both for Paulinus himself and for the government by presenting his retirement as a choice rather than something he was forced into. It seems likely that Seneca himself was already, even in 55, considering the fact that he might one day, perhaps soon, be forced out of Nero's court or find himself desperate to leave. So from his own point of view also, it was a useful move to make a public statement about the value of retirement: it helped lay the groundwork for the day that was sure to come.

The writing of these treatises also allowed Seneca to articulate many of his negative feelings about the life of the palace. He vividly evokes the bustle of contemporary life and gives us a clear sense of what was he looking for in his later years:

> Among the rest of our troubles, this one is the worst of all, that we even change our vices. We don't even get to stick to a familiar vice. First this one, then that one is a favorite, and our problem is that our choices are not just bad, but also fickle. We're tossed around, grasping at one thing and then another; we abandon the things we tried to obtain, we search out the things we've abandoned, in a state of constant oscillation between desire and regret.
>
> (*On Leisure* 1.2–3)

His goal is not simply a state of greater moral purity (though it is that) but, above all, a place of security where he can feel that his actions and his intentions are in tune with one another—an escape from the schizophrenic jostle from one style of behavior to another.

In this same passage, Seneca goes on to hint at a third problem with public life—namely, that it is extremely dangerous. Seneca, even in the early years of service but increasingly as time went on, could hardly have been unaware that his life hung in the fickle and temperamental young emperor's hands. He comments that "we do not consider whether the way itself is good or bad, but we just count the crowd of footsteps; but none of those footsteps come from people coming back" (*On Leisure* 1.3). This is an allusion to Aesop's fable of the fox and the sick lion. The fox warily approaches the lion's cave, and the lion encourages him to enter; after all, a sick lion could hardly hurt a lively young fox. But the fox refuses: he has noticed that many animals' footsteps lead into the lion's cave, and none lead back—because, of course, the lion has eaten them all.

One might think that the fable just tells us, in a vague way, that society is dangerous; if one becomes a follower of the crowd, one can lose one's individual identity and become unable to hang on to one's own goals and ideals. The lion is the crowd, as well as the devourer of that crowd. But there is a suggestion of a more specific and more material kind of danger, namely that those who flatter and praise and gather around the emperor may find that he is not always so safe; even a sick lion can bite. The hint of political danger is reinforced when we remember that Seneca is here alluding to an earlier Roman writer who used the same fable to discuss the dangers of a writer submitting to popular opinion— specifically, of submitting to the dangers of a close relationship with an imperial regime. A generation earlier, Horace, writing to his patron Maecenas, the friend and advisor of the then-emperor Augustus, made a similar appeal to the story:

> And if the people of Rome should ask me why
> I love the colonnades they love, but do not share
> in their opinions, nor do I seek or reject
> the things they do, I'd answer as the wary fox once answered
> the sick lion: "Because the footsteps scare me:
> they all go into your den, none go away."

(Horace, Epistles, 1.1.70–75)

Horace, like Seneca, shies away from suggesting that the emperor himself may be dangerous to those who do not share his views, but both writers hint that the danger comes from a singular, powerful individual, and that the masses may be victims themselves.

Horace returns to the Aesopic fable form in another poem a little later in the same collection, and here the fox is less wary:

> A slim little fox once crept through a narrow gap
> into a corn barrel, and after he ate all the rats,
> he tried to get free; but it was no use; his stomach was swollen.
> A nearby weasel said, "If you want to get out,
> you have to go back skinny, through the narrow gap your skinny self came in by."

(Horace, Epistles, 1.7)

Horace's promise—or perhaps threat—to his patron is that he is willing to give back all the things that he has received through his patronage, including his lovely Sabine farm: if that's what it takes to reclaim his in-dependence, then Horace (who boasts of his modest background as a freedman's son) is willing to give back everything and get out as poor as he came in. He defends his right to stay away from Rome and the court, all year if he so chooses; he insists that, though grateful for what Maecenas has given him, he is no paid lap dog, and he can get out any time he likes. But the juxtaposition of the two fox fables in the same collection expresses a submerged anxiety about whether things are always so easy. The fox can easily get out of the barrel: all it takes is some dieting. But the animals that have chosen to go into the sick lion's cave no longer have a choice; they will never come back out. As Horace says in another poem, "Cultivating a powerful friend is sweet to people who have never done it. Those who have, fear it" (*Epistles* 1.18.86–87).

Seneca, who knew Horace's poetry well, transferred the problem into his own terms in the speeches he made to Nero in begging for retirement from the court. After Burrus died, more and more voices were raised against Seneca to Nero. Gossips reported to the emperor that Seneca was greedily still increasing his private fortune and abrogating to himself honors that really belonged only to Nero—including literary honor as well as vast wealth. They presented Seneca as deliberately copying and challenging Nero's greatest accomplishments; for instance, they told him that Seneca "was writing poetry more often now that Nero had developed a love of it" (Tacitus 14.52). And, even worse, they reminded the emperor that Seneca was always scolding him about his most enjoyable activities, such as chariot racing and singing. Seneca's intellectual and cultural talents, which had once been an asset in Nero's court, had now become a liability: he was too productive, too clever, too talented. "How long was nothing to be believed glorious at Rome, unless it originated from Seneca?" they asked. Nero was a man now, these critics reminded him; he could afford to cast off his tutor.

Seneca was highly conscious of how hazardous his position now was. Tacitus gives us a wonderfully satirical account of Seneca's attempt at a strategic exit speech in 62, which is worth quoting at length. Seneca asked to speak to the emperor face to face, was admitted, and began:

> It is now fourteen years, Caesar, since I was joined to your hope, and eight years since you became emperor; in the meantime, you have piled such honor and wealth upon me, that nothing is lacking for my happiness, except moderation in its enjoyment.

He cites the examples of others who have helped emperors, such as Agrippa, advisor and general to Augustus, and acknowledges how little, in comparison, he has been able to offer Nero:

What have I been able to offer to your generosity, except my learning, which was trained, so to speak, in the shade, and which has become famous only because people see me as having helped the early stages of your youth? A vast reward for such a thing. But you have given me an enormous influence, huge amounts of money, so much that I often ask myself, "Is this me? Am I, born from a simple equestrian, provincial background, counted among the most important people of the state? Among those noblemen of ancient families, has my new name begun to shine?"

At this stage of the speech, Seneca still seems to be treating Nero's bounty as more or less a good thing, despite being undeserved and unfitting for one of his station. But then he shifts to suggest that he has been morally corrupted by too much wealth:

Where is that soul that was happy with moderation? Has it laid out such gardens, walked through such suburban mansions, grown fat on such vast acres of land and such far-flung investments? I have just one defense to make: I had a duty not to stand in the way of your gifts.

But now, Seneca suggests, the emperor's generosity has extended far enough: "We have both filled up the measure, both you of what a prince should give a friend, and I, of what a friend should take from a prince; anything more will increase envy." The only solution is for Nero to take it all back:

I ask for help: I can no longer bear my riches. Order for my estates to be organized by your own procurators, to be taken back into your own wealth. I will not beat myself down to poverty, but I will give back the things whose splendor dazzles me, and the time I used to devote to gardens and villas, I'll turn back to the soul.

(*Annals* 14.53)

It was a fine effort, but Nero saw through it. His reply was brilliant and cruel. Nero declared: "If I am able to meet the practiced rhetoric of your speech right away, that is the first of my debts to you"; at last, by this stage of his reign, Nero was able to give his own speech, with no need of Seneca's help as speechwriter. He went on to pretend that they were still friends, that he still genuinely felt grateful to Seneca, and that he did not realize how desperately Seneca wanted to be away from him. At the same time, he insisted that there was no possibility of going back on the arrangement. The first reason was that Seneca had given him such imperishable gifts that the small things Nero could give in return—a handful of villas, a few miles of parkland, some millions of coins—were nothing in comparison. It was, frankly, embarrassing to think of how little he had managed to give his greatest benefactor: he had not even made him the richest man on earth: "I blush that you, who are first in my love, are not yet excelling everyone in fortune."

The second and more truthful reason Nero gave for refusing to let Seneca retire was that it would look bad for himself:

> Not your moderation, if you give back your money, not your retirement, if you leave your prince, but my avarice and the fear of my cruelty will be on everyone's lips. Even if your abstinence is praised to the skies, it would not be fitting for a wise man to get glory from the bad reputation of his friend.

So saying, he kissed Seneca, "being used by nature and practice to veil his hatred under a show of affection." Seneca expressed his gratitude, as of course he had to do if he wanted to survive. But he then, Tacitus tells us, moved into a much more retired mode of life, while still being officially under the emperor's service. Without leaving the city, he banished callers and mostly stayed at home, reading, writing, and claiming to be too ill to go out. Illness was, again, a useful excuse to deal with an impossible social position.

It was in this period that he worked on the two great works of his old age: the *Natural Questions* and the *Letters to Lucilius* (*Epistulae Morales*). Neither of these deals in any direct way with Seneca's own life, but both hint at a long meditation on issues that were deeply intertwined with Seneca's relationship with Nero and with the political power struggles of the past years. The *Letters* construct a self that is both public and private. They deal with a self that is stylized, an "everyman." But they also evoke, in appealing intimacy, the details of daily life that seems very much like Seneca's own life. He is conscious of his slaves, his rides in his cart, carriage, or litter, his baths, the noises of the city, the daily round, the dilemmas of what to do with each hour of every day, reading habits, the problems of illness and fatigue and the annoyance of other people. *Natural Questions,* Seneca's major work of natural history and science, can be read as an attempt to turn his attention away from the anxieties of political, human life toward the relative simplicity of natural phenomena.

But this text, too, shows the complexity of Seneca's political attitudes and position.

LUCAN AND PETRONIUS

Any slave leaving the house without his master's permission will receive one hundred lashes.[4]

Before we turn to these works, we should note how differently Seneca positions himself as a writer from his literary contemporaries. As we have seen, Seneca had introduced his nephew, Lucan, to Nero and had presumably helped educate him and train him as a writer, as well as teaching him the fundamentals of Stoicism. Lucan and Nero were initially good friends, but at some point, presumably around this same period (the early sixties CE), the relationship soured. The ancient sources give inconsistent reasons for the falling out. Tacitus (*Annals* 15.49) tells us that Nero was jealous of Lucan's poetic talent and success and had tried to suppress his poems, ordering him not to publicize them. Suetonius says that Nero just lost interest in Lucan and began ignoring him, which made Lucan begin writing satirical poems against the emperor ("Life of Lucan").

It is likely that, whatever the literary and personal sources of the tension, there was also a strong political element: Lucan became hostile to the whole institution of imperial government. His great poem, the *Pharsalia,* which was begun around 60 CE (and probably left incomplete at the time of his death in 65), is an epic about the central battle of the Roman Civil War between Julius Caesar and Pompey, from an obviously anti-imperialist perspective: the world disintegrates as soon as Caesar crosses the Rubicon and destroys the Republic. The only really admirable character amid the madness and blood lust and confusion is Cato, the Stoic defender of the old Republican values, who alone sticks to principle and a life in accordance with nature, even when everyone else has descended to chaos.

Lucan's literary work is thus far more explicitly opposed to Nero's regime than anything written by Seneca. Cato, a highly politicized Stoic, represents a more active and more clearly dissident version of philosophy from that of Lucan's uncle. But the *Pharsalia* is not without its ideological contradictions. Most obviously, the poem begins with lavish, not to say

fawning, praise of Nero himself, whose presence on the throne should
be more than enough compensation to the world for all the bloodshed
of the civil wars, and who seems on the point of ascending to heaven as
another Apollo. If only this god will turn his gaze to Rome and adopt
the median position in the sky, then world peace can follow:

> *If you should press on either part of the enormous sky,*
> *the universe will feel your weight; adopt the middle spot,*
> *as weight to the well-balanced heaven; let that space*
> *of calm air still be peaceful, let no clouds get in the way*
> *of Caesar. Then let the human race lay down its arms and turn*
> *to thoughtful planning; may all races love each other;*
> *may Peace, sent through the world, shut up the iron gates of warrior Janus.*
>
> (*Pharsalia* 1.55–62)

It is possible that these lines were composed before the falling out between Nero and Lucan, although that does not explain why he retained
them in the later version of the poem. A more plausible reading is that
Lucan was struggling with a similar problem to that of his uncle: how to
articulate some kind of resistance to Nero's regime without being destroyed in the attempt. Perhaps Lucan hoped that Nero would not get
through more than the first couple of pages of his poem and would
therefore imagine that the whole thing was equally flattering to himself.
Perhaps, too, readers with greater attunement to Lucan's political position could be expected to read between the lines here, taking the apparent flattery as ironic dissimulation.

The most prominent other writer of the period was a very different
figure, even more distant from Seneca in ethos, style, and ideology. Petronius was some thirty years younger than Seneca: he was born around 27
CE, so would have been in his thirties in the sixties. Petronius was dubbed
the "arbiter of taste" (*arbiter elegantium*), known for his risky, witty speech
and his love of parties. Unlike Seneca, Petronius rose to the senatorial class.
He held a number of official positions in government, including acting as
a provincial governor and then as a consul—tasks that he was said to do
remarkably well, to the surprise of those who saw him only as a hedonist.

His only surviving work is a fragment from a much longer piece, the
Satyricon—a proto-novel in both prose and verse, which evokes the wanderings and misadventures of a young man in pursuit of his aberrant
boyfriend, and the many comic characters he meets along the way. The

Figure 4.1 Trimalchio's dinner.

only section that survives more or less intact is called "Trimalchio's Dinner," and it gives a vivid satirical portrait of an upstart freedman's crazily lavish banquet (Fig. 4.1). The joke is mostly against Trimalchio, who is too nouveau riche to see the absurdity of his displays of wealth and extravagance. His food is all show, a feast for the eyes and mind more than the belly: he serves dishes prepared to look like all the twelve signs of the Zodiac, eggs with birds apparently hatching from them, and sausages on pomegranate seeds, to affect the impression of meat cooking on hot coals, a pig ready-stuffed with cooked innards. The main theme of all these displays is the passage of time, of which Trimalchio is paranoically conscious: the centerpiece of his dinner is a silver skeleton, brought in to remind the diners of mortality, and after much conversation over expensive wine (brought in from estates that Trimalchio owns but never sees), Trimalchio reads out his will and creates a dramatic enactment of his own funeral, complete with mourners and a trip down to Hades.

Petronius' jokey, snobbish, vivid description of Trimalchio's absurd pretensions is entirely consistent with the tradition of hostility to freedmen among the Roman Senate. But there are touches of sympathy as well as mockery in the portrait of this Roman Gatsby.[5] Moreover, Trimalchio's crazy, autocratic ways, and especially his love of the arts, poetry, and the theater, are not so distant from those of Nero himself. His combination of threats and intimacy in his interactions with his slaves evokes the life of the imperial court—and in this house, too, it is easier to enter than to leave alive. It is tempting to trace a parallel between this upstart, super-rich provincial, who is deeply obsessed with death and who spouts pseudo-philosophy, and Seneca himself. If so, the portrait would have been deeply unwelcome to Seneca. The two writers must have known one another, and indeed, they were to die accused of conspiracy in the same plot against Nero; but there is no record of a friendship, and the chances are that there was no love lost between the senatorial *arbiter elegantarium* ("judge of tasteful things"), with his mocking, distanced attitude to the absurdities of contemporary court life, and the equestrian philosopher, once known as the *magister principis* ("teacher of the prince").

Petronius' satirical narrative, for all its absurdities, is deeply engaged with the texture of physical, material, human life in his own social milieu. He is interested in capturing the details of how people from different classes talk, and in evoking crude sexual and scatological humor—for instance, Trimalchio tries to be a generous host by assuring his guests that they can go ahead and fart at dinner, if they feel the need. The text may invite us to laugh at him, but at least it engages with his world. This level of interest in how other people live stands in sharp contrast to Seneca's work of this period, especially the *Natural Questions*, which can be seen as an extensive attempt to get beyond the confines not merely of Neronian Rome but of all individual human life, to find some larger, more sublime point of view from which to understand nature, the universe, and everything.[6]

THE CONTEMPLATION OF HEAVENLY THINGS: *NATURAL QUESTIONS*

Natural science had long been a concern for the Stoics, and Seneca used earlier works on the subject in composing his own (including Aristotle as well as Stoic discussions). But he is also willing to make his own judgments between theories, including rejecting the standard Stoic view at times. The subjects of meteorology and physics are fields in which he obviously took an intense, and personal, interest. Science itself provides a vantage point from which to consider ethical and social problems from a quite different angle. One of Seneca's major themes in this text is the relativity of vision and perspective: "mountains [like the Apennines and the Alps] are high, as long as they're compared with us; but really, when you look at the whole world, the lowness of all of them becomes clear" (*NQ* 4b11.2). The problem of how to deal with social hierarchies, which Seneca had dealt with much more directly in *On Benefits,* recurs here through geology: looking at the mountains reveals how the illusion of rank masks an ultimate equality.

Seneca addresses the question of whether it is proper for a philosopher to ignore moral problems and focus on science. He imagines an interlocutor asking why he wastes time analyzing how snow is formed rather than inveighing against the moral aberration of rich people buying snow to cool their drinks—a practice to which Nero was notoriously addicted: "Why do you bother to devote all that effort to studying those silly things, which don't make anybody a better person, just more 'educated'?" (*NQ* 4b11.13.1). Seneca's answer is that in fact, the examination of natural science is utterly relevant to a program of moral reform. If we investigate the natural properties of water, we will see immediately the shame of spending large sums of money on iced water or snow, which is not even composed only of water, but is "mostly air." This passage, like several in the *Natural Questions*, makes a clear criticism of Nero's luxurious habits at the time. The emperor had begun to take midnight swims in a pool chilled by ice or snow in order to increase his endurance for partying (Suetonius, *Nero,* 27.2). Seneca exclaims—without naming Nero directly—that, "the snow in which you are now swimming has come to take the place of water!" (*NQ* 4b13.11).

Actual instances of naming the emperor in this text are usually flattering, but in ways that are easy to read ironically: for instance, in discussing the source of the Nile, Seneca claims that Nero just sent two centurions to discover it, because "just as he is very devoted to other virtues, so too he is utterly committed to the truth" (*NQ* 6.8.3). Of course, readers would be quite aware that Nero had actually sent the soldiers to investigate the terrain while planning an attack on Ethiopia—not out of disinterested concern for scientific truth (Pliny 6.181). Seneca's flattering remarks can be read as a covert jibe against Nero for failing to live up to his old teacher's standards. Similarly, Seneca digresses from earthquakes to discuss Callisthenes, a philosopher who studied earthquakes and was killed by Alexander—clearly hinting that even the greatest of emperors look bad when they kill their intellectual friends (*NQ* 6.23.2–3). It is thus wrong to read the *Natural Questions* simply as a rejection of the life of politics. Metaphors of politics are used to discuss physics, and conversely, physics is described in terms that constantly revert to Seneca's favorite moral and political themes.

The text of this work is problematic, and the traditional ordering of the books is now not thought to reflect the order in which Seneca wrote them; most scholars agree that the earliest section is the one listed in the manuscripts as Book 3, on rivers. This book begins programmatically, with a partial acknowledgment that Seneca himself, in old age, looks back with regret and repentance on his earlier existence, seeking study as way of redeeming a misspent life (*NQ* 3. Pref. 1). He suggests, too, that measuring out the universe in his mind may help take his mind off his anxieties (punning on the words *metior*, "to measure," and *metus*, "fear"). He has chosen to write about science rather than history, because it teaches us what really matters: not the conquests of emperors and kings, but the contemplation of divine things, with an unconquered mind. As the book continues, it becomes clear that the study of rivers and other large bodies of water is not an abstruse pursuit, not divorced from the personal, human concerns Seneca was facing while writing, but a way of approaching them by other means. The central topic is how to deal with loss. Seneca discusses the various theories about how rivers and streams maintain their water levels and insists that this water does not come from rainfall; rather, it is kept up by a constant process of exchange between the four elements (earth, air, fire, and water), such that particles of earth and air are constantly adding to the rivers, at the same time as the rivers are constantly evaporating and flowing toward the sea. The importance of all this from an ethical and personal standpoint is that it allows Seneca to insist that gifts do not only come from above (like rain into a river) but, rather, are maintained through a nonhierarchical process of mutual exchange. Moreover, there is a deeply comforting suggestion that real change between states and between elements is always possible: "all things are in all things," he declares (*NQ* 3.10.4). Rivers can find a new channel if they lose an old one; water can be replenished even without rainfall. For Seneca, having lost his position at court, his social status, and any sense he might have had of personal security, it was good to be able to see in the physical realm around him an image of change and trans- formation, without cost and without limits. The discussion of waterways allows him to inveigh against luxury: a vivid instance of extravagant cru- elty on which he spends a lot of attention here is the current elite prac- tice of having surmullet fish brought to the table in glass jars to die in front of the guests, so they can exclaim at the beauty of watching the fish's color turn from red to white as it dies (NQ 3.18.1). The study of water turns into a study of the corrupt effects of empire, which chal- lenges even the freedom of this most liberated of all elements (NQ 3.30.7–8).

The next books (4A, on the Nile, and 4B, on clouds, rain, hail, and snow) are concerned again with favorite Senecan themes and again are deeply relevant to his own current life: the topics are escapism and retire- ment, and, again, the corruptions of luxury (since the excessive consump- tion of snow and ice is a classic instance of excessively demanding elite tastes). Book 5, on the winds, is concerned with freedom and with the proper reach of empire, since the topic allows Seneca to examine the clas- sic question of whether it is a good thing for the winds to have carried naval and merchant ships from one corner of the world to another for conquest and trade. We learn that it was not nature but greed that made humans act in this way: "it was not enough for us to be crazy in our own part of the world!" Book 6 takes us to earthquakes, a topic that Seneca tells us he already wrote about in his youth. It allows him to return to his pre- occupation with fear and freedom: there is nothing more terrifying than the rumble of an earthquake, but knowledge of its causes allows us to sur- mount these fears and face death bravely—than which there is nothing more important (NQ 6.32.5). Book 7, on comets, allows for a discussion of the limits of human knowledge, and the power of the gods, who "have not made everything for humans." This topic again has a strong political dimension, since comets were supposed to portend the destinies of kings and emperors, and a famous comet was seen "in the very happy principate of Nero" for six months, moving in the opposite direction from a comet associated with Claudius (7.21.3). While apparently trotting out the standard Neronian line here, Seneca manages also to suggest that it is mere narcissism for an emperor to think a comet has anything to do with himself. Nero's comet was lured with the desire for "food," just like fire, which follows where it has fuel to feed on, not motivated by a need to respect the young leader. The *Natural Questions* thus implies that Nero, too, would benefit from taking a view from above.

The last two books in order of composition are the most intensely focused on questions of human life in general, and Seneca's in particular—while at the same time taking on a vast canvas of the natural world. Book 1 (the penultimate book composed) discusses rainbows, meteors, and other lights in the sky, but it is ultimately about human self-knowledge, self-deception, and desire. The rainbow, Seneca argues, is created by the reflections of innumerable raindrops, which create mirrors; the same is true, *mutatis mutandis*, of clouds. All these natural mirrors create various kinds of optical illusions, since rainbows, for example, have no real substance but look like a great arc in the sky: "what is shown in the mirror does not exist" (*NQ* 1.15.7).

This leads to an extensive discussion of somebody called Hostius Quadra, a rich man obsessed with sex, who was eventually killed by his slaves in revenge for the degradations he had put them through. Hostius, Seneca tells us, enjoyed having group sex with both men and women and also set up mirrors all around while he was in the act, which would exaggerate the size of his male partners' genitalia. He used mirrors to increase his corrupt desires and failed to realize that nature gave us mirrors "so that a human being can know himself."[7] Hostius, in his obsession with watching himself (and especially with watching himself being penetrated) can be seen as the opposite of Seneca, in his idealized literary persona. Seneca maintains firm and vast boundaries around himself, making both body and soul impenetrable; and he looks for a mirror to reflect his own life, not in the luxurious mirrors created for the perversities of elite Roman life but in the clouds and raindrops of the divine sky.

Seneca presents his studies in physics as giving meaning to his life and allowing him a perspective that goes beyond the confines of his own body: "If I had not been allowed access to these fields, it would not have been worth it to be born. What reason could I have to be happy for being admitted to the number of the living? Just to eat and drink?" (*NQ* 1. Pref. 4). This sentiment is a variation on the philosophical trope that is most vividly expressed by Plato's Socrates in the *Apology*: "the unexamined life is not worth living by a human being." The Platonic line suggests that human beings ought to devote their lives to the study of ethics: a human being should spend his or her life in self-examination. But in Seneca's version, there is a striking shift of emphasis away from a human behavior toward the study of the vast universe of nature: "Ah, how despicable humans are, unless we rise above the human!" (*NQ* 1. Pref. 5). Seneca draws a sharp contrast between the kind of philosophy that deals with man—moral philosophy—and the "loftier, more intellectual" kind, which deals with the gods and the works of heaven, which "leads us up out of darkness, to source of shining light." The mystical language suggests that the study of physics can provide a refuge or sanctuary far from the taint and sickness of human affairs. The study of science is not, for Seneca, motivated by merely practical considerations; it is a source of spiritual regeneration and redemption.

In the *Natural Questions*, Seneca worked to turn his attention away from the anxieties of political, human life toward the broader, vaster view of natural phenomena. He implies that his addressee, Lucilius, can escape not only from the evils of the external human world but also from himself by releasing his mind to the study of the heavens, which is the ultimate form of liberation. This, we are told, "unchains the mind, prepares it for the contemplation of heavenly things, and makes it worthy to associate with God" (*NQ* 1. Pref. 6).

But we could also see it as an attempt to put his personal, political, and moral struggles into a larger perspective. Seneca expands a theme popular among Roman Stoics: that there is a distinction to be drawn between the small state or city in which an individual may live (such as Carthage, or Rome: these are examples of the lesser republic, the *republica minor*) and the large community of which we are all a part. Seneca's shift toward the big picture is an acknowledgment of a larger reality, a world of which his life is one small part.

The shift to a view from above allows Seneca to present even the Roman empire itself as just a pinpoint on a far more immense canvas. In the tragedies, characters like Hercules and Medea and Juno feel cramped even in the largest world they can imagine; the biggest empire the world has ever known is still too small for their ambitions and their guilt. Now, through moving through the heavens as a scientist and astronomer, Seneca presents his mind as capable at last of rising above all the limitations of political ambition and material desire:

The mind cannot despise colonnades, and paneled ceilings gleaming with ivory, and carefully clipped topiaries and streams landscaped to flow toward the house—until it goes around the whole world, and looks down on the earth from above, and sees how tiny it is; how most of the earth is covered up by sea; how even the part above sea level is mostly wilderness, or scorched desert, or frozen ice; and the mind tells itself: "Is this that pinpoint which is divided by sword and fire among so many peoples? How absurd are the boundaries of mortals!" (*NQ* 1. Pref. 7)

The absurdity Seneca points to here is not merely that humans overestimate the importance of their own possessions on earth, or that they think themselves more important than they are. Nor is the problem only that humans overvalue things that are actually close to worthless, although they do that too. It is also that we waste our lives in fighting and struggling for things that are no more than anthills from the perspective of the heavens: "This army of yours is only a scurrying of ants, struggling in a tiny plot of land" (*NQ* 1. Pref. 10).

Seneca's phrasing here is largely impersonal: he speaks not of "I" and "you," but of "the mind" and of "humans." The speaker of the *Natural Questions* is aspiring to a point of view that goes beyond any mere human individual and can span the whole compass of the universe. In doing so, he transcends the messy personal struggles of a Spanish-born philosopher entangled in the Roman imperial court. Spain itself appears as an example of a place that seems like the boundary of a great empire—but that is not so far away in the long run: "After all, how great is the distance from the farthest shores of Spain all the way to India? Only a very few days' journey, if you have a good wind for your ship" (*NQ* 1. Pref. 13). Seneca thus liberates himself from the perspective he was forced to adopt when fawning to Nero, of emphasizing the vast distance he has climbed from provincial obscurity to the heart of the empire; he is able to see that the distance was hardly anything, a mere instant of time.

The final book in the original order, Book 2, is concerned with thunder and lightning and provides an opportunity for an extensive discussion of a climactic topic: the divine order of the universe. Seneca insists that "there is an order in things" (*NQ* 2.13.3) and that everything is fated—although we still have freedom to choose our own actions. People say that lightning is sent by the gods to punish the wicked, only in order to terrify us into good behavior (*NQ* 2.42.3); but the real ruler of the universe, the real Jupiter, is also identifiable with nature, with fate, with fortune, with providence, and with any number of other abstractions, and is always benevolent in his exercise of power—a model for kings and emperors on earth. The study of the divine order leads Seneca to conclude, yet again, that we must reconcile ourselves to the inevitability of death, which will come when it will—if not by lightning, then by some other means. "Take courage from this very source of despair," he declares: "That's how it is, Lucilius: we're all saved for death" (*NQ* 2.59.6). By seeing his own imminent death, constantly threatened by Nero, as part of the universal cosmic pattern and universal human destiny, Seneca could feel far less alone.

Having lost his colleague Burrus and at least one other dear friend, Serenus, to death, Seneca builds up his friendship with another friend, Lucilius, the addressee of both the *Natural Questions* and *Letters to Lucilius*. Little is known about Lucilius himself. Seneca is our only source for his life, and the letters do not give much substantial information about him. He was, we gather, of equestrian status, a native of southern Italy, a frequent visitor to Pompeii, slightly younger than Seneca himself, and working as a procurator (an imperial administrator) on Sicily. It is possible that he was the author of a poem on volcanoes (*Aetna*), a subject that could have been easily studied by one living near Mount Etna, and whose author seems to have a strong knowledge of Seneca's *Natural Questions*. Lucilius is presented as setting out to make progress in philosophy, in search of advice from one who has progressed just a little further down the same road. He is, we learn, considering giving up his political life for philosophical retirement—a situation suspiciously like Seneca's own recent past, such that some commentators have suspected that Lucilius may be an imaginary friend. His name, again suspiciously, seems reminiscent of Seneca's own: Lucilius is a diminutive form of Lucius.[8] Lucilius is like Seneca's own smaller, younger self.

At times, Seneca seems to present Lucilius as an idealized counterpart to himself. He is the man who would never be tempted by ambition to turn away from his studies: "I know how distant you are from ambition, how dearly you love leisure and book-learning" (*NQ* 4. Pref. 1). Immediately, however, Seneca turns to a characteristic meditation on how rare this quality of self-sufficiency is. Most of "us," he declares, are tormented by our own combination of self-love and self-hatred: "sometimes we suffer from self-love, sometimes self-disgust." The worst result of all is that we cannot live at peace alone with ourselves: indeed, "we are never alone with ourselves." Seneca's narrator, as so often, occupies an ambiguous position, fluctuating between the moralist and the sinner. He seems able to analyze the torments of psychological inauthenticity but has no consistent capacity to avoid them himself. He assures Lucilius that he must, above all, avoid flattery and mistrust flatterers; but he does so in such overblown terms that one cannot help suspecting that the narrator himself is flattering Lucilius.[9] The passage ends with a characteristic twist: Lucilius is urged, finally, to ask himself whether the flattering picture is true or not, and Seneca allows that it may well not be. The advantage, however, of doing this exercise alone is that "if they are false, you can be ridiculous without anybody seeing!" The benefits of living with only imaginary friends are, by the time of the *Natural Questions*, all too evident to Seneca.

The problem that recurs in both *Natural Questions* and the *Letters to Lucilius* is one that will be familiar to readers of Marlowe's *Doctor Faustus* or Milton's *Paradise Lost*: Seneca knows he can withdraw from the world, but he is left with the problem of how to live with himself. "Fly—what, from myself? / Which way I fly is hell; myself am hell," asks Satan (*Paradise Lost* 4.75). Seneca suggests that this impossible fantasy is actually achievable: "Therefore one must flee and withdraw into oneself; but one must withdraw even from oneself" (*NQ* 4. Pref. 20). Lucilius, Seneca's addressee in these works, is part of his solution to the problem: through evoking his friend, he is able to imagine and inhabit his best self, unencumbered by either the material world or the burden of his particular personal history. "We will be together, where we are best. We will give each other advice, independent of the face of a listener" (*NQ* 4. Pref. 20). It is as if the face (*vultus*) in itself connotes, for Seneca, the possibility of deceit: a face can always be a mask. The page is, then, the only place where he can feel or be his own best self and best friend.

Contemplating clouds and thunderstorms is not just escapism. The weather system can also be seen as analogous to the threats of life in court: tyrants, like thunder, are something we must learn not to fear. On another level again, the issue is human agency, including Seneca's own. Can a philosopher influence or even understand a tyrant, any more than he can influence the rain? On yet another level, there is a comfort in watching monumental forces that act with violence and power, but without cruelty, and always in accordance with a divine order of things.

THATCHED COTTAGES AND GOLDEN PALACES

While Seneca was struggling to remove himself to the view from above, there were important developments in Nero's court. After Burrus and Seneca were both out of the way, a member of the Praetorian Guard named Tigellinus took over control of the guard from Burrus and became increasingly influential with Nero. Tacitus tells us that he worked to get rid of a number of rivals at court, including Rubellius Blandus Plautus, a rich young man who was a member of the Julian family and therefore had a dangerously good claim to power, as well as one Sulla, brother of Claudius' wife, Messalina. Both had tried to keep a low profile and had withdrawn from Rome—Sulla to Gaul, and Plautus to Asia. But Tigellinus persuaded Nero that they were probably gathering support for their treason at a distance: the only safe way was assassination. Six days later, Sulla's head was brought back to Rome, and Nero laughed at his ugly, prematurely gray hair (Tacitus 14.57). Tigellinus cited Plautus' interest in Stoicism as a proof of his treasonous intentions—itself a marker of how far the pendulum had swung since the early days of Seneca's tutorship of Nero. Soon Plautus, too, was tracked down. He knew death was coming and waited for the soldiers, naked as if for exercise. His head, too, was taken back to Nero, who laughed at the sight, exclaiming, "Nero, why did you fear a man with such a big nose?" (Tacitus 14.59). In such circumstances, it is not surprising that Seneca continued to keep a low profile and struggled to find things to take his mind off the current times.

A close friend of Seneca's may well also have been among the victims of the purge. Serenus, who had (presumably thanks to the intervention of Seneca himself) been appointed as prefect of the night-watch under Nero, died suddenly, soon after Seneca's first bid for retirement, in 62 or perhaps 63 CE. The cause was poisoned mushrooms, the same means that had been implicated in the death of Claudius. It is not clear whether the poisoning was accidental or on purpose, but it seems perfectly possible that it was part of the general attempt by Tigellinus and his cronies to eliminate all the people associated with the old crew of advisors, including Burrus, Seneca, and all the rest. We are told that all those dining on the mushroom dish—a whole group of tribunes and centurions—dropped dead (Pliny, *NH*, 22.96). Seneca was devastated by the loss. He notes how unphilosophical he became in his grief, failing to stick by the precepts he offered to others in times of grief: "I wept so much too much for my dearest friend Annaeus Serenus, that I myself am among the examples of those conquered by grief—not what I wanted" (Epistle 63.14). The attempt to distract himself by contemplating the great divine order of the universe did not always succeed.

In 62, the same year that Seneca first pleaded with Nero for permission to give back his wealth and retire from public life, Nero's longtime concubine Poppaea, wife of his friend Otho, got pregnant. This was the last prompt Nero needed to divorce his long-unloved wife, Octavia, accusing her of having an affair with a slave. She was exiled to Campania. This caused a public outcry and Octavia was temporarily reinstated, only to be cast off again, under the pretext that she had supposedly been sleeping with a member of the Guard. The twenty-year-old girl was killed by having her veins cut open by soldiers, and then being suffocated in the bath.

This was a time when any person seen as a threat or even an irritation by Nero was in danger for his or her life. Two powerful freedmen were killed: Doryphorus for being opposed to the marriage with Poppaea, and Pallas—who, we remember, had wealth comparable with that of Seneca himself—simply for being too rich (Tacitus 14.65). Seneca narrowly escaped death at this time: Tacitus tells us that in the year 62, a man called Romanus accused him of conspiring against the government with Gaius Piso, although Seneca managed, on this occasion at least, to turn the accusations around on Romanus. Seneca had lost none of his strategic cunning in old age, but he knew very clearly that any day might be his last.

When Poppaea's baby was born, a girl, the Senate rushed to Antium to attend the celebrations. Thrasea was forbidden to attend and took it rather well. Nero, it was said, told Seneca that he was now reconciled with Thrasea, and Seneca congratulated the emperor. Tacitus comments that this increased both "the glory and the danger for these famous men" (15.23). In a world so deeply committed to flattery and double-speak, even Thrasea's failure to suggest bitterness at being excluded, and even Seneca's congratulations at Nero's obviously ironic claims of friendship with Thrasea, could be interpreted as expressions of dissent. Saying anything at all, or even not saying anything at all, was now dangerous.

The baby lived only four months, and grief did nothing for Nero's mental stability. And yet Seneca managed to hang onto life. The secret of his survival lay in his ability to be both there and not there at the same time. He was supposedly still in the emperor's service but withdrawn from society, sometimes actually sick (with the usual bronchial complaints) and sometimes feigning illness. He ate and drank even more moderately than usual in these last years: dry bread, figs, and other fruit made a suitable diet for a philosopher and were also harder to poison than more elaborate fare. Although Seneca was a keen viticulturalist and owned vineyards on several of his estates, he was always a moderate wine drinker. Now, he gave up wine more or less entirely, drinking spring water instead—which helped him to escape from the fate of Britannicus. He traveled around the country, visiting one of his country estates after another; he owned several, including one particularly well-loved one at Nomentum, and another in Alba. He traveled to various tourist destinations, such as the well-known seaside pleasure-resort of Baiae, in the Gulf of Naples, as well as to Naples itself, to Campania, and to villas once owned by the famous general Scipio, and the famous voluptuary, Vatia. He even at one point (if we are to believe his own report) took boarding rooms above a noisy bathhouse in the city, temporarily enjoying the challenge of trying to study through the bustle below: the grunts of the weightlifters, the patter of the masseur as he wielded his paddle on the oil of the customers' backs, the high-pitched camp voice of the hair depilator and the screams of his clients as they got their armpits and legs plucked, the songs of those who liked to sing in the bath, the splash of the more enthusiastic swimmers, and the various cries of the food vendors, the sausage seller, the candy man, and the cake seller, each hawking their wares (Epistle 56.1–2). Eventually, the noise was too much even for the self-professed philosopher and he was off again, back to the country. The vividness with which Seneca evokes his various locations is one of the major joys of the *Letters to Lucilius*. He hardly ever gives any indication of why exactly he is traveling, presenting his movements as simply whims. But clearly, there was a reason why Seneca had to keep moving in these years: he was trying to stay below Nero's radar.

The *Letters* give a vivid picture of his daily life in this period. In response to the shakiness of all human careers and attempts to establish oneself in security and prosperity, Seneca suggests that the only solution is the lifestyle of ascetic philosophy: "Let your food relieve hunger, your drink quench your thirst, your clothes keep out the cold, and let your home be just a protection against the enemies of your body. It is unimportant whether you live in a hut made of turf, or one built of many types of colorful marble; remember that thatch keeps a man sheltered, just as well as gold" (7.5). The image of the person sheltered by gold is not merely a fanciful exaggeration: rich Romans of the period, presumably including Seneca himself at the height of his wealth, did live in houses whose walls and ceilings were inlaid with gold leaf, as well as other luxurious decorations (such as wall paintings, mosaics, statues, and stucco); Nero built a magnificent palace of this type for himself in 64, the Golden House.[10] Seneca's simple life in quasi-retirement allowed him enough distance to criticize the kind of pampered lifestyle that he himself had lived for most of his middle years, and to be quietly critical of Nero's increasingly extravagant and autocratic ways. At the same time, as always, Seneca remained open to the possibility that wealth, in itself, is no bad thing: "He is a great man who uses earthenware dishes as if they were silver; but he is equally great who uses silver as if it were earthenware" (5.6). His goal was not poverty or even voluntary simplicity, but rather, peace of mind; he seeks ways to limit the psychological damage caused to rich people by wealth. Living at subsistence level, he acknowledges, is simply "what many thousands of slaves and many thousands of poor folks do all the time." Rich people should emulate them, not so that they can see how hard their lives are, but in order to see how easy it is to bear.

He reports his battles with his health, especially when struggling with intense attacks of asthma, which he dubs the "little death" (54). He presents himself as old and physically weak: traveling in the bay of Naples, he gets violently ill from seasickness (53), and he reports that he is now particularly prone to the cold, far more so than in his youth. In one letter, set at the start of spring, he tells Lucilius that he is still cold: "I can hardly thaw out even in mid-summer... As a result, I spend most of the time all bundled up" (67).

In another letter (83), he gives a vivid description of his daily routine, on an ideal day in which he has managed to devote himself to reading and writing, without interruption: "Leisure without study is death; it's burial for a living man" (82.3). Seneca was a lifelong exerciser who had always favored efficient workouts that would tire him out without taking too long—like jumping, running, or weightlifting (15.2). Now in his sixties, he tires easily, so he used a young slave as his trainer, Pharius, who is at an age when he—like his master—is starting to lose his teeth (presumably a five- or six-year-old; one wonders what the child thought of the old man). The slave functions here as a mirror for his master, who ruefully discovers his own physical vulnerability matched by that of his human property. Seneca says that he is now getting so frail that even Pharius is too fast for him, and of course, the boy gets stronger every day while the master gets weaker; soon he will have to find an even younger slave.

After the workout, Seneca would take a lukewarm bath. Again, he notes his intolerance to cold in old age, which contrasts with his earlier love of bathing in cold water:

> I, such a *psychrolutes* in the past [Greek for "cold-water washer"], I who used to celebrate New Year by plunging in the canal... have switched over, first to the Tiber, then to this tank warmed by the sun—even when I'm at my strongest and everything is in good shape.
>
> (83.5)

The bath was followed by a simple breakfast of dry bread, eaten with no table or plate; then a tiny power nap (the routine of an infant), just enough to "take off the yoke." "Sometimes I know I have slept, sometimes I just suspect" (83.6). Then he would be ready to begin his day of reading and writing. He insists that the two activities must be alternated: "we should not confine ourselves to either reading or writing: continuous writing makes one depressed and exhausted, while continuous reading makes one lax and weak" (84.1).

Seneca's daily routine was regularly interrupted by his frequent relocations. He notes the inconveniences and disruptions caused by constant switching around from place to place, and comments that there are some things he can't research or write about while riding around in a carriage (72.2). When he is curious to look at a particular villa from a nice beach, he insists on being carried longer than usual in his litter and then complains at the jolting, which is more exhausting than a hard workout (55).

One might wonder whether it was not rather more exhausting for the slaves carrying the litter than for the elite occupant. Seneca's "simple" peripatetic life had to be sustained by a large number of people, mostly slaves—albeit fewer slaves than he would have owned in his previous life at court. Presumably Seneca was a reasonably humane slave owner: one of his most famous works is Epistle 47, on slaves, in which he appeals to Lucilius, and other elite Romans who would be reading the collection, to treat their slaves with compassion and gentleness, and with recognition that slaves are just as human as their masters. He speaks out against cruel masters who keep their slaves standing all night at their luxurious dinner parties, forbidding them to eat or drink or say a word, or even cough or sneeze involuntarily. As so often, Seneca loves the rhetorical effect of a fictional dialogue, imagining an interlocutor objecting: "'He is a slave!' But maybe free at heart. 'He is a slave!' Will that hurt him? Show me a person who isn't a slave! One man is slave to lust, one to greed, one to ambition, all to fear..." (47.17).

Seneca's rhetoric is impressive, such that it is hard not to believe that he is addressing a real social problem in a new, even revolutionary way. But the views Seneca espoused were actually quite common, even normal, among the Roman elite of his time. His Spanish contemporary, the agricultural writer Columella, claims that he jokes and talks in a friendly manner with his rustic slaves and treats humanely even those who are kept imprisoned and chained up (sic; Columella 1.8). Seneca's attitude to slavery and to his own slaves was no more enlightened than that of his contemporaries: he thinks that masters ought to treat their human property reasonably well, but—like almost everybody else in the ancient world—he takes the institution of slavery entirely for granted, and most of the time, he gives minimal consideration to the actual lives of his own slaves.[11] Moreover, Seneca's insistence, in this same letter, that all of us, even slaves, have a "free" soul is actually used, in this same letter, to justify the material conditions of slavery; being a slave does the slave no real harm, since being enslaved is merely an indifferent thing that does not touch the soul's virtue.[12]

Seneca's slaves are of interest to him insofar as they help him understand himself better. In evoking a life of hardships, and the proper philosophical attitude toward it, he always looks from the perspective of the master, never the slave: "My household slaves are sick, my income is reduced, my home is creaky; loss, wounds, labors and fears come upon me; well, it's a normal thing" (96.1). The sickness of slaves is a test to the master's philosophical composure, not a problem for the sick people themselves. Similarly, when he visits one of his villas and finds that the slave he remembers as a little boy is now grown old, he thinks immediately of his own old age and imminent death (12)—rather than, for example, pausing to consider the hard life that has worn this person out at such a young age. Slavery is usually treated not as a specific (and unjust) social institution affecting particular individuals, but as a useful metaphor for various philosophical tropes: for instance, we should not be slaves to the body (14), but being a slave to philosophy means real freedom (8.7). "Fearing is being a slave" (66.17). In his discussions of wealth and poverty, Seneca is focused on how a rich person can free himself from the fear of becoming poor; he has no interest in alleviating or challenging the conditions of slavery or poverty (17). By living below one's means, one can realize that wealth is less necessary than one might otherwise think. Voluntary poverty enables the rich to stay rich, but with a greater feeling of inner peace.

There are revealing moments in the letters where one can see how very privileged Seneca's position was, even when he is living the "simple life." Sometimes he himself is conscious of and a little embarrassed by his inability to set aside the values of the elite. When, on one occasion, he rides in a "farmer's cart," drawn by mules, with a barefoot, poor driver, his response is to feel ashamed, in case any rich people see him riding in this unimpressive style—although he knows he ought to see this asceticism as superior to flamboyant extravagance: "I can scarcely get myself to wish this cart to be seen as mine" (87.4). He reports at one point that "My friend Maximus and I have had a very happy couple of days, taking very few slaves, only one carriage-full, and no luggage except what we were wearing" (87.2). If a whole carriage load of slaves was "very few," one can imagine how many slaves Seneca was accustomed to. He goes on to explain that his diet is equally ascetic: "Nothing could have been taken away from our lunch: it took less than an hour to prepare" (87.2). The hour's labor devoted to baking the master's bread and preparing the fruit for his lunch was again performed by slaves, allowing the great man plenty of time to contemplate the universe and write about it all.

The minimalist retinue of slaves would have included a secretary or secretaries to note down his thoughts, as well as a doctor to tend to the master's constant ailments, the little boy to act as his physical trainer and jogging companion, others to wash, massage, and dress him, as well as people to clean his house and at least one cook and baker to prepare his meals. More slaves would have been stationed at each of his villas, taking care of the estate in his absence and ready to care for the master when he stopped by. Seneca vaunts his fine philosophical forbearance for not flying into a rage when he arrives at his Alban villa late at night, finding nothing ready for him. His baker slave has failed to make him fresh bread, but he can fall back on getting inferior bread from one of his other underlings: his tenants, estate manager, or housekeeper can rustle up something, which will be enjoyable if he is hungry enough (123.2). Seneca's standards of what counts as moderate are clearly formed by comparing himself only with the most privileged sectors of Roman society. He says, for example, that, "everyone [sic] now has mules laden with cups of crystal and myrrhine and hand-carved by the greatest artisans" (123.7); the artisans are not included in "everyone." Seneca was, even in his difficult last years, a wealthy and pampered gentleman.

As well as his own slaves, he was also accompanied by his wife, Paulina, and her slaves, who would have included maids to wash and dress her and do her hair, as well as an old female clown named Harpaste, inherited by Paulina from a dead relative, who is all the funnier (and all the more useful as a philosophical *exemplum*) because she is blind and doesn't realize why the rooms are getting so dark (50).

Just one passage in the *Letters* evokes Seneca's relationship with his wife, and it suggests an intimate and affectionate, albeit deeply narcissistic, attitude toward her. Seneca tells Lucilius that he has gone to his villa at Nomentum to escape a fever. He insisted on going, inspired by the example of his older brother, Gallio (Novatus), who got a fever while governor of Achaea and "took ship at once, insisting that his sickness was not in his body, but in his location" (104.1). Paulina, Seneca tells us, tried to stop him, apparently in fear for his health; Seneca overrode her but also acknowledges that her concern for him is important to him:

> Because I know that even her breath is turned with mine, I'm starting to be considerate of myself, in order to be considerate of her. And although old age has made me braver in many respects, I'm losing this benefit of age, since it comes to my mind that inside this old man is a young man, who needs compassion. So, since I can't persuade her to love me more bravely, she manages to persuade me to love myself more devotedly. You see, one must indulge real feelings: and sometimes, even if there are pressing reasons, one must call back one's breath, even at the cost of torture, in respect for one's family; breath must be kept back even on the lip. After all, a good man must not live the length of life he wants, but the length he ought. One who doesn't

value his wife or friend so much as to wait longer in life, who insists
on dying: that man is a hedonist.

(104.3)

The passage recalls the earlier letter in which Seneca reports that he was
tempted to kill himself, due to his coughing and bad health, but restrained only by the pleas of his old father (78). In youth, Seneca stayed
alive for the sake of his father; in old age, he stays alive for the sake of his
devoted wife. Life is forced upon him by his family; it is not what the
death-driven philosopher would have chosen.

Despite claiming to be deeply affected by Paulina's love and wishes
for his safety, Seneca presents himself as having entirely ignored or resisted her actual request, which was for him to stay in the city. Paulina's
anxiety is used as a marker of Seneca's own thoughtfulness, and also as
proof that he himself has no dishonorable desire to live any longer than
he should. But the narrative goes on to prove that she was entirely wrong
to think that his health would be better if he stayed: rather, as soon as he
escaped from the "terrible smell of smoking kitchens" in the city and
reached his own beloved vineyards, he felt far better: "I've found myself
again," he declares (104.6). The relationship is thus entirely asymmetrical,
since Seneca succeeds in taking care of Paulina (by taking care of himself), but she fails to take care of him. Inspired by the lovely villa at Nomentum, Seneca goes on to insist that one should regard all losses, even
the death of those we love most dearly, as simply the falling of leaves
from a flourishing plant: loved ones cannot grow again like leaves, "but
they can be replaced" (104.12). Much though he may love his wife, or at
least love her attentiveness to him, Seneca insists that the really important relationship is always with oneself: "The things you run from are
inside you" (104.20). We may well wonder whether Paulina was really
quite as devoted as Seneca presents her here. It is at least possible that she
had other motives for encouraging her rich, pompous, and much-older
husband to stay in the city: maybe she feared not his death but his survival.

CURING THE SORES OF THE SOUL

All these details about Seneca's life in his last years, and many more,
come from his last and greatest work: the *Moral Letters*, also known as the

Letters to Lucilius. We have seen how vividly this text evokes the details of Seneca's external daily routines in his last years; it is time now to consider how the letters present his state of mind as he looked back on his eventful and complicated life.

The first important thing to note about the letters is that they are letters: their form necessarily implies distance from the addressee. Seneca emphasizes the fact that he is communicating with a friend who is separated from himself; he is not writing a diary for his own future self, but a carefully crafted presentation of his life and thoughts for the edification of another particular person. The epistle is an ostensibly personal, private form of communication—although clearly Seneca intended the collection for publication. The fragmentary form, with the opportunity to leap from one topic to another, and the constantly shifting locations are eminently suitable for the last, peripatetic years of Seneca's life.

The second important fact is that the *Letters to Lucilius* are addressed to Lucilius, as are the *Natural Questions.* Their specified target readership is not Nero, nor anybody in a central position of political power. This in itself is a mark of how much Seneca's public position had changed since the days of *De Clementia*, when he could write in direct address to the young prince.

The *Letters to Lucilius* conjure up a paradoxical relationship between writer and addressee. On one hand, Seneca sets out to give advice to his friend, suggesting that he himself is at least somewhat further along the road toward philosophical perfection. On the other, he constantly acknowledges that the real work has to be done by each person for himself: only Lucilius can teach Lucilius. He urges him in the very first epistle to "persuade yourself that what I write is the case" (1.1); it is not the writer's job to teach, but that of the reader himself. But Seneca constantly works in the *Letters* to undermine the distinction between the reader and the writer; we are supposed to become so closely involved that this distinction disappears. If you can find a true friend, he suggests, you can talk to him as if to a second self (3.3). Seneca manages to invite us to think of the text as a transparent window into his thoughts, even as he carefully constructs his own image. He claims his letters have "nothing strained or artificial" (75.1): "I feel whatever I say, in fact, I don't just feel it, I love it!" (75.3). Even if we may be skeptical of Seneca's claims to be utterly authentic and natural in these very well-crafted pieces of prose, it is a likeable gesture. The focus on the inner life, and on the mind as a safe sphere in which one can withdraw from any kind of adversity, was both one of the most original and one of the most influential aspects of the collection.

Seneca insists that he himself is imperfect. He claims that the main focus of his life in retirement is curing his own moral ulcers: "What, then, am I myself doing with my leisure? I am trying to cure my own sores...There is no reason why you should desire to come to me for the sake of making progress. You are mistaken if you think that you will get any assistance from this quarter; it is not a doctor that dwells here, but a sick man...I prefer you to pardon rather than envy my retirement" (64.3–4). Seneca presents himself as a patient rather than a doctor, a student as much as a teacher. Whatever philosophical insights he may share, they have come only to him intermittently and only late in life. He argues that learning of moral goodness, in particular, is much slower than other kinds of learning. "Just as wool takes up certain colors right away, but others it won't absorb unless it is soaked and steeped in them many times," so too it takes many years truly to absorb the truths of Stoicism. But there is hope, because "the main part of progress is wanting to progress" (61.36). "Whatever my work is like, read it as if I were still seeking the truth, not as if I knew it" (45.4). This character of Seneca as seeker is used as justification also for his philosophical eclecticism. He constantly cites Epicurus, as well as other philosophers from different traditions (such as Socrates and Diogenes the Cynic): "I have sold myself to no-one; I have no master's name" (45.4).

Moreover, his sickness is literal as well as metaphorical. Both pathos and a sense of urgency are generated from the constant reminders that the writer and his addressee are old and sick; time is running out, and there is little life left in which to learn how to live. Seneca acknowledges that being an old man without having achieved wisdom is an embarrassing position to be in: "What is more undignified than an old man who is only just beginning to live?" (13.17). There is a real possibility that each day may be the last, either for Lucilius or for Seneca himself— if not from old age, then from Nero. But there is also a repeated acknowledgment that wisdom does not come all at once, as if through a single moment of insight or inspiration; it is a product of practice, of daily, repeated, developed habit.

The structure of the text itself helps to make this point, since Seneca does not offer his readers a single, unified treatise on philosophy, which might give the impression that one could absorb it all in a single reading. Rather, the format of the *Letters* suggests that each day will mean making a new beginning at the attempt at moral progress. The text is framed into small chunks, tiny pieces, because that is how we experience our lives— episodically. This is not a philosophy of abstractions, but of habit formation, which happens from day to day.

The *Epistles*, even more than most of Seneca's work, are deeply resistant to biographical interpretation, while at the same time inviting the reader to contemplate Seneca's life as well as his or her own. Seneca resists the idea that a "life" is a period of some sixty or seventy years, with a narrative involving birth, childhood, youth, and maturity, and conflicts, journeys, and realizations along the way. Human life is, on the one hand, viewed from a cosmic perspective: as in the *Natural Questions*, viewed from above, as a mere pinpoint of time within eternity. But more commonly, the *Epistles* present life as something that happens not by the lifespan, but by the day. What matters, then, is not what Seneca did over his years as Nero's advisor, but rather, what he did today: "I will keep watching myself all the time, and I'll go back over my day—which is the most useful habit" (83.2). Moreover, even that "dailiness" is often presented in a generalized way: what Seneca realizes as he looks back on his day is that now, as always, he is dying. What we all do, every day, is begin to die—*Cotidie morimur* (24.20):

> We die every day. You see, every day a little bit of our life is taken away from us, and even at the moment we are growing, our life is decaying. We lose our infancy, then childhood, then adolescence. Even up to yesterday, all past time is gone; even this day that we are spending now, we share with death. It's not the last drop that empties the water-clock, but whatever has flowed out before.

The major theme of the collection is how to deal with the passage of time. Seneca's most vivid discussions are of the way time slips away without our even being aware of it: "What man can you give me who puts any value on time, who counts a day, who understands that he dies daily? This is our big mistake: to think we look forward to death. Most of death is already gone. Whatever time has passed is owned by death" (1.2).

But there are at least hints that Seneca was also looking back rather further, to his own past life. Occasionally there is mention of his long-lost childhood: "it was just a moment ago that I sat at the feet of Sotion the philosopher as a boy; a moment ago that I began to plead in the courts, a moment ago that I stopped wanting to do so, a moment ago that I stopped being able to do so" (49.2). Seneca mostly recommends looking back only over one's past day rather than the whole lifespan. He recommends that Lucilius should "think of each day as a separate life" (101.10). This highly episodic mode of living discourages long autobiographical reminiscences. Seneca lives not in the lifetime span, but in the day and hour of the moment, and also in the eye of eternity: "the soul looks out from the height and laughs at the succession of time" (101.9). The soul is not bounded by a single lifetime: " 'All years are mine', says the soul" (102.21). Sometimes he suggests a longer view: in the face of loss, he argues, the best comfort is to keep one's memories intact: "Having is taken away; having had, never" (98.11). Memory thus allows us always to maintain at least a vestige of what we have once had, forever. He recommends looking back on the good parts of your own life (78.18): "consider in your mind your own best roles." This way, you can live without needing an audience to praise you: "Be your own spectator; praise yourself" (78.21). Even in relative solitude (apart from wife, friends, and a cartful of slaves), Seneca can find an active audience for himself, in his mind and his memory.

It is frustrating from a biographical perspective that Seneca says so little about what, exactly, causes him most joy and most pain as he looks back on his life. When his memories bring him nothing but grief, he is never specific about what he most minds or most regrets: "I was just feeling disgusted at myself, I was despising the fragments of my broken lifetime, on the point of crossing over to that vast time and possession of eternity—when suddenly I was woken by your letter" (102.2). The letter format itself marks a series of breaks in time, as we begin each one again; it provides an ever-present opportunity to change the subject.

Seneca hints at his own life story a number of times in the *Epistles*, but never explicitly or with any specificity. Often Seneca applies to other people—the addressee, or people in general—stories that seem particularly applicable to himself. In Epistle 19, for example, he tells Lucilius what a shame it is that he—Lucilius—ever rose up beyond his humble provincial origins to such heights of prosperity: "If only you'd had the chance to grow old in the modest manner of the family into which you were born, and fortune had never raised you to such heights!" (19.5).

The career up the Roman ladder of success is presented as a condition of permanent slavery, although not to a human master but to one's own desires: once one starts on the path of ambition, there is no end to more wants: "from the end of one desire springs up another." Power and prosperity are, then, vehicles of enslavement: "Take your worn-out neck from the yoke; better to have it severed once and for all, than be pressed down forever."

Seneca makes it sound very easy to escape from prosperity and power. He imagines Lucilius asking how to extricate himself and responds: "*Utcumque!*" ("Any old way!"). There is some disingenuousness here: Seneca is presenting as easy something that he himself manifestly found extremely difficult. It is presumably no coincidence that the following letter takes up the central Senecan theme of inconstancy. Seneca suggests that his greatest concern is not that he might act against his true beliefs, or speak words he does not really believe, but rather that his beliefs, and thus his words and actions, might be in a constant state of flux. "The greatest proof of an evil mind is fluctuation, and constant wavering between the pretense of virtue and the love of vice" (120.20). Only a good man can be always the same as himself, and thus only a good man can be truly known. The fragmented, episodic form of these letters itself may suggest a lack of coherent, consistent selfhood—or may suggest that the speaker can be constant only for a paragraph or two, no more. A buried worry running through the text is whether their author is able to maintain a stable persona: has he changed, since the early days with Nero, or has he not? Either one is a bad answer.

There are discussions of teaching and learning, which inevitably suggest that the one-time tutor of Nero was still preoccupied with the question of whether he did any good in his position—and whether, if he failed, it was his fault or that of the pupil. He emphasizes the importance of the living teacher, who inspires his student not so much by words as by action, by the model of his own life. Useful though books may be for some purposes, they are far less important than a real-life teacher: "the living voice and the intimacy of a common life will help you more than the written word" (6.5). But what if the teacher himself is unable to live up to his own precepts? This is a recurrent anxiety in the letters. Seneca argues that it is essential that one's life should match one's teaching: "this is the most essential duty and proof of wisdom: that one's actions should match one's words, and that a person should always, everywhere, be the same, and himself" (20.2). A philosopher, Seneca insists, is not simply a purveyor of wisdom in mere words: he is also, and most importantly, a person who teaches by example. "He is not only a teacher of truth, but a witness to the truth" (20.10.) There is an unresolved tension between Seneca's admissions that he himself is imperfect, full of moral sores, a patient rather than a doctor, and his insistence that one must live up to what one teaches.

In more positive spirit, he suggests that he is still on his way toward wisdom. He relates that he is, even in old age, going to lectures on philosophy, designed for young men embarking on their education in preparation for beginning a career; he insists that actually this is a far better use of an old man's time than the more traditional pursuits of going to the theater or the wrestling or the gladiatorial games (76.3–4).

A repeated question in the *Letters* is whether philosophical teaching is worthwhile. Seneca imagines an argumentative opponent who claims that it is a waste of time; for one thing, the advisors will always fail to follow their own advice: "those who give this advice most assiduously cannot follow it themselves" (94.9). For another, nobody is ever changed by precepts: either you teach somebody who already knows how to behave well, or else you teach somebody who does not know, and precepts will not be enough to change him (94.11). But Seneca responds by redefining the goals of his writings and teachings: "Just because Philosophy can't cure everything, doesn't mean it can't cure anything" (94.24). The central point is that giving advice is not the same as giving factual information, where one simply conveys a piece of knowledge to another person. Rather, the point of moral philosophy is to make its practioners feel and take to heart the premises that they may, subliminally, already know: "We sometimes know but don't pay attention" (94.25). The point of Seneca's own precepts and, in particular, of his aphoristic, punchy style is that it is the most effective way to make the point hit home and become memorable or noticeable: "Virtue is aroused by a touch or a shock" (94.29).

But he is conscious that sometimes teaching just won't work. This theme sometimes emerges in surprising places. Nomentum (Fig. 4.2), where Seneca owned one of his villas, was one of the places he enjoyed growing vines—a hobby he found deeply sustaining, and also informative as a way to think about how cultivation can be achieved. The vines were his ideal pupils, the ones who responded to his attempts at grafting

Figure 4.2 Nomentum (Mentana) today.

and shaping their growth, but even here he acknowledges that not all will be good students: "Not every vine accepts grafting; if it's old and decayed, or weak and slim, the vine will not receive the cutting, or won't nourish it and make it part of itself, nor accommodate itself to the qualities and nature of the grafted part" (112.2). This is as close as Seneca ever comes to discussing his failure at teaching Nero.

Another major theme of the collection is wealth, luxury, and profit. Seneca looks back with very mixed feelings on his life as a rich man with massive sociopolitical influence. The language of ownership recurs constantly, but Seneca insists the real way to be wealthy, to be powerful, and to make a profit that will last is to contemplate philosophy: "Everything belongs to other people, Lucilius; only time belongs to us" (1.3). The gifts of fortune are not really gifts at all: "Do you call these things the gifts of fortune? They are traps!" (7.3–4). Seneca names the temporary, false "benefactor" fortune; he might equally well have cited the name Nero, but "fortune" makes the process sound more passive—as if wealth simply came to Seneca without his having to lift a finger for it.

Some of Seneca's most vivid writing is inspired by the emptiness of consumer goods:

Suppose you acquire, heaped up, the property of many ultra-rich people. Imagine that fortune carries you far beyond mere private wealth: you get a golden roof, purple clothes, and so much luxury and wealth that you can bury the earth beneath your marble floors. So much that you don't just possess wealth: you trample on it. Let's say you also have statues, pictures, any of the most modern and fancy kinds of artwork. All you learn from this is how to desire more stuff."

(13.8)

Consumerism provides no psychological satisfaction, because there is no limit to our desires for things that we never needed in the first place. Moreover, it is not only pointless, but spiritually damaging. We acquire property that actually robs us of the power to know ourselves and live in accordance with nature, and we believe that losing it will be a real pain—a belief that is pure illusion: "One who owns himself has lost nothing" (42.10). Hunger for food is satisfied by enough food to fill the stomach, but hunger for something we don't actually need (like nice clothes or big houses or piles of gold) has no natural limit, because there is no natural need that these things satisfy: "Natural desires are limited; but those that spring from false opinion can have no place to stop" (16.9).

Seneca constantly reverts to the theme first taught him by his old tutor Attalus, that "money never makes one rich" (119.9); true wealth comes from being satisfied with enough. "Enough is never too little" (119.7). He insists that we need to remind ourselves that the world is vast, but our actual needs are small and easily satisfied: we do not need crops planted all the way down in Sicily or Africa to fill a single belly; we should measure not only the world, but ourselves, and realize "how little we can consume, and for how short a time" (114.27). Seneca's Stoicism is the philosophical response to an elite society that has grown increasingly consumerist and materialistic as a result of the vast growth of the Roman empire. "How tiny a part of those banquets of yours, prepared by so many hands, do you taste with your mouth that is already tired by pleasure? . . . How tiny a part of that shellfish, brought here from so far away, slips down your insatiable throat? Poor things, don't you know that your hunger is bigger than your stomach?" (89.22). "Prosperity is a restless thing: it troubles itself" (36.1). The only way to escape this bad temptation is retirement to a life of pure contemplation. Seneca insists that riches that may seem to be a lucky gift, that land easily or apparently for free in our laps, always bring a terribly heavy cost: "we would belong to ourselves, if those things were not ours" (42.8). We think these things are cheap, but they are horribly expensive, paid not in money but in far more valuable assets: "a cost of anxiety, of danger, of lost honor, freedom and time" (42.7).

There is a strikingly modern (and quasi-Buddhist) ring to Seneca's insistence on practicing "voluntary simplicity" or minimalism as a response to the unhealthy psychological pressures of a materialist, consumerist culture.[13] Seneca does not appeal to the damage done to natural resources by excessive human production, consumption, and waste. But he does emphasize that our drive for material wealth leads us far away from a life in accordance with nature. Moreover, like many modern advocates for a curb on consumerism, Seneca insists that there is an affinity, not a contrast, between the real needs of humans and the integrity of the natural world. It is good for "nature," in the sense both of external nature (the external world that is pillaged by excessive consumption) and internal nature (our real needs, to which we may become blind through false kinds of acculturation).

One can see hints in the *Letters* of Seneca's attitude toward the world of political power from which he was struggling to disentangle himself. Autonomy is a major theme. Virtue, Seneca stresses, is the only way to achieve real freedom and independence from external control. Virtue is also the only way out from the falsehoods and entrapment of desire and ambition. All our other desires necessarily go unsatisfied: a person in this kind of society (or, rather, Seneca) achieves the height of power and influence and wealth only to want more—more power, more security, more money. However, "the power and greatness of virtue cannot rise to greater heights, because what is already the greatest can't get bigger" (66.8).

Epistle 73 is important for its extensive discussion of the relationship of philosophers to those in power—a topic that allows Seneca to look back, implicitly, on his own career. Seneca insists that the wise man will always be grateful to those who have helped him along the way and allowed him to put his theories into practice (73.4–5). Philosophy teaches us, above all, to be grateful (73.10). Presumably the epistle is partly designed as a plea to Nero to see Seneca not as an ungrateful former dependent, or as a threat to his own power, but rather as a thankful recipient of the emperor's favor. But it also continues the task of trying to explain and justify to the emperor his (exalted) reasons for giving up many of his gifts. We must recognize, Seneca insists, that riches are preferable to poverty, but they are not essential and are not part of ourselves, and wealth must be used with moderation: "Few men have been allowed to put aside prosperity gently" (73.18). As so often, Seneca shows his intense awareness that one's own good fortune can became a trap. Even people, he insists, are not essential to the core of happiness. You can lose your whole family, your spouse, children, friends, everyone you ever knew and loved: and still, if you are virtuous, you can be happy. Virtue "takes hold of the whole soul, and takes away any longing for anything" (73.25).

Seneca insists on the wise man's imperturbability and lack of anxiety about the future: "What is more crazy than to be anguished by the future, and not save oneself for the real suffering, but invite misery and bring it upon oneself?" (74.33). The sentiment is perfectly sensible, but it seems likely that Seneca would not insist on it so adamantly and so frequently were he himself not constantly troubled by apprehension about his own future. His attitude toward retirement from society—his own and other people's—remains complex. He suggests that retirement is the best and safest way to retain one's own integrity, but he also argues that the wise person ought always to be engaged with others wherever he may happen to be. Public life may offer more temptations than a life of simplicity and quasi-solitude: "Who uses gold plate when he dines alone?" (94.70). But the wise person ought ideally to participate and set an example to others of moderation even in the midst of excess. On festival days, for example, Seneca suggests that the hardest but wisest way is not to avoid the crowds of merrymakers but to join in with moderation, setting an example of abstinent behavior even in the midst of excess: "It shows greater self-control to refuse to withdraw oneself, and to do the same things as the crowd, but in a different way" (18.4). The resolution to this apparent contradiction can be found in the claim that a life of retirement and a life of social engagement can actually be the same thing. Even in solitude, the philosopher engages with others: "My purpose in hiding myself and locking the door is to help more people" (7.1). The wise man, we learn, "is not apart from the state, even if he retires; no, in fact he has left one tiny little corner, and crosses to bigger, broader realms, and set in the sky, he understands how low the seat he was sitting on was, when he mounted the currule seat [used by senior magistrates] or tribunal chairs" (67.2). As in the *Natural Questions*, Seneca takes the line that the real engagement with the world that is recommended by Stoicism can best be practiced in what may look, to outsiders, like retirement.

Meanwhile, in Rome, Nero was erecting triumphal arches for his victory over the Parthians in the eastern part of the empire—despite the fact that the war was still ongoing. He was also trying to maintain public confidence in the grain supply by dumping rotten food into the Tiber. He embarked on building projects, setting up a new gymnasium in the city. Without Seneca as his public relations manager and advisor, Nero's foreign and domestic policies tended more and more toward the theatrical. He sang in public theaters across the empire and provided public banquets in Rome. One of his most notorious performances was a "marriage" with a man dressed up as a woman. In July 64 CE came one of the most famous disasters of Nero's rule: a great fire broke out in Rome, which burned for six days solid, killed many citizens, and destroyed whole neighborhoods around the Circus, including houses, temples, and porticos, all reduced to ash. Some muttered that Nero himself had started the blaze; others, that he capitalized on its theatrical value by appearing on stage while the fire raged to sing about the burning of Troy.

Seneca was presumably out of Rome at the time, but one of his letters, probably composed immediately after the Great Fire, discusses "our friend Liberalis," whose town of Lyons has been devastated by fire.[14] He gives a vivid description of a city of "so many beautiful buildings ... ruined in just one night" (91.2). Archaeologists have searched in vain for any evidence of an actual fire at Lyons from this date, the summer of 64 CE. The obvious conclusion is that Seneca is fabricating a fire at Lyons in order to allow himself a space to discuss the fire at Rome and to suggest that the Rome from which he has withdrawn is far less solid, and far less magnificent, than his own mind. Discussing the fire at Lyons, Seneca branches out to consider the transience of all the mighty cities of the world: "time blots out even the traces of all the cities that you hear of as magnificent and grand" (91.10). He acknowledges that a vast destruction may leave room for rebuilding, as it did in Rome: "May it be built to endure, and under better auspices, founded for a longer existence!" But he also suggests that the real rebuilding work has to happen inside the mind. Seneca's philosophical and literary creation in the *Letters* is more powerful and more enduring than the emperor's burned city: "We are in the power of nothing when death is in our power" (91.21).

Nero's response to the fire was rather different: he embarked on an even more lavish building project, a palace for himself named the Golden House (*Domus Aurea*), a vast complex of apartments, their walls inlaid with gold and jewels and images of lakes, rivers, and fields—which was never actually completed (Figs. 4.3 and 4.4). Nero's comment on the palatial building, we are told, was that "he was at last beginning to be housed like a human being" (Suetonius, *Nero,* 31). The response of the Roman elite was predictably less positive; the Golden House was seen as the absolute nadir of imperial self-indulgence. Nero also tried to appease the gods, who must have had something to do with the fire, by proprietary ceremonies. We are told that he found a new category of human scapegoats in the Christians, who were crucified or thrown to the beasts in the arena, condemned both as arsonists and as misanthropes.[15]

To pay for all this construction and for the expensive entertainments at the theater and the circus, Nero had to raise a lot of money from the provinces. We are told that "the provinces had been completely ruined" and that "throughout Asian and Achaea it was not simply the temple offerings but the statues of the gods that were being plundered" (Tacitus 14.45). Of the two men sent to retrieve this plunder for the emperor, one, Secundus Carrinas, was trained in Greek philosophy, and it was apparently suspected that he used his philosophical background as a justification for this sacrilegious temple robbing. In this context—or so it was rumored—Seneca came under increased suspicion, and he made yet another plea to be allowed to retire permanently to the country. We are told that he again attempted to give back his wealth to Nero, to help with the building projects after the fire (Dio). When that failed, again, Seneca claimed to be sick from a "muscular disease" (Tacitus 14.45) and locked himself in his bedroom. Some said (and again, Tacitus does not wholly endorse the rumor) that Nero gave orders for Seneca's freedman, Cleonicus, to give him poison; but, either thanks to the freedman's loyalty or Seneca's own suspicions, he did not consume it. Seneca thereafter became even more careful about restricting his diet: even bread was dangerous.

For somebody who wrote so frequently about the importance of facing death bravely and readily, Seneca was extremely good at avoiding it. He himself acknowledges the difficulty, even for the most philosophical of us, in eliminating all fear of death: "Death is in the category of the things that are not evil; but it has the appearance of evil" (Epistle 82.15). Seneca's central preoccupation is with trying to make death his own, something

Figure 4.3 The Domus Aurea ("golden house") was built by Nero after the Great Fire of Rome. It was an extremely lavish palace building, of three hundred rooms, designed to accommodate huge parties; the walls were decorated with elaborate frescoes, ivory, and gold leaf.

Figure 4.4 The Domus Aurea (exterior view).

that belongs to him and is in his power, not something that might threaten his autonomy. He is on a constant quest to reinvent death as a sphere where he can be in control and can express himself, rather than simply at the mercy of somebody else. Death, he suggests, is a great leveler, since ownership of death is available to everybody, no matter how he or she dies: "nobody does not die his own death." On the other hand, death is deeply personal, and Seneca clearly wanted to be able to manage his last moments for himself rather than have them come upon him suddenly by poison: "The best death is the one you like" (70.3). This kind of line makes a partial acknowledgment that one may in fact be unable to die in the manner one might have chosen; but that fantasy remains essential. He meditates obsessively on other famous philosophical deaths in history, most especially those of Socrates and of Cato the Younger (who disemboweled himself rather than survive the death of the Republic). These each give examples of how a death can be both imposed from outside, by an external political power, but also can be performed exactly as the agent himself desires. By owning death, Seneca manages to see it as a path to freedom: we have "only one way into life, but many ways out" (70.14). Death is also the ultimate test of whether we can put our moral training into practice: "for this one thing the day will come when we have to be tested" (70.18).

THIS COURAGEOUS DEATH

At the start of 65 CE, a conspiracy to kill Nero began, centered on a man called Gaius Piso, who had been exiled under Caligula but recalled by

Claudius (Dio 59.8.7). Piso was a well-born and popular man, good-looking and skilled in rhetoric, although, as Tacitus snootily remarks, he indulged in frivolity, luxury, and immoderate pleasures (15.48). The roots of the conspiracy are unclear: Tacitus tells us that he does not know who the prime mover was (15.49). It seems likely that the conspirators' motives were mixed: some, including Seneca's nephew Lucan, joined the group because of their personal hatred for Nero, while others were driven by a sense that the empire was going downhill under Nero's reign. A large number joined the group: Tacitus names no fewer than eleven elite men, along with several from military positions, including, most importantly, Faenius Rufus, who was joint head of the Praetorian Guard along with Tigellinus. Tigellinus, we are told, persecuted Faenius Rufus, trying to bring him down by making false accusations against him to Nero (such as that he had once been a lover of Agrippina); Rufus therefore had a strong motive to change the status quo.

The plot was unfortunately vague in its practicalities, and the conspirators failed to keep their intentions secret. A woman called Epicharis, Tacitus tells us, got wind of it, and in an attempt to get things moving, she tried to enlist various members of the navy; one of these, Proculus, told Nero of the conspiracy. He had no witnesses, but Epicharis was detained in custody, and Nero's suspicions were now aroused. The conspirators hoped to waylay Nero on the day of the Circus, where one of them would fall at his knees, then tussle him to the ground, at which point the others would leap upon him and stab him to death. But the night before, Scavinus, one of the plotters, had his freedman sharpen the knife he planned to use for the assassination, and—either because the master had let slip the secret, or because the man guessed—the next day, the freedman told Nero, and Scavinus was brought in for questioning. Under threat of torture, he gave the whole plot away, naming his fellow-plotters. Epicharis, too, was tortured and questioned, although she stood up against it far better than he had done and died rather than give the secret away.

Everyone suspected of involvement in the plot—rightly or wrong—was either condemned to death or forced to commit suicide. Seneca was also convicted. He certainly knew many of the conspirators and may well have known of the plot. Piso, like Seneca, had been exiled and then recalled under Claudius, and the two men would have shared many friends and associates. Dio asserts, implausibly, that Seneca was a "ringleader" in the group, "publicly making great talk about the glory of tyrannicides, and full of threats, even going to the length of offering Caesar's head to all his friends." He and Rufus together were motivated, Dio says, by Nero's "disgraceful behavior, his licentiousness, and his cruelty" (62.24.1). Tacitus also reports the rumor that some of the conspirators had plans to kill Piso also, once Nero was dead, and then put Seneca in charge of the empire, as a way of giving the coup more moral legitimacy—he would seem to have been "chosen for supreme power by innocent men, for the sake of the outstanding nature of his virtues" (Tacitus 15.65.1). All this may be mere gossip; but it is fascinating to consider the alternative history of the Roman empire that might have taken place had Seneca actually become emperor, and gained the greatest *imperium* in the world, as opposed to the great *imperium* of the self. Would he have done any better than Nero himself?

But the evidence that Seneca was directly involved in the plot is fairly circumstantial. Only one of the conspirators, Natalis, denounced him, and his sole piece of proof was a brief exchange when he went to visit Seneca's house when he was sick (or claiming to be sick). Natalis asked, "Why do you close your door on Piso?" Seneca replied, "Frequent conversations with him are not to his advantage or mine; but my own health depends on that of Piso" (Tacitus 15.60.1). This could mean that Seneca was involved in Piso's plot, and that was the way that Nero chose to interpret it. But it could equally have been a vague piece of politeness, or a failed attempt to distance himself from the plotters.

Seneca was tracked down on the journey back from Campania to Rome. He was staying at his lovely, well-tended estate at Nomentum, with his wife, various close friends, and his household of slaves and freedmen. He was there cross-examined by a tribune about his remark about Piso. Seneca insisted that he never said his health depended on Piso's: such a thing would have been entirely false, and Seneca claimed that he never uttered empty words of politeness. "Nobody," he said, "knew that better than Nero, who had more often experienced Seneca's freedom of speech, than his servility." If this claim of total sincerity was intended to convince Nero to spare his life, it was futile. When the tribunes reported back to Nero, the emperor asked if Seneca was preparing to kill himself. Since they said he looked perfectly calm and cheerful, Nero instructed them to go back and pronounce the death sentence on his old tutor.

Our sources for the death of Seneca give rather different depictions of how honorably he died. Dio, using a source hostile to the philosopher, tells us this:

> It was his wish to end the life of his wife Paulina at the same time as his own, since he said that he had taught her both to despise death and to desire to leave the world with him. So he opened her veins as well as his own. But as he had a hard time dying, the soldiers hastened his end; she was still alive when he died, and so she survived. He did not kill himself, however, until he had revised the book he was writing, and had deposited his other books with some friends, fearing that they would otherwise fall into the hands of Nero, and be destroyed.
>
> (62.25.1–3)

If a person's death is, as Seneca insisted, the image of his life, this version of the death gives a particularly unflattering reflection of the man. He was, on Dio's telling, even willing to kill his own wife in order to enhance the reputation of his own teaching. Moreover, he was obsessed to the end with his own reputation and with the survival of his own works. Narcissism, rather than philosophical calm, is the keynote of this death scene.

Tacitus' account of the same event seems to follow a much more sympathetic source: a (lost) narrative written by a friend of Seneca's named Fabius Rusticus, possibly within a larger history, or as part of a complete biography of Seneca. He tells much the same story but gives it a more positive interpretation, although he still points very clearly to the egotism and showiness of the performance.[16]

A crucial difference between the two accounts is that in Tacitus's version, Paulina herself is the one who wants to die with her husband. Seneca embraces her and begs her not to grieve for him forever; Paulina answers that she chooses to die with him. Seneca, "not hostile to her glory, and also out of love, to avoid leaving her, his only-beloved, to be harmed," then falls in line with her wishes. He declares to her, "I showed you how to make life go easy, but you prefer the glory of death; I will not begrudge you the example. May we both have the same steadfastness for this courageous death, but may your end be more famous" (15.63). Thereupon, they cut their wrists with a single cut. Tacitus presumably intends his readers to see these words as self-important and at least partially fake: for most of the death scene, his Seneca is far too concerned with managing his own postmortem reputation to be concerned about that of his wife.

Moreover, the notion that Paulina would inevitably have faced "harm" or "outrage" after her husband's death is belied by the care with which Nero looks out for her. Tacitus does not explain how the emperor—who was presumably at Rome rather than actually in the villa—knew that she planned to kill herself. But he tells the story that Nero gave orders for the suicide to be stopped, since he had no grudge against her and did not wish to make himself look too cruel (15.64). The soldiers then bandaged up her arms, and she lived on for several years, "admirably faithful to her husband, and pale in face and limbs, showing how much life-blood she had lost." Tacitus also reports, without entirely giving it credence, another rumor: that she offered to kill herself with Seneca only when she thought herself doomed under Nero anyway. She was happy to have her life saved as soon she realized it was an option. So much for philosophical teaching.

Seneca himself had been preparing for his death for many, many years, in practical, spiritual, and rhetorical ways. He had a will that was prepared long ago, when he was "still super-rich and super-powerful" (*praedives* and *praepotens*). He hoped to read it out loud to his friends, to impress them with his generosity and gratitude toward them; when the soldiers refuse to let him do so, he offers them instead, as his last gift, "the image of his life" (*imago vitae suae*). This is "both his only remaining possession, and the most beautiful one of all." Such sentiments, one might think, would be rather more fitting from the mouth of a friend than from the man himself. But it is clear that the purpose of these "friends"— none of whom are named, and none of whom speak—is to act as an audience for Seneca's final drama and to ensure that his words and actions are preserved for an even wider public to enjoy and admire. As well as "friends"—many were presumably old clients or other dependents— Seneca was surrounded by a large apparatus of household slaves, including secretaries to note down whatever he said, as well as a doctor and bath attendants. Obviously modeling himself on the dying Socrates in Plato's *Phaedo*, he urges the friends not to cry but to be brave, inspired by his own philosophy: "Where," he asks, "are your philosophical maxims? Where is the rationality, cultivated over so many years, as a counter to imminent dangers?"

So far, so Socratic; but then Seneca shifts abruptly but characteristically from philosophy to common sense, and suggests that the real reason his friends ought not to cry for him is simply that they could easily have seen it coming: "Who didn't know about Nero's cruelty? There was nothing left after killing his mother and brother, than to add the murder of his guardian and tutor" (15.62). Seneca had worked hard to whitewash the murders of Britannicus and Agrippina at the time, but he must always have known that Nero's aggression would likely one day turn to himself. Seneca's death scene is thus a moment when the veil is stripped away, when the philosopher can finally, at last, speak truth to power (Fig. 4.5).

But even now, Seneca's attitude toward Nero's rule is conciliatory rather than revolutionary: he presents the emperor's murderousness as inevitable and does nothing to suggest that he, or his followers, either could or should stop him. The philosopher is concerned with creating an impression for a large audience and for his admiring readers in years to come, rather than influencing the political future. Tacitus wryly remarks that his words about Nero "seemed to be meant for the general public," even though he was supposedly addressing only a small group of friends. Similarly, even after he and Paulina have slashed their wrists, Seneca manages to keep talking to the public: "he called his secretaries and dictated a long speech, which has already been published in his own words, so I will hold back from summarizing it." Tacitus is quietly mocking Seneca's attempt to control the script of his own death, implying that there is something a little unseemly about this master of rhetoric making a public relations exercise even from his own dying hour.

The vein slashing did not work for Seneca. Perhaps he had suspected that this method might not be successful when his time came: he wrote in the *Natural Questions* that when veins are cut, "the blood continues to ooze either until it all flows out, or until the cut in the vein closes and shuts off the bleeding, or some other reason keeps the blood back" (3.15.5). In his own case, the blood failed to flow out because his body was too old and skinny, emaciated from long years of fasting. He cut behind his knees as well, but to no avail. Fearing that the sight of his suffering might upset his wife, "and he himself might slip from his purpose at seeing her agonies," he sent her off to the bedroom, where the soldiers bandaged her arms and saved her life. It is telling that Seneca feared being distracted from his purpose by his wife's pain, a detail that marks the difference from Socrates' death scene as clearly as anything. Seneca was not blessed with perfect philosophical calm and resolution at all times: he had a constant struggle to abide by his moral purpose.

Figure 4.5 Seneca was forced to commit suicide by Nero and finally died by suffocating in a steam bath. This painting, evocative of the muscular effort Seneca put into the attempt to die, is based on two ancient sculptures, neither of which is now believed to represent Seneca.

When even the legs would not bleed enough, Seneca again emulated Socrates by calling for hemlock. His hemlock, however, was not administered by the public executioner, but by his own private doctor, Statius Annaeus (whose name suggests he may have been a relative but was more likely a freedman who had perhaps begun serving Seneca as a slave but had been manumitted). He had bought it long ago, presumably at some expense, in readiness for a death he knew was likely to come in this forced manner. However, even the hemlock did not work on his cold, feeble body. He stepped into a dish of hot water, spattering the poor slaves standing nearby: this spill was, he said, a libation to Jupiter the Liberator. Finally he had his slaves lift him into a hot bath, and he suffocated in the steam. They cremated him immediately, according to his wish.

The death Seneca had anticipated for so long had finally arrived. It was, like his life, a highly theatrical moment, composed of a series of compromises. The failure of each successive method of death is both terrible (he could not even kill himself successfully) and blackly funny, as Tacitus surely intended. Seneca's wish to control his final moments was highly visible here, but so too was the impossibility for him of achieving the Stoic ideal of perfect constancy and calm within the pressures and violence of Neronian Rome, and given Seneca's own frailties. One can sneer at a death that took so long and that was so difficult to achieve; Seneca failed repeatedly at something that everybody manages, in the end. But one can also admire the ways that he kept trying, despite his failures—just as he had done in life, in his constant attempts to continue along the path of philosophical virtue.

We might also note that the repeated attempts to die each required a new set of props, all of which cost money. This death was also an appropriate end for one who had lived the life of a rich man and who had become Rome's most perceptive analyst of consumerism and the psychology of luxury. It may be remembered that Seneca in old age complained of feeling constantly cold and enjoyed warm baths. The bath in which he died was an instrument of pain and loss; but also it was a luxury item, heated and administered by slaves, offering this elite man his final path to freedom. Seneca's death, despite and because of his own best efforts, can be seen as a vivid image of his life. It was a slow, painful, highly theatrical and rhetorical confrontation between philosophical idealism and human weakness in the face of political power.

After Seneca's death, Nero rounded up everybody associated with the conspiracy: the year 65 was devoted to a long series of executions and forced suicides, of which Seneca's was in many ways the least impressive. The tribune, Subrius Flavus, died a less dramatic but no less brave death than that of Seneca, and Tacitus does him the honor (which he denied to Seneca) of recording his last words, in which he explains why he came

to hate Nero: for being the murderer of his wife and mother, and a charioteer, an arsonist, and an actor (15.67). In the same year Nero also killed
his latest wife, Poppaea, probably accidentally, by kicking her in the belly
during pregnancy. Numerous other exiles and deaths followed. Musonius Rufus was exiled. Lucan, Seneca's nephew, and later, in 66 CE, Mela,
his father, were denounced on more charges of conspiracy. Lucan, Suetonius tells us, was "easily forced to confess, and descended to the most
abject pleas, even naming his own mother as one of his companions
despite her innocence. He hoped this unfilial behavior would benefit
him with the parricidal emperor. But when he was allowed free choice
of the manner of his death, he wrote a letter to his father with edits for
some of his verses, and after a large meal, offered his arms to a doctor, for
cutting his veins" (*Life of Lucan*).

Petronius, envied by Tigellinus because Nero found him so amusing, was
also condemned: he opened his veins, then partially bandaged them, to
enjoy a last evening chatting with friends over dinner, before dozing into
death during the meal (Tacitus 16.19). The most impressive of this series of
forced deaths belong to Barea Soranus and, especially, Thrasea, who was accused of being contemptuous of the emperor. Thrasea echoed and trumped
Seneca's death: as he cut his arteries he sprinkled not bathwater but his own
blood on the ground and exclaimed: "To you, Jupiter the Liberator, I pour
this libation!" Whereas Seneca had carefully downplayed the political sig-
nificance of his death, Thrasea did the opposite. This was the first in a series
of reappropriations of the life, death, and work of Seneca.

Seneca's former student, patron, emperor, and enemy, Nero, died less
than four years later. High taxes, bad management, and poor public relations led to an inherently unstable situation for the empire. Trouble had
been brewing in the provinces of Germany and Spain, and the Praetorian
Guard, who were nominally on the side of the emperor, switched their
allegiances over to Galba, the governor of one of the Hispanic provinces.
Nero now found himself, like his old tutor before him, wandering in fear
of his life. After some desperate hours of indecision, he fled Rome for his
villa in the north, riding barefoot and with a cloth to cover his face, and
with only a few loyal freedmen as companions. Finally despairing of
safety, he ordered them to dig his grave right by the roadside, weeping at
the thought of the world's loss of himself: "What an artist dies with me!"
he exclaimed. Hearing the thunder of his enemies' horses drawing near,
he stabbed his dagger into his throat, with the help of his freedman.[17]

Rome was then plunged into a series of conflicts over the succession: the following year is known as the Year of the Four Emperors, since no candidate as heir managed to last more than a few months. Nero's theatrical death is like that of his old tutor Seneca in its grisly humor and in its narcissism—although unlike Seneca, Nero had no loyal wife or family members or friends to stand by his side in death, since he had killed them all.

EPILOGUE

I n the immediate aftermath of Seneca's death, the dead philosopher was a controversial figure. The central question was the extent to which he could be blamed for what was wrong with the Julio-Claudian dynasty—or, conversely, could be praised for having stood out against it. Some viewed him as at least partly responsible for the worst excesses of Nero's reign; the negative assessment made its way into Dio's *Roman History*. Others—including some of those who had benefited from Seneca's patronage—saw him in much more idealized terms, as a virtuous man who tried his best to speak out against the wickedness of his times; this was presumably the picture painted by the lost work of Fabius Rusticus. Seneca would continue to be a polarizing figure throughout much of the next two thousand years.

Our earliest surviving response to Seneca's life, character, and relationship with Nero is a play that has come down to us among Seneca's own tragedies: the *Octavia*.[1] This fascinating work was clearly written by somebody who knew Seneca's dramatic and prose oeuvre very well; the author draws heavily on the *De Clementia*, and uses the vocabulary and tropes of Senecan tragedy—the obsessions with power, empire, death, guilt, reversals of fortune, and unnamable dread; the supernatural, exile, wealth, prophecy, murder, and revenge. But these are all applied not to a Greek mythological subject, but to Seneca's own lifetime. The play is set during three days in 62 CE and covers Nero's divorce of his first wife Octavia (presented as an innocent victim of the tyrant's crazy passions), his cruel act of exiling her, and his remarriage to Poppaea. Seneca features as a character in the play, a counselor who offers all the right advice but goes unheeded by the despotic Nero. The author uses Nero and Seneca to make a larger political point: that the power of the emperor must be limited and must yield to law and the community. The "Seneca" of the *Octavia* is notably more optimistic about all this than the real Seneca had been. There is a scene in Seneca's *Thyestes* in which the murderous, power-hungry Atreus is advised to moderate his plans by an Attendant— but the Attendant soon caves to Atreus' unstoppable will. In the *Octavia*, the same motifs are replayed in a scene between "Seneca" and "Nero," and this time around, the Attendant-figure ("Seneca") sticks to his guns and quotes his own *De Clementia* to urge moderation on "Nero," unsuccessfully but with consistency and dignity. Nero's wickedness is revealed all the more by his refusal to yield to his old tutor, claiming, rather, "I can do what Seneca disapproves of!" (*Octavia* 569).

In literary terms, Seneca had a huge influence on Latin style. The great writer on rhetorical technique and education Quintilian—who lived a generation after Seneca—famously criticized Seneca's style for being "corrupt" and a bad influence on the youth of his own time. Seneca, he insists, is a dangerous model for the young because his writing is full of unnatural turns of phrase, "faults" that are all too easy to imitate.[2] Quintilian's criticisms hint at just how popular Seneca's style of writing became soon after his death.

As the Roman world gradually became Christianized, Seneca took on a new importance as a pagan who could, more readily than almost any other, be assimilated into the Church. A fascinating thread in the reception of Seneca after his death is the apocryphal Latin correspondence between Seneca and the apostle Paul. It is clear from their (postclassical) language that this set of letters cannot possibly be genuine; they were probably composed in the third century CE, or perhaps early in the fourth. But the fact that somebody went to the trouble of faking them suggests how desirable it seemed to find a pagan author who could be assimilated into the Christian tradition. The legend was not without a certain plausibility; Seneca's brother Novatus was governor of Achaea and in around 52 had dismissed the charges brought against Paul by the Jews (Acts. 18.12–17).[3] Novatus himself was presumably motivated by the usual Roman governor's desire to keep the Jewish people in order, but it was possible to interpret the move as deliberate siding with the Christians, and this helped Christian readers in late antiquity and the

Middle Ages interpret Seneca's moralizing, death-oriented version of Stoic philosophy as a kind of Christianity *avant la lettre*. "Seneca," in this correspondence, calls Paul his "brother" (*frater*) or "my dearest Paul" (*Paule carissime*) and is made to realize instantly that Paul is inspired by true divine spirit, articulating thoughts that "were expressed not by you, but through you" (Ep. 1.10–11). In actuality, the current of influence between Pauline Christianity and Roman Stoicism ran in the other direction. Paul was deeply influenced by Stoic philosophy, if not directly by Seneca. He borrowed the notions of indifferent things, of what is properly one's own (*oikeiosis*), the ideal of freedom from passion, and the paradoxical notion of freedom through slavery, fairly directly from the Stoics.[4] The affinities between Stoicism and Christianity thus ran fairly deep and were ripe for further exploitation by later Christian thinkers.

In the third and fourth centuries CE, when Christianity was only just beginning to gain widespread acceptance and when paganism still lingered, the apocryphal correspondence was useful for ecumenical relations between pagan and Christian. Seneca could be seen as the representative pagan philosopher, fit to engage in dialogue with the first proponent of the Christian worldview and ripe for conversion. It was claimed in late antiquity and the Middle Ages that Seneca converted to Christianity and was, as it were, baptized by the bath of his death. Lactantius (advisor to the first Christian emperor, Constantine) urges anyone who wants to know about justice to "take up the books of Seneca, who both described public ethics and vice very truthfully, and condemned them with the utmost spirit" (*Inst.* 5.9.19). Tertullian called Seneca "often ours" (*saepe noster*), although he also noted that his work is not always compatible with the Christian truth. Jerome went further, calling him "our Seneca" (*Seneca noster*) (*Ad Jovinian* 1.49). In his *On Famous Men* (*De Viris Illustribus*) of 393, he claims that the correspondence of Paul and Seneca, "which is read by many," justifies including Seneca "in the company of the saints"—although he otherwise would not qualify (Chapter 12). This passage does not necessarily suggest that Jerome—who could certainly tell the difference between classical and contemporary Latin—actually believed the correspondence to be genuine; rather, it was useful to have a justification for presenting the learned pagan and the great apostle as good friends.

Augustine was also aware of the supposed correspondence of Paul and Seneca (Letter 153), but his attitude toward Seneca was definitely critical;

indeed, his critique of Stoicism in general, and of Seneca in particular, was a crucial building block in his construction of Christian theology in *City of God*.[5] Augustine notes Seneca's criticisms of conventional Roman religion (or rather "superstition"), although he describes him as failing to live by his true beliefs: he had freedom "as a writer, but lacked it in life" (6.10). He claims that Seneca pretended to respect the religious practices of his contemporaries while really disbelieving in them (1.10). The more substantive criticism Augustine makes is that Stoic ethics depend on human pride. The Stoics, including Seneca, claimed that the wise man can be entirely free from vice and can live in a state of total tranquility, undisturbed by false emotions. This claim, according to Augustine, is fundamentally false: since the Fall, no human being could ever achieve such a state in this world, and if anybody—like the Stoics—believes that he can live without sin, "he does not avoid sin, but rather forfeits pardon" (14). The Stoic ideal of the wise man is both empirically false (no such person could ever exist in a postlapsarian world) and morally wrong, since it suggests that fallen humans have the power, through mere will, to control their own happiness. The charge of pride is one that recurs again and again in later responses to Seneca's work.

In the later Middle Ages, Seneca was known mostly through the *Letters to Lucilius*, with the longer essays and the plays being relatively underread in this period.[6] He was respected as a moral teacher (dubbed "*Seneca morale*" by Dante), but in a rather vague way: medieval intellectuals tended to think of themselves as following the traditions of Christianized Aristotelianism developed by Aquinas rather than any Stoic author. Despite this, it has been well said that Stoicism was "everywhere and nowhere" in the Middle Ages:[7] Stoic logic and Stoic ideas about God and nature actually had a large but mostly unacknowledged influence in this period. Seneca's account in *On Anger* of the passions, and especially of the distinction between "first movements" in response to a stimulus (by blushing or shivering or bursting into tears) and actual emotions, was transformed into a list of eight sins based on temptations to yield to bad thoughts[8]—a list that was then transformed again, by Pope Gregory the Great in the seventh century, into the Seven Deadly Sins that we know today. Seneca's careful analysis of "first movements" that were absolutely not worthy of moral blame had thus been transformed into its opposite: they were bad thoughts that revealed humanity's fallen nature.[9] The fact that Senecan Stoicism could be so wildly distorted is one mark of how little it was studied for several hundred years. Seneca's life story was popularized in the thirteenth-century bestseller "The Golden Legend" (*Legenda Aurea*), which was a compilation of hagiographical accounts of famous saints—Seneca being included by virtue, again, of his association with Paul. The book includes a lurid account of the death scene involving a face-to-face showdown between Nero and Seneca, after which Seneca opens his veins in the bath—thus fulfilling his name, the author tells us, since *se necans* means "killing oneself."[10]

In the early modern period, there was a great expansion of interest in the Stoic tradition in general, and Seneca in particular. The humanists produced new editions and commentaries on his work,[11] and it began to be translated into vernacular languages, including English, by Thomas Lodge (1612). Erasmus produced one of the earliest complete editions, in 1562 (second edition) and included a preface that suggests an interestingly ambivalent attitude toward his author in literary terms: he criticizes his excessive use of "too rhetorical a style" (450) and his tendency to be long-winded and muddled, although he praises the letters, in particular, for offering "a true reflection of a real situation" (569). The combination of admiration with reservations would recur in many later assessments of our author.

Seneca was important in the time of the Renaissance in three sometimes interrelated but conceptually distinct ways.[12] First, his prose work—along with the philosophical writings of Cicero, which were even more widely read—was one of the primary sources for ancient Stoicism and had a major impact both on early modern political thought and early modern metaphysics and theology. Since the Greek Stoics were lost, the Roman Stoics provided the main means of access to the whole school. Secondly, Seneca's punchy, aphoristic writing style had a major impact on the trend toward a snappy, polished literary style adopted by some writers in the sixteenth and seventeenth centuries. And thirdly, Senecan tragedy was rediscovered in this period after a long period of neglect and had a major impact on the formation of early modern drama.

The figure of Seneca as advisor to an autocratic emperor haunted the imaginations of intellectuals and courtiers who found themselves in similar positions: the life story of Thomas More, scholar, philosopher, writer, and advisor to Henry VIII, who was then beheaded by the king, has been well compared to that of Seneca.[13] Seneca as a historical character (rather than as a writer or philosopher) often did come across rather badly in early modern literature and drama—moving beyond even the not-very-sympathetic portrayal in Tacitus. In Monteverdi's *L'Incoronazione di Poppaea*, an innovative historical opera from 1643, Seneca warns Nero not to cast off Octavia and marry Poppaea; for this reason, Nero orders Seneca to kill himself. After the philosopher's elaborate suicide bath, Nero and the courtiers cheerfully sing: "Now that Seneca is dead, now let me sing!" (*Hor che Seneca è morto, cantiam!*), and later Poppaea and her maidservant pick up the melody: "Now that Seneca is dead, Love, I appeal to you!" Seneca could easily be portrayed as a spoilsport.

The focus on individual, autonomous, or "autarkic" selfhood was one of the most appealing features of Seneca's work for a period often associated with the formation of modern notions of selfhood and modern forms of "self-fashioning."[14] Seneca was a key figure for the development of new understandings of psychology and ethics. Self-assertion, self-correction, and autonomy were crucial to the development of an idea of secular individuality in the early modern period; Seneca helped form these concepts.[15] Moreover, Seneca was particularly useful for thinking through the (problematic and permeable) boundaries of political communities, as well as of individual human bodies and selves. The question of how the two kinds of *imperium* might relate had a particular resonance at the period of the formation of modern nation-states and during the rise of absolutist models of monarchy. Seneca's *De Clementia*, in particular, shaped the whole "mirror for princes" tradition, a genre represented by such works as Castiglione's *Book of the Courtier* (1528), which focused on the correct behavior of kings and other elite groups. Machiavelli's *Prince* (1513) was both a participant in the tradition and an attack on its (Senecan) basis: Machiavelli tries to show that Seneca's appeal to the ideal that a ruler should be merciful is entirely misguided. Princes should not spare those they conquer; rather, they should kill them. Machiavelli disputes not only Seneca's ethics but also his metaphysics in insisting that the strong man should not submit to the will of providence nor be constant against the alterations of fortune, but should be himself willful, *impetuoso*, and violent.[16] But Stoicism, including Senecanism, could seem liable to provoke sedition when employed not by the ruler but against him. The future James I of England objected in *Basilikon Doron* to those who imitate "that ancient sect."[17]

It is often difficult to disentangle specifically Senecan elements in the Neo-Stoicism of this period, although Seneca (along with Cicero) was certainly one of the dominant influences. Montaigne, who has often been seen as more of a Skeptic than a Stoic, was deeply influenced both by the style and format of Seneca's work, especially by the meandering, personal mode of the *Letters to Lucilius*. The modern genre of the "essay" (leading from Montaigne to Robert Burton, Francis Bacon, and Thomas Browne to the great eighteenth-century essayists like Addison, Steele, and Johnson) could not have developed without the model of Seneca's epistles. Montaigne rejected the Stoic ideal of the perfect sage, but he defends the man against the usual accusations of hypocrisy ("Defense of Seneca and Plutarch") and engages deeply both with Seneca's notion of constancy (which he reinterprets as primarily a military virtue, not one to be adopted by a private citizen)[18] and most importantly with his ideal of clemency, from Seneca's *Letters* and especially from *De Clementia*— which Montaigne transformed into a modern ethics of flexible, humane kindness, to contrast with the heroic, rigid code of his contemporaries.[19]

A very different response to Seneca as an ethical model for the war-torn Europe of the late sixteenth century was Justus Lipsius' *De Constantia* (*On Constancy*) from 1584, which has been seen as an attempt to reclaim a Senecan, organic model of government against the assaults on it from Machiavelli.[20] Lipsius, a Belgian Catholic scholar, produced an edition of the complete works of Seneca while working at the University of Leiden. His attempt to produce a version of Stoicism ("Neo-Stoicism") that would be compatible with a generalized form of Christianity was recognizably a response to the French Wars of Religion; Stoicism, unlike the Bible, was not tainted by the various theological disagreements between Protestants and Catholics, and it offered a path back to a pristine, ancient model of steadfastness in a time of crisis. Neo-Stoicism allowed for a kind of cosmopolitanism that would transcend the boundaries of nationalities and of specific religious sects.

Reconciling Senecan Stoicism with Christianity remained a problem in the sixteenth and seventeenth centuries. Simon Goulart, a pastor from Geneva who sympathized with Lipsius' Neo-Stoicism, warned that "If you read Seneca as a pagan, he seems to have written as a Christian, but if you read him as a Christian, you feel that it is a pagan speaking."[21] Goulart suggests that Seneca's correspondence with Paul must have been a forgery, since Seneca clearly knew nothing of God, and his supposedly perfect sage is an arrogant, morbid fantasist: "he is defiant in his virtue, and looks for all his sources of happiness within himself; in other words, he paints castles in the air and looks for life in death."[22] A common objection was that Seneca and the other Stoics showed too little humility and detracted from God's power in claiming that human beings alone could achieve happiness through virtue alone, without divine grace. Joseph Marston wrote in 1598, "Peace, Seneca, thou belchest blasphemy / To live from God, but to live happily / (I heare thee boast,) from thy Philosophy."[23] In *Paradise Regained* (1671) Milton's Jesus speaks out against the Stoic's "philosophic pride":

> *Much of the Soul they talk, but all awry;*
> *And in themselves seek virtue; and to themselves*
> *all glory arrogate, to God give none.*

(4.313–315)

Descartes has often been seen as the father of modern philosophy and modern scientific thinking. But in his ethical thought, at least, he looked back closely to the ancients and especially to Seneca's *On the Happy Life*, on which he gave an extensive commentary in his letters to Princess Elizabeth in 1645. Descartes insisted—like Seneca and other Stoics—that the proper use of reason was essential for happiness. But he parted company with Seneca in his claim that the ultimate goal is not virtue or a life in accordance with nature, but happiness—which results from virtue but is not identical with it. For Descartes, the passions are not dangerous or misleading; they are "all by nature good."[24]

In the later seventeenth and eighteenth centuries, Stoicism, drawn largely from Seneca, was appealing in its promise of salvation in this world, not the next, and in its focus on the human capacity to achieve happiness without a need for external, supernatural aid. Rousseau took the epigraph to *Emile* from Seneca: "We are sick with evils that can be cured; and nature, having brought us forth sound, itself helps us if we wish to be improved."[25] In *Pantheisticon*, John Toland equipped his pantheists with chants drawn directly from Seneca: "To lead a happy Life Virtue alone is sufficient," they declare.[26] Stoicism had a new kind of political importance at the time of the Enlightenment because it promised "to restore man to his ethical dignity." It has been claimed that Thomas Jefferson was, perhaps unknowingly, using "the language of Stoic philosophy" when he drafted the Declaration of Independence, with its claim that "all men were created equal";[27] the masculine language ("men") is very much in tune with the Stoic emphasis on manly virtue (*virtus*) and on a model of social equality that has few implications for material or institutional change.

For some Enlightenment thinkers, the Stoics could be reinterpreted as Deists or even atheists; Diderot described them in his *Encyclopédie* as "materialists, fatalists and, strictly speaking, atheists"—which was all to the good.[28] Hume, by contrast, criticized the Stoics as being all too susceptible to irrational superstition in their belief in providence and a benevolent nature: "The STOICS join a philosophical enthusiasm to a religious superstition."[29]

Diderot's positive attitude toward Seneca aroused a great deal of controversy in France. In 1778 he published his last great work, the "Essay on the Reigns of Claudius and Nero," which incorporated his earlier "Life of Seneca." In it, he carefully defended Seneca against criticisms both ancient and modern. He identified closely with Seneca—the beleaguered philosopher who had tried and failed to guide the public and the ruling powers that were, who was persecuted by wicked detractors and dishonored in his lifetime, but whose heart was always in the right place and who clearly saw the distinction between life and art: "Seneca's detractors bear a striking resemblance to those of the *philosophes*," he wrote. Seneca could be assimilated into the same model as Socrates, whom Diderot had earlier admired. Seneca was essential to Diderot's last-ditch attempt to insist that philosophers ought indeed to have a public role and a public voice—and that even if the public were deaf to them (as Nero was to Seneca), their teaching was no less valuable. The peculiarity of Diderot's interpretation was not lost on his contemporaries; indeed, some have referred to the "Querelle sur Sénèque" ("Quarrel on Seneca"), with Seneca taking center stage in Enlightenment debates about the relative values of the new intellectuals versus the old political and religious establishment.

The influence of Seneca as a dramatist has a mostly distinct history from Seneca the political, theological, and philosophical writer. It was believed for many generations that *Seneca philosophicus* was actually a different author from *Seneca tragicus*; some theorized that Seneca the Philosopher was the father and Seneca the Tragedian the son. Seneca's dramas had an enormous impact on the early development of European and British drama.[30] Greek tragedy remained almost unknown to much of the general public in the sixteenth century, whereas Senecan drama became an essential element in the school curriculum and shaped the plays composed for the new forms of theater that took over from the old medieval mystery plays. A performance of Seneca's *Phaedra* in Rome in

1485 can be seen as the starting point of early modern drama. Italian early modern drama was deeply influenced by Seneca and gave rise to a new form of tragedy all over Europe, spreading to Spain, France, and Britain in somewhat different ways. In purely formal terms, much in early modern drama was modeled on Senecan tragedy, including the five-act structure. Early works like *Gorbodoc* even borrowed the classical chorus, although that was soon dropped. Moreover, sixteenth-century drama took from Seneca its obsession with revenge (as in Kyd's *Spanish Tragedy*, the *Revenger's Tragedy*, or later, *Hamlet*) as well as its ghosts, its violence, and its characters driven by overweening ambition to commit ever-more-splendid acts of aggression and dominance—like Marlowe's Tamburlaine or Faustus. In terms of language, too, the marvelous bombast and quick, aphoristic repartee of Senecan tragedy had an enormous impact on the way that characters on the early modern stage learned to talk. Dramatists of the period often read Seneca in the original Latin, but he was also newly available in English translation, in the collection edited by Thomas Newton, *Seneca His Tenne Tragedies*, of 1581. Seneca was so fashionable that Thomas Nashe satirized it in his preface to Robert Greene's *Menaphron* in 1589:

> English *Seneca* read by candle light yeeldes manie good sentences, as *Bloud is a begger*, and so foorth; and, if you intreate him faire in a frostie morning, he will affoord you whole Hamlets, I should say handfulls of tragicall speaches. But O griefe! *tempus edax rerum*, what's that will last alwaies? The sea exhaled by droppes will in continuance be drie, and *Seneca* let bloud line by line and page by page at length must needes die to our stage.

Seneca on stage was, Nashe suggested, getting old by the late sixteenth century—but it had a long way still to go. Senecan drama continued to have a major impact on Jacobean tragedy in the seventeenth century, in the works of Webster and others: the Duchess of Malfi's famous line, "I am Duchess of Malfi still!" is a clear recollection of Seneca's Medea: "*Medea nunc sum!*" ("Now I am Medea").

One might imagine that Senecan tragedy appealed to readers, writers, and audiences in the sixteenth and seventeenth centuries largely because Greek tragedy was relatively unknown; Shakespeare would perhaps have written rather differently if he had read Aeschylus, Sophocles, or Euripides. But this is to put it too negatively. It is striking that, of the Greek tragedies that were fairly widely read, the most popular were those that were the most Senecan: Euripides' *Hecuba,* which features both a revenge plot and a ghost, was one of the most widely translated into Latin, and therefore widely read, in the time of Shakespeare. Senecan drama was popular and influential because it spoke to a specific set of cultural preoccupations. People at this time had a particular interest in the self-assertion and rage that were articulated so well in Senecan tragedy. The "constancy" that was found by Lipsius in Seneca's prose work had its counterpart in the terrible insistence on individual identity, the desperate aspirations to world dominance and revenge, and the schizophrenic will to power, that could be found in Atreus, Medea, or Seneca's mad Hercules—the imperialist spirit gone crazy. Power, self-assertion, violent revenge, and the construction of a non-Christian universe in which the wheel of fortune was constantly tipping around—these themes dominated the drama of the period and were discovered through Seneca. It has been rightly recognized that the interest in Senecan drama was partly inspired by the fact that early modern Europe, like imperial Rome, was a society that institutionalized the spectacle of violence; both of these powerful, self-consciously novel cultures looked for ways to watch and enact visions of destruction.[31]

In France, Senecan influence led to a rather different and more formally controlled kind of drama, which adhered to the classical "rules" of time and space and which was, far more often than in Britain, based on classical plots. Pierre Corneille drew heavily on Seneca's prose works as well as his tragedies: his great play *Cinna,* for example (1641), is an extensive dramatization of an anecdote from the *De Clementia* about Augustus' mercifulness. Racine modeled his masterpiece, *Phèdre,* on Seneca's *Phaedra* as well as Euripides' *Hippolytus.* But Racine's relationship with Seneca was complex and somewhat adversarial. Even where Racine dramatizes the events of Seneca's own lifetime—as he did in the *Britannicus*—Seneca himself is excluded from the picture: he chose to focus on Burrus, not Seneca, as the moral center of the play because, he reminds us, it was Burrus who was known for "the severity of his morals"; Seneca's virtues were the more superficial ones of "elegance and affability."[32]

Seneca had an important but mostly buried influence on the political and cultural life of the eighteenth and nineteenth centuries. As a primary representative of what was now known as "Silver Latin," he began to be treated increasingly with suspicion, or not read at all. His highly artificial,

bombastic dramas seemed too distant from the more naturalistic contemporary literary forms in drama and the novel. Whereas in the early
modern period readers had assumed that Senecan tragedy was performed
(and had performed it), scholars in the nineteenth century insisted that
these dramas were composed only for recitation, not the theater—and
used that idea as further evidence to condemn the author for mere arti-
fice. Moreover, his prose writings began to be dismissed as the postur-
ings of a hypocrite who failed entirely to practice what he preached.
The shift away from Seneca was tied up with the assumption of new
requirements of "truth," both for literature and for life, and perhaps also
with a diminished faith in the possibilities of intellectual advisors changing the world for the better. Even when Seneca did play a part in culture, it was often a bit part: in the novel *Quo Vadis*, he is only a minor
character.

T. S. Eliot's influential essays "Seneca in Elizabethan Translation" and
"Shakespeare and the Stoicism of Seneca" (both 1927) helped perpetuate a deeply hostile attitude toward, specifically, Seneca's tragedies while
claiming to buck the trend. Eliot notes the "censure" heaped on these
works and comments that it is well deserved. These plays are, he argues,
bombastic and "rhetorical" in all the wrong ways: "his characters all seem
to speak with the same voice, and at the top of it."[33] His central claim in
both essays is that Seneca was rather less influential on Elizabethan drama
in general, and Shakespeare in particular, than had been believed. For
Eliot, being un-Senecan was to the credit of the Elizabethans.

But by the later part of the twentieth century, a rather different picture of Seneca had begun to emerge. In Germany in particular, retellings
of Seneca's doomed relationship with Nero and forced death became a
particularly popular way of trying to think through the legacy of Nazism
and collaboration.[34] Seneca was still sometimes seen as a mere brown-
noser to Nero—as he is in the enjoyable 1956 Italian movie, "Nero's Big
Weekend," which goes back again to the story of Poppaea. But he began
to be taken rather more seriously. In Britain, Ted Hughes created a
stripped-down version of his *Oedipus* in 1968, which emphasized the
horror and bleakness of the original.[35] Seneca gradually began to seem
relevant again, not (as in the early modern period) as an advocate of
mercy or champion of autocracy but as a writer whose concerns with
empire and its discontents prefigured the experiences of globalization
and totalitarianism.

Moreover, Seneca's pragmatic model of ethics became increasingly interesting to intellectuals and philosophers, and even psychotherapists. Foucault, in *The Care of the Self* (1984—the third and final volume of his *History of Sexuality,* Foucault 1985), was particularly interested in Seneca's account of daily self-examination and his model of selfhood as something to be practiced and brought into being by action—an "interlocutory" and "social" kind of self, which he thought was a superior alternative to the dualist self of Descartes and his heirs. Some critics, like Pierre Hadot, argued (quite plausibly) that Foucault distorted Seneca's concept of selfhood by overidentifying with it; Hadot developed his own interesting account of Seneca's importance as a philosopher of the "interior."[36] But for our purposes, the important thing is not whether Foucault was wrong about Seneca, but the fact that he found Seneca so useful for reimagining his own notions of individual identity. Foucault's focus on the "care of the self" built on Seneca (and Epictetus) to recognize that the gaps between psychotherapy, political activism, identity politics, and ethical philosophy might be less wide than had once been believed.[37] Seneca's discussion of anger, and of the emotions in general, bears comparison with modern analysis of emotional disturbance and mental health, having particular affinities with the cognitive therapy movement in psychology.

There has been a rise of interest in Stoicism in American culture in recent years, as well as in British and European cultures. For those seeking ancient self-help guidance, Epictetus and Marcus Aurelius tend to be the favored models.[38] The possibility of guilt and pollution looms larger in Seneca and might provide rather less comforting reading. It is the Stoicism of Marcus Aurelius, not Seneca, that provides the moral center of Ridley Scott's movie *Gladiator* (2000), and it is Epictetus, not Seneca, who inspires the supposedly admirable workingman character, Conrad Hensley, in Tom Wolfe's long-winded novel *A Man in Full* (1995). In this book, Stoicism of a specifically Epictetan kind can act as a useful way of getting through the dark times of late capitalism—dishonor, the loss of vast wealth, and the onset of an economic recession. Seneca's own vast wealth and largely privileged life make him less useful as a model for these purposes, and his love of dialogue and paradox undercuts his value as self-help, as do his constant harping on death and suicide and, most importantly, his insistence that he may not be the perfect wise man but may be only beginning, every day, to advance toward the goal.

But this complexity is precisely why we ought to pay close attention to Seneca, in times that resemble his own in many ways. Some of these connections are suggested in Suzanne Collins' bestselling trilogy, *The Hunger Games*, whose popularity speaks to the relevance of Seneca's age to ours. *The Hunger Games* is set in a dystopia that combines the United States (in an exaggerated but highly recognizable future era) with imperial Rome. Collins emphasizes the massive inequalities of wealth, status, and power and the use of violent death in the "arena" as a spectacle to entertain and subdue the populace (by providing them with "bread and circuses"—*panem et circenses,* Juvenal 10.81). The books meditate on Senecan themes, including the emptiness of life in the service of elite pleasure, and the central Senecan question of how to maintain integrity when trapped in horrible circumstances. One of the characters (Peeta) says before entering the arena, "I want to die as myself"—a deeply Senecan desire. The books trace a familiar set of impossible choices, between retirement, rebellion, or assassination and collaboration with an oppressive and murderous regime. The man who devises the Games in which the heroine first participates is named, not coincidentally, Seneca Crane. He plays a fairly small part in the books, but his role is much expanded in the film adaptation of the first novel in the trilogy (*The Hunger Games,* 2012), where his intimate but dangerous relationship with the evil President Snow is closely modeled on Seneca's relationship with Nero. Seneca Crane is an ambassador and spokesman for the government, whose success depends on his ability to create elaborate scenarios in which teenagers can slaughter each other for entertainment. However, he has what the president calls "an unfortunate sentimental streak," which tempts him to allow the two protagonists to survive the Games. Like his historical predecessor, he is troubled by his position as Head Gamemaker for the regime; like his predecessor again, he is forced to kill himself. In the second novel, our heroine, Katniss Everdeen, marks her resistance to the regime, and her awareness of its point of vulnerability, by writing "Seneca Crane" on a dummy she hangs from a noose.

The consumerism, the massive social inequalities, and the vast global reach and global trade of modern Western countries has obvious similarities with imperial Rome. Elite people in our societies—and even less elite ones—struggle, as did Seneca, with the psychological pressures created by an excess of material wealth, combined with a deficit in individuals' sense of autonomy and involvement in the political process. Pride is not seen as a problematic category for contemporary U.S. or British society, as it once was for Christian Europe, but Seneca's dark, tentative, and morbid version of Stoic self-assertion provides a useful corrective to the mindless optimism that can be passed off as self-confidence.[39] Senecan Stoicism can be appropriated by monotheistic religions, but it can also be appropriated by secular cultures: Larry Becker's "New Stoicism" attempts to strip the school of its reliance on providence and reinvent it for people with a "scientific" outlook, coping with adversity in the modern world.[40]

Seneca has been dubbed the "conscience of the Empire,"[41] although it would be more accurate to see him as its unconscious—but an unconscious with a public voice and a beautiful literary style. His wide-ranging and contradictory body of work articulates the psychological contradictions and pressures of consumerism, globalization, and empire—all themes of enormous importance for the modern Western and non-Western worlds. The theme that one can find peace only within oneself—and quite likely not even there—is an idea that is particularly attractive in a fragmented and frightened society. Seneca's difficult negotiations between interior and exterior, and between center and periphery, have a strikingly modern feel. We may well wonder whether the notion that only the truly virtuous person can be happy is either true or helpful, politically or ethically. But even Stoic-skeptics can acknowledge the continuing fascination of Seneca's contradictory psychology, lurid life story, and complex, paradoxical, rich literary work.

NOTES

Introduction

1. The best and most thorough account of Seneca's death (and its later reception) is Ker 2009 (*The Deaths of Seneca*).

2. On which, see my *Death of Socrates*, 2007.

3. I allude here to the title of the most informative modern scholarly account of Seneca's political life: Miriam Griffin's *Seneca: A Philosopher in Politics* (Griffin 1976).

4. Rubens himself was deeply influenced by Seneca, through the Neo-Stoicism of his friend Lipsius: on this see Morford 1991.

5. Seneca's exile will be discussed in more detail in Chapter II.

6. The most sustained attempt to do this is Griffin 1976—who provides a nuanced and detailed account, which fully acknowledges the problems inherent in the quest. On the difficulties and desirability of looking at all Seneca's extant work together, see especially Volk and Williams 2006.

7. See Bartsch and Wray 2009.

8. On the term see Rudich 1993 and 1997. See also Bartsch 1994.

9. The best account of Cicero's life story is Rawson 1975.

10. See especially Tacitus, *Dialogus.*

11. Much of our information about early Stoicism comes from the (unreliable and anecdotal) account in Diogenes Laertius' *Lives of the Philosophers.*

12. See Asmis 1996.

13. See especially Lucian's *Hermotimus, or the Choice of the Schools*, which is a (presumably imaginary) dialogue between a stand-in for the writer himself and a foolish friend who has been taken in by the Stoics. Lucian's alter ego insists, over and over, that the Stoics are misleading in their claims to teach wisdom, and suggests to his friend that life is too short to waste on their shenanigans.

14. See Long and Sedley 1987.

Chapter I

1. Cf. Horace, *Serm.* 1.4.

2. See Edwards and Woolf 2003, on Roman notions of the capital city and its peripheries.

3. Valerius Maximus 4.4.4; Livy 3.26–29.

4. See Keay 1988; Curchin 1995.

5. Knapp 1983.

6. There has been quite a lot of debate among historians about what exactly the status of the new city was, in terms of Roman law: Knapp 1983; Griffin 1976.

7. Knapp 1983.

8. Griffin 1976.

9. The *iugerum* was about two thirds of an acre, and "sacks" are *cullei*—the total is over four thousand liters.

10. See Griffin 1976, 287, and Griffin 1972 on Seneca's devotion to vineyards and olive groves.

11. An epigram from the *Anthologia Latina*, 409, whose authenticity has been doubted: see Knapp 1992, 103, for arguments for and against. Knapp sees it as authentic.

12. For more on educated Roman women, see Hemelrijk 1999; Levick 2002.

13. On performance aspects of declamation see Gleason 1995.

14. See Winterbottom 1974, introduction.

15. See Vassileiou 1973, as well as Sussman 1978, and especially the discussion of Fairweather 1981.

16. On exemplarity, see Roller 2004; on Valerius Maximus, Bloomer 1992.

17. As argued by Sussman 1978, 27–28.

18. See Sussman 1978, 28. Cf. Epistle 108 (on which, see below) and *To Helvia* 17.3–4.

19. Scheidel, W., and Meeks, E. (May 2, 2012). ORBIS: The Stanford Geospatial Network Model of the Roman World. Retrieved Dec. 31, 2012, from http://orbis.stanford.edu.

20. Morley 1996, 33–39.

21. Succinctly discussed in Volk and Williams 2006; see Morford 2002 for more detailed cultural and philosophical analysis.

22. On the Sextians: Manning 1987 makes the most careful distinction between the Sextians and other sects (such as Pythagoreans and Stoics). See also Lana 1959, Griffin 1976.

23. Tacitus, *Annals* Book 2. 85.

24. On this passage, and its resonances with the similar scene in Seneca's *HF*, see Wilson 2004.

25. *General Introduction to Psychoanalysis*, Chapter 25: "Fear and Anxiety."

Chapter II

1. *On the Good Life* 20: "I will know that the whole world is my country, and that the gods, my guardians, stand above me and around me as judges of my words and actions" (*Patriam meam esse mundum sciam et praesides deos, hos supra me circaque me stare factorum dictorumque censores*).

2. There is a strong revisionist account of Caligula in Winterling 2011. Winterling argues that many of Caligula's supposedly insane actions were actually very sane and calculated political moves designed to consolidate imperial power against the threat of the hostile Senate and aristocracy.

3. See *On Constancy* 18, where he describes how Caligula's brutal behavior toward his subordinates aroused a corresponding rage in them and led to his assassination; *On Anger* 1.20, evoking Caligula's insane belief that he was more powerful than the gods; *On Anger* 3.18.1, describing Caligula going for a nighttime stroll with some senators and their wives, and suddenly chopping off their heads; *On the Shortness of Life* xviii.5; *To Polybius* 17, on Caligula's lack of grief for his dead sister; *To Helvia*, on his extravagance and crazily expensive dinner parties; *On Benefits* 2.12. on his outrageous treatment of a senator; *On Benefits*. 7.10 on his attempts at bribery; Epistle 94.64 on his (evil) motives for warfare.

4. Bartsch 1994.

5. Julius Canus also appears in Plutarch, fragment 211.

6. See Rudich 1993.

7. Griffin 1976.

8. Rudich 1997, 27–35.

9. See Bougery 1936.

10. They are gathered, with extensive commentary in Italian, by Vottero 1998.

11. The Epicurean view is actually somewhat complex, and evidence for it hinges on a disputed passage of Diogenes Laertius' *Life of Epicurus*, DL X.119, which seems to say that a wise man ought to marry and have a child—but has sometimes been amended to say that the wise man ought NOT to marry and have a child. For scholarly discussion of the text of this passage, see Chilton 1960.

12. Tacitus, *Annals*, 12.60; Suetonius Claudius 29.

13. This is suggested by Josiah Osgood's recent study of the reign of Claudius, Osgood 2011.

14. See discussion in Osgood 2011. Crispus Passienus died in 55 and was mourned by Seneca in a spurious epigram; he is also referred to in *NQ* 4. pref. as "a dear friend."

15. Josephus 19.4.

16. *To Polybius* 13; Griffin 1976, 5–6.

17. See Fantham 2007, 175–176.

18. Griffin 1976.

19. See especially Wallace-Hadrill 1996.

20. See Stini 2001. More bibliography on exile can be found in Kelly 2006 and Gaertner 2007.

21. Orbis.

22. As Griffin 1976 notes (p. 288), the legal penalty "under the Lex Julia for adultery was certainly relegation, and the Scholiast on Juvenal 5. 109 attests that Seneca was relegatus on this charge."

23. The law against adultery, the Lex Iulia, ruled that a convicted adulterer should be stripped of half his assets. Cf. Seneca's allusion to his loss of property in *To Helvia* 10.2.

24. See Fantham 2007.

25. *On Providence* and Epistle 24.

26. *P. L. M.* vol. iv. 3.

27. *P. L. M.* vol. iv. 2.

28. Gregorvius 1855: vol. 1. 217.

29. *To Helvia* 6.5, 9.1. Cf. Theophrastus 5.8.2; Pliny, *NH*, 16, 71; Diodorus 5.13.1.

30. Gahan 1985.

31. Claudius, Suetonius, 28.

32. 60.10.

33. It was certainly written after the death of Caligula (to whom it is very hostile—something that would hardly have been safe if he had still been alive), and before the adoption of Seneca's brother Novatus by Junius Gallio (which also cannot be dated securely: it was sometime between 41 and 52 CE).

34. See Griffin 1976, Appendix note C, p. 398, who rightly criticizes the view that all of *On Anger* was written before the exile in 41; as she argues, the tropes discussed in *On Anger*, including the disparagement of court life, are paralleled in other Senecan texts of the post-exile period (such as *On Benefits*).

35. The word "passions" is generally used to translate the Stoic terms *affectus* (Latin) and *pathos* (Greek). But the terminology is potentially misleading, since "passion" tends to suggest a particularly intense form of emotion. The problem, for the Stoics, is not emotional intensity: indeed, the ideal Stoic wise person will experience intense joy, according to the theory. The problem with *affectus* is rather that these are emotions based on a false perception of reality, which will inevitably cause disruption of our tranquility, and hence will make us miserable.

36. Graver 2007.

37. Compare Bourdieu 2008. The issue in Rome in this period is well articulated by Osgood 2011.

38. *On Anger* 1.20.4–5, also cited in *De Clementia*.

39. Inwood 2008.

40. A distinction discussed in detail at 2.2.1ff.

41. *Hercules Oetaeus* is probably not by Seneca, and *Octavia* obviously is not.

42. *Hercules Furens* 612: *morte contempta redi.* The words are spoken by Hercules, who has returned home from the labor of bringing Cerberus from the underworld and rescuing his friend Theseus. He does not know what horrors await him on his return: he is afflicted by madness sent by Juno and kills his wife and children, thinking they are the family of his enemy, the tyrant king Lycus.

43. At Ostia, assisting at a sacrifice (Tacitus, *Annals,* 2.37) or inspecting a grain supply (Dio 60.48).

44. The scholiast to Juvenal 5.109.

Chapter III

1. *Phoenissae* 618–619.

2. . . . *hoc sedent alti toro*
quibus superba sceptra gestantur manu,
locus hic habendae curiae—hic epulis locus.
Libet reuerti. nonne uel tristes lacus
incolere satius?

3. Scholiast on Juvenal 5.109.

4. For an excellent account of the passage see Ker 2009.

5. Rumor questioned by Grimm 1991.

6. See Leach 1989.

7. Cf. *Annals* 13.11; Suetonius also praises Nero's intention to rule in the manner of Augustus and notes his early measures designed to appeal to people and Senate alike (*Nero* 10).

8. The text's form and content—mixing prose and verse, and mixing serious with comic and fantastical elements—puts it in the category of Menippean satire, on which see especially Relihan 1993.

9. The best analysis is Leach 1989. See also the edition with introduction, Eden 1984.

10. Tacitus 13.2.

11. Griffin 2000.

12. On the tradition, see Murray 2007, who points out how limited and disappointing our evidence for Hellenistic kingship treatises really is.

13. See Barnes 1974 on the relationship of the consulship to *nobilitas*.

14. See Lindsay 2009.

15. *Ex Ponto* 4.2. For discussion of Novatus' adoption see Lindsay 2009, p. 156.

16. Pliny, *NH,* 31.62.

17. Pliny, *NH,* 31.62.

18. *Annals* 13.4.

19. On Pallas see Oost 1958.

20. Seneca tells Nero that he is now "just turned eighteen" (1.9.1), and since Nero's eighteenth birthday was December 15, 55, the obvious conclusion is that *De Clementia* was composed soon after that (in late December 55, or January 56)—hence, some ten months after the killing of Britannicus.

21. Braund 2011.

22. Leach 1989.

23. All well argued by Leach 1989.

24. *Venenum in auro bibitur. Thyestes* 453. The line is spoken by Thyestes as he is trying to resist his brother's lavish hospitality. He soon changes his mind, accepts the invitation, and is taken inside, where he is tricked into eating his own children.

25. On Seneca's wealth, see Griffin 1976, Chapter 9: "Seneca praedives." Also Levick 2003, and Fuhrer 2000.

26. Macmullen 1974.

27. Scheidel and Friesen 2009.

28. For more examples of Roman individuals with vast fortunes, see Duncan-Jones 1994, pp. 343–344.

29. Rutledge 2001.

30. Rutledge 2001, pp. 270–271.

31. 59 CE; it must be later than 58, because it calls the brother Gallio—a name he received only after his adoption, which had certainly taken place by 59.

32. Cf. the biting critique of Stoic attitudes toward poverty and social justice in Nussbaum 2004.

33. For extensive discussion of this text, see Griffin 2013. Griffin rightly emphasizes that *On Benefits* shows relatively little interest in patronage or in social justice; rather, it deals with a "Roman aristocratic code of beneficence" and "insists on the inclusion of the Princeps within aristocratic society" (168).

34. The *fasces*, literally a bundle of sticks carried by officials on ceremonial occasions, are a symbol of magisterial power.

35. *On Benefits* 3.7.3: If we make gratitude compulsory, "we spoilt two things which are more beautiful than anything else in human life: a man who is grateful, and a man who is kind in giving favors."

36. On this text, see the excellent study by Griffin 2013.

37. Scholars once thought his main source was Hecaton of Rhodes' lost work on the subject, but Inwood 2008 has rightly questioned the assumptions behind this view.

38. This is emphasized by Griffin 2013.

39. Fear 2007.

40. *Troades* 1125: "A valley slope with a gentle rise encloses the intervening space and sprouts up like a theater." This is the location in which the crowd gathers to watch the sacrificial murder of the young girl Polyxena on the tomb of Achilles.

41. Dio 62.10.3.; Tacitus notes only Burrus' encouragement, not Seneca's, at 14.15.

42. See Edwards 1993, Chapter Three: "Playing Romans."

43. Epictetus 4.1.45–50; the passage is discussed by Long 2004.

Chapter IV

1. *On Leisure*, 1.4: *Dices mihi: "Quid agis, Seneca? Deseris partes?"* The term used for "party" can also connote a part in a play: Seneca imagines retirement as a change of theatrical role, but with implications of desertion of a political duty or military post.

2. Date disputed; it could have been composed almost any time before the addressee, Serenus, died, which was 64, but likely Neronian but pre-retirement; see Griffin 1976.

3. This is Griffin's argument (Griffin 1962, and Griffin 1976, 319–320).

4. Petronius, 28. This is the notice on the door of Trimalchio's house.

5. The original title for F. Scott Fitzgerald's *The Great Gatsby* was "Trimalchio in West Egg."

6. See especially Williams 2012.

7. On this passage see Bartsch 2006.

8. Ker 2011, p. 33.

9. This is the same passage in which Seneca launches into a self-justificatory account of his own biography, in which he insists on his loyalty to his friends as the reason why he suffered exile (on which, see Chapter II).

10. See below: the Golden House was built after the Great Fire at Rome.

11. See Bradley 2008, who rightly objects to the idealizing readings of Sørensen 1984 and others.

12. Nussbaum 2004 gives a brilliant account of the ways in which this logically inconsistent and morally repugnant view still lurks behind many modern discussions of international aid to people in poorer nations.

13. Wimbush 1998 gives useful background on the various different ancient movements toward rejection of materialism. In the United States, there is a growing movement toward "voluntary simplicity": practitioners call themselves VS-ers, minimalists, or participants in simple living. There are several complementary movements toward buying, producing, or amassing unnecessary material goods. Some focus less on the simple lifestyle than on modes of acquisition other than purchase ("freeganism," "up-cycling," "dumpster diving").

14. Closs 2013.

15. The killing of Christians by Nero in the wake of the Great Fire is attested to only by Tacitus and is impossible to verify. The numbers were presumably fairly small compared to the many other types of undesirables who were thrown to the lions in the same period.

16. Dyson 1970.

17. This is the account of Suetonius, *Nero*, 47–49; for assessment of the various sources, see Champlin 2003.

Epilogue

1. The dating of the play is the subject of much scholarly dispute. Some argue that it was composed very soon after Seneca's death, perhaps in 68, under the emperor Galba; others favor a much later dating. See discussion in Ferri 2003, 5–30.

2. On Quintilian's response to Seneca, see Taoka 2011, who argues that Quintilian is actually imitating Seneca (Epistle 114) while supposedly attacking him.

3. See also Abbott 1978, who argues—not very convincingly—that Seneca may well have met Paul in Rome.

4. See Engberg-Pedersen, 2004 and 2000.

5. There is a vigorous account of Augustine's rejection of Stoicism in Chapter 14 of *City of God*, in Brooke 2012, 1–11.

6. On this material, Colish 1985.

7. Ebbensen 2004, 108.

8. Through Origen, by a monk named Evagrius in the fourth century.

9. The story is well told by Sorabji 2004.

10. The passage is discussed by Cunnally 1986, 316.

11. The most important were by Erasmus, the French humanist Marc-Antoine Muret, and Justus Lipsius. On Muret, see Kraye 2005.

12. This is well articulated by Monsarrat 1984, 6.

13. Edwards 1997.

14. "Self-fashioning" is a term popularized by Stephen Greenblatt's 1980 study, *Renaissance Self-fashioning*, which focused on Thomas More, among others; its relevance for Seneca, and the link between More and Seneca, is made by Edwards 1997. For more on Seneca's relevance for modern understanding of selfhood, see Long 2006.

15. Braden 1985.

16. Stacey 2007 analyzes Machiavelli's response to Seneca; built on by Brooke 2012.

17. See Brooke 2012, 67–69.

18. Montaigne, *Essays* i. 12: "On constancy" ("*De la constance*") (Montaigne 1993).

19. Quint 1998 shows how Montaigne's ideal of opposition to cruelty emerged from his study of Seneca.

20. On Lipsius, see Lagrée 2004 and Brooke 2012, 12–36, who emphasizes the ways that the Lipsian prince is an alternative, and more Senecan, figure than the Machiavellian autocrat.

21. *Oeuvres Morales Mêlées*, 12, cited in Lagrée 2004, 160.

22. Cited in Lagrée 2004, 165.

23. Quoted in Oestreich 2008, 70.

24. *The Passions of the Soul*, cited in Rutherford 2004, 191.

25. From *On Anger* 2.13. The Rousseau passage is discussed in Brooke 2012, 189.

26. Cited in Brooke 2012, 125.

27. Cassirer 1961, 166–170, cited in Brooke 2012, 1.

28. Discussed in Brooke 2012, 148.

29. *Natural History of Religion*, 174, quoted in Brooke 2012, 180.

30. On this much-studied topic a good starting point is Boyle 1997.

31. The affinity between early modern and Roman forms of violence is noted in Boyle 1997, 409.

32. Racine, vol. 1, 390, citing Tacitus. The relationship of Racine to Seneca is well discussed by Levitan 1989.

33. Eliot 1932 p. 54.

34. Ziolowski 2004.

35. Hughes 1983.

36. Hadot 1995.

37. Foucault 1985. See Long 2006 on the particular contemporary resonances of Seneca's presentation of the self.

38. James Bond Stockdale, a U.S. Navy officer who spent seven years in captivity (mostly in solitary confinement) in Vietnam, has written and spoken extensively about the use he made of Epictetus (with a dash of Marcus Aurelius) during those years and as a guide for his men. Despite his commitment to ancient Stoicism, Stockdale shows no interest in Seneca, and the reason is that Seneca is much less useful as a guide to Stockdale's macho military "will" and "self-respect," even in times of extraordinary suffering and apparent failure. Stockdale's model of Stoicism involves a belief that "your good and your evil are of your own making" (1995, 240) and an insistence on the total rightness of one's own actions at all times. He is dismissive of those who wonder whether he ever feels that he has "blood on his hands"; pity, guilt, and fear are, in his view, a distraction to be dismissed.

39. Compare Ehrenrich 2010 on the dangers of modern U.S. optimism.

40. Becker 1999.

41. Grimal 1978.

FURTHER READING

This is a good time to read Seneca in English. There are a number of excellent recent translations, including a series published by Chicago University Press that will eventually include his complete works. Oxford World's Classics has published a fine selection and translation of the *Letters*, by Elaine Fantham (*Selected Letters*, 2010), a collection of the *Dialogues and Essays*, translated by Tobias Reinhardt (2009), and a selection of the tragedies, translated by me (*Six Tragedies of Seneca*, 2010). For those interested in Seneca's prose works, the Cambridge translation and commentary *Moral and Political Essays* (J. F. Procopé, John M. Cooper, 1995) includes the essays *On Anger, On Mercy, On the Private Life,* and the first half of *On Benefits* and has excellent notes.

The most accessible and exciting ancient source on imperial Rome is Tacitus' *Annals*, of which there is a good recent Oxford World's Classics translation (J. C. Yardley, 2008). Suetonius' gossipy *Life of Nero* is also very much worth reading (in *Lives of the Caesars*, translated by Catherine Edwards, Oxford World's Classics 2009).

The best modern scholarly study of Seneca in English is Miriam Griffin's *Seneca: A Philosopher in Politics* (1976), which may be rather dense for nonspecialists but has a host of useful information.

Edward Champlin's *Nero* is a fine and lively study of the emperor and his time; Miriam Griffin's *Nero* is also useful.

For those wanting to know about a very different Stoic philosopher, A. A. Long's *Epictetus: A Stoic and Socratic Guide to Life* (2004) is highly recommended.

BIBLIOGRAPHY

Abbott, Kenneth M., 1978. "Seneca and St. Paul." In *Wege der Worte: Festschrift für Wolfgang Fleischhauer*, ed. D. C. Riechel, pp. 119–131. Köln: Böhlau.

Asmis, Elizabeth, 1996. "The Stoics on Women." In *Feminism and Ancient Philosophy*, ed. Julie K. Ward, pp. 68–92. New York, NY: Routledge.

Barnes, T. D., 1974. "Who Were the Nobility of the Roman Empire?" *Phoenix* 28.4, 444–449.

Bartsch, Shadi, 1994. *Actors in the Audience.* Cambridge, MA: Harvard University Press.

Bartsch, Shadi, 2006. *The Mirror of the Self: Sexuality, Self-Knowledge and the Gaze in the Early Roman Empire.* Chicago, IL: Chicago UP.

Bartsch, Shadi, ed., with David Wray, 2009. *Seneca and the Self.* Cambridge, UK: Cambridge University Press.

Becker, Larry, 1999. *A New Stoicism.* Princeton, NJ: Princeton University Press.

Bloomer, W. Martin, 1992. *Valerius Maximus and the Rhetoric of the New Nobility.* Chapel Hill, NC: University of North Carolina Press.

Bougery, A., 1936. "Le mariage de Sénèque." *Revue des études latines* 14, 90–94.

Bourdieu, Pierre, 2008, translated by Richard Nice. The Bachelors' Ball: The Crisis of Peasant Society in *Béarn.* Chicago, IL: Chicago University Press.

Boyle, A. J., 1997. *Tragic Seneca: An Essay in the Theatrical Tradition.* New York, NY: Routledge.

Braden, Gordon, 1985. *Anger's Privilege: Renaissance Tragedy and the Senecan Tradition.* New Haven, CT: Yale University Press.

Bradley, K. R., 2008. "Seneca and Slavery." In *Seneca*, ed. J. G. Fitch, pp. 335–347. Oxford: Oxford University Press.

Braund, Susanna Morton, ed. 2011. *Seneca: De Clementia.* Oxford: Oxford University Press.

Brooke, Christopher, 2012. *Philosophic Pride: Stoicism and Political Thought from Lipsius to Rousseau.* Princeton, NJ: Princeton University Press.

Champlin, Edward, 2003. *Nero.* Cambridge, MA: The Belknap Press of Harvard University Press.

Chilton, C. W., 1960. "Did Epicurus Approve of Marriage?" *Phronesis* 5.1, 71–74.

Closs, Virginia, 2013. "While Rome burned: Fire, leadership, and urban disaster in the Roman cultural imagination." Dissertation submitted at the University of Pennsylvania: http://repository.upenn.edu/dissertations/AAI3594781.

Colish, Marcia, 1985. *The Stoic Tradition from Antiquity to the Early Middle Ages.* Leiden, Netherlands: E. J. Brill.

Cunnally, J., 1986. "Nero, Seneca, and the Medallist of the Roman Emperors." *The Art Bulletin* LXVIII, 314–317.

Curchin, Leonard A., 1995. *Roman Spain: Conquest and Assimilation*. London, UK:
    Routledge.
Duncan-Jones, Richard, 1994. *Money and Government in the Roman Empire*. Cambridge, UK:
    Cambridge University Press.
Dyson, S. L., 1970. "The Portrait of Seneca in Tacitus." *Arethusa* 3, 71–83.
Ebbensen, Sten, 2004. "Where Were the Stoics in the Late Middle Ages?" In Steven J.
    Strange and Jack Zupko, editors, *Stoicism: Traditions and Transformations*, pp. 108–131.
    Cambridge, UK: Cambridge University Press.
Eden, P. T., ed., 1984. *Apocolycyntosis*. Cambridge, UK: Cambridge University Press.
Edwards, Catherine, 1993. *The Politics of Immorality in Ancient Rome*. Cambridge, UK:
    Cambridge University Press.
Edwards, Catherine, 1997. "Self-Scrutiny and Self-Transformation in Seneca's Letters."
    Greece and Rome 44, 23–38.
Edwards, Catherine, and Gregory Woolf, editors, 2003. *Rome the Cosmopolis.* Cambridge,
    UK: Cambridge University Press.
Ehrenrich, Barbara, 2010. *Bright-Sided: How Positive Thinking Is Undermining America*.
    London, UK: Picador.
Eliot, T. S., 1932. "Seneca in Elizabethan Translation." In T. S. Eliot, *Selected Essays
    1917–1932*, pp. 51–88 (first pub. 1927). New York, NY: Harcourt, Brace.
Engberg-Pedersen, Troels, 2000. *Paul and the Stoics.* Edinburgh: T&T Clark.
Engberg-Pedersen, Troels, 2004. "Stoicism in the Apostle Paul." In Steven J. Strange and
    Jack Zupko, editors, *Stoicism: Traditions and Transformations*, pp. 52–75. Cambridge, UK:
    Cambridge University Press.
Fairweather, Janet, 1981. *Seneca the Elder*. Cambridge, UK: Cambridge University Press.
Fantham, Elaine, 2007. "Dialogues of Displacement." In *Writing Exile: The Discourse of
    Displacement in Greco-Roman Antiquity and Beyond*, ed. J. F. Gaertner, pp. 173–192. Leiden,
    Netherlands: Brill.
Fear, Trevor, 2007. "Of Aristocrats and Courtesans: Seneca, 'De Beneficiis' 1.14." *Hermes*
    135, 460–468.
Ferri, Ronaldo, 2003. *Octavia*. Cambridge, UK: Cambridge University Press (Classical
    Commentaries).
Foucault, Michel, 1985. *The Care of the Self* (History of Sexuality, Volume 3). New York, NY:
    Vintage Books.
Fuhrer, Thérèse, 2000. "The Philosopher as Multi-Millionaire: Seneca on Double
    Standards." In Karla Pollmann, *Double Standards in the Ancient and Medieval Worlds*, pp.
    201–219. Göttingen: Duehrkohp & Radicke.
Gahan, John J., 1985. "Seneca, Ovid and Exile." *Classical World* 78, 145–147.
Geartner, J. F., 2007. *Writing Exile: The Discourse of Displacement in Greco-Roman Antiquity
    and Beyond*. Leiden, Netherlands: Brill.
Gleason, Maud, 1995. *Making Men: Sophists and Self-Presentation in Ancient Rome*. Princeton,
    NJ: Princeton University Press.
Graver, Margaret, 2007. *Stoicism and Emotion*. Chicago, IL: Chicago University Press.
Greenblatt, Stephen, 1980. *Renaissance Self-Fashioning: From More to Shakespeare.* Chicago,
    IL: Chicago University Press.
Gregorvius, Ferdinand, 1855. *Wanderings in Corsica*. London, UK: Cortland.
Griffin, Miriam, 1972. "The Elder Seneca and Spain." *Journal of Roman Studies*, 62: 1-19.
Griffin, Miriam, 1976. *Seneca: A Philosopher in Politics*. Oxford, UK: Clarendon Press.
Griffin, Miriam, 2000. *Nero: The End of a Dynasty*. London, UK: Routledge.
Griffin, Miriam, 2013. *Seneca on Society: A guide to De Beneficiis*. Oxford, UK: Oxford
    University Press.

Grimal, P., 1978. *Sénèque, ou la Conscience de l'Empire*. Paris, France: Fayard.

Grimm, Veronika, 1991. "On the Mushroom that Deified the Emperor Claudius." *Classical Quarterly* 41.1, 178–182.

Haase, F., 1852. *Seneca: Works*. 3 volumes. Leipzig, Germany: Teubner.

Hadot, P., 1995. *Philosophy as a Way of Life*, trans. Michael Chase. Oxford, UK: Oxford University Press.

Hemelrijk, Emily A., 1999. *Matrona Docta: Educated Women in the Roman Elite from Cornelia to Julia Domna*. New York, NY: Routledge.

Hughes, Ted, 1983. *Seneca's Oedipus*. London, UK: Faber.

Inwood, Brad, 2008. *Reading Seneca: Stoic Philosophy at Rome*. Oxford, UK: Oxford University Press.

Keay, S. J., 1988. *Roman Spain*. Oakland, CA: University of California Press.

Kelly, Gordon P., 2006. *A History of Exile in the Roman Republic*. Cambridge, UK: University Press.

Ker, James, 2009. *The Deaths of Seneca*. New York, NY: Oxford University Press.

Ker, James, 2009. "Seneca and Self-Examination." In *Seneca and the Self*, eds. Shadi Bartsch and David Wray, pp. 160–187. Cambridge, UK: Cambridge University Press.

Ker, James, 2011. *A Seneca Reader: Selections from Prose and Tragedy*. Mundelein, IL: Bolchazy-Carducci Publishers.

Knapp, Robert C., 1983. *Roman Córdoba*. Oakland, CA: University of California Press.

Knapp, Robert C., 1992. *Latin Inscriptions from Central Spain*. Oakland, CA: University of California Press.

Kraye, Jill, 2005. "The Humanist as Moral Philosopher: Marc-Antoine Muret's 1585 Edition of Seneca." In *Moral Philosophy on the Threshold of Modernity*, eds. Jill Kraye and Risto Saarinen, pp. 307–330. Dordrecht, Netherlands: Springer.

Lagrée, J., 2004. "Constancy and Coherence". In Steven J. Strange and Jack Zupko, editors, *Stoicism: Traditions and Transformations*, pp. 148–176. Cambridge, UK: Cambridge University Press.

Lana, I., 1959. "Sextiorum Nova et Romani Roboris Secta." *Rivista di Filologia e di Istruzione Classica* 31, 225–232.

Leach, Eleanor Winsor, 1989. "The Implied Reader and the Political Argument in Seneca's *Apocolocyntosis* and *De Clementia*." *Aretheusa* 22, 197–230.

Levick, B., 2002. "Women, Power, and Philosophy at Rome and Beyond." In *Philosophy and Power in the Graeco-Roman World*, eds. G. Clark and T. Rajak, pp. 134–155. Oxford, UK: Oxford University Press.

Levick, B., 2003. "Seneca and Money." In *Seneca, Uomo Politico*, eds. Arturo de Vivo and Elio lo Cascio, pp. 107–114. Bari, Italy: Edipuglia.

Levitan, William, 1989. "Seneca in Racine." *Yale French Studies*, 76, 185–210.

Lindsay, Hugh, 2009. *Adoption in the Roman World*. Cambridge, UK: Cambridge University Press.

Long, A. A., 1987, and David Sedley. *The Hellenistic Philosophers*. Cambridge, UK: Cambridge University Press.

Long, A. A., 2004. "The Socratic Imprint on Epictetus' Philosophy." In Steven J. Strange and Jack Zupko, editors, *Stoicism: Traditions and Transformations*, pp. 10–31. Cambridge, UK: Cambridge University Press.

Long, A. A., 2006. *From Epicurus to Epictetus*. Oxford, UK: Oxford University Press.

Long, A. A., 2009. "Seneca and the Self: Why Now?" In *Seneca and the Self*, edited by Shadi Bartsch and David Wray, pp. 20–36. Cambridge/New York, NY: Cambridge University Press.

Macmullen, Ramsay, 1974. *Roman Social Relations, 50 BC to AD 284*. New Haven, CT: Yale University Press.

Manning, C. P., 1987. "The Sextii." *Prudentia* 19, 16–27.

Monsarrat, Gilles D., 1984. *Light from the Porch: Stoicism and English Renaissance Literature.* Lyon, France: Didier Erudition.

Montaigne, Michel de., 1993. *Essays.* Translated by John M. Cohen. London, UK: Penguin.

Morford, Mark, 1991. *Stoics and Neo-Stoics: Rubens and the Circle of Lipsius.* Princeton, NJ: Princeton University Press.

Morford, Mark, 2002. *The Roman Philosophers: From the Time of Cato the Censor to the Death of Marcus Aurelius.* New York, NY: Routledge.

Morley, N. 1996. *Metropolis and Hinterland.* Cambridge, UK: Cambridge University Press.

Nussbaum, Martha. 2004. "Cicero's Problematic Legacy." In Steven J. Strange and Jack Zupko, editors, *Stoicism: Traditions and Transformations*, pp. 214–249. Cambridge, UK: Cambridge University Press.

Oestreich, Gerhard, 2008. *Neostoicism and the Early Modern State.* Cambridge, UK: Cambridge University Press.

Oost, S. V., 1958. "The Career of M. Antonius Pallas." *American Journal of Philology* 79 (2): 113–139.

Osgood, Josiah, 2011. *Claudius Caesar: Image and Power in the Early Roman Empire.* Cambridge, UK: Cambridge University Press.

Quint, David, 1998. *Montaigne and the Quality of Mercy.* Princeton, NJ: Princeton University Press.

Rawson, E., 1975. *Cicero: A Portrait.* Bristol, UK: Bristol Classical Press.

Relihan, Joel, 1993. *Ancient Menippean Satire.* Baltimore MD: Johns Hopkins University Press.

Roller, Matthew, 2004. "Exemplarity in Ancient Rome: The Cases of Horatius Cocles and Cloelia." *Classical Philology* 99, 1–56.

Rudich, V., 1993. *Political Dissidence Under Nero.* New York, NY: Routledge.

Rudich, V., 1997. *Dissidence and Literature Under Nero.* New York, NY: Routledge.

Rutherford, D., 2004. "On the Happy Life: Descartes vis-à-vis Seneca." In Steven J. Strange and Jack Zupko, editors, *Stoicism: Traditions and Transformations*, pp. 177–197. Cambridge, UK: Cambridge University Press.

Rutledge, Steven, 2001. *Imperial Inquisitions: Prosecutors and Informants from Tiberius to Domitian.* New York, NY: Routledge.

Scheidel, Walter, and Steven Friesen, 2009. "The Size of the Economy and the Distribution of Income in the Roman Empire." *Journal of Roman Studies* 99, 61–91.

Sorabji, Richard, 2004. "Stoic First Movements in Christianity." In Steven J. Strange and Jack Zupko, editors, *Stoicism: Traditions and Transformations*, pp. 95–107. Cambridge, UK: Cambridge University Press.

Sørensen, Villy, 1984. *Seneca: The Humanist at the Court of Nero.* Chicago, IL: Chicago University Press.

Stacey, Peter, 2007. *Roman Monarchy and the Renaissance Prince.* Cambridge, UK: Cambridge University Press.

Stini, F., 2001. *Plenum exiliis mare: Untersuchungen zum Exil in der Römischen Kaiserzeit.* Stuttgart, Germany: Franz Steiner.

Stockdale, James, 1995. *Thoughts of a Philosophical Figher Pilot.* Stanford, CA: Hoover Institution Press.

Sussman, Lewis A., 1978. *The Elder Seneca.* Leiden, Netherlands: Brill.

Taoka, Yasuko, 2011. "Re-Reading Institutio Oratoria 10.1.125-31." *Aretheusa*, Winter, 126–127.

Vassileiou, A., 1973. "A propos d'un passage de Sénèque le Père (Contr. 2. Pr. 4): La psychologie d'un père ambitieux pour ses enfants au 1er siècle ap. J.-C." *Latomus* 32, 162–165.

Volk, K., and G. D. Williams, 2006. *Seeing Seneca Whole: Perspectives on Philosophy, Poetry and Politics.* Leiden, Netherlands: Brill.

Vottero, Dionigi, 1998. *Lucius Annaeus Seneca: I Frammenti.* Bologna, Italy: Patron.

Wallace-Hadrill, Andrew, 1996. "The Imperial Court." In A. K. Bowman, E. Champlin, and A. Lintott, eds., *Cambridge Ancient History X: The Augustan Empire, 43 B. C.–A. D. 69,* Cambridge, UK: Cambridge University Press, pp. 283–323.

Williams, Gareth D., 2012. *The Cosmic Viewpoint: A Study of Seneca's Natural Questions.* New York, NY: Oxford University Press.

Wilson, Emily, 2007. *The Death of Socrates: Hero, Villain, Chatterbox, Saint.* London, UK: Profile Books, and Harvard, MA: Harvard University Press.

Wilson, Emily, 2004. *Mocked with Death: Tragic Overliving from Sophocles to Milton.* Baltimore, MD: Johns Hopkins University Press.

Wimbush, Vincent L., 1998. *Ascetic Behavior in Greco-Roman Antiquity.* Minneapolis, MN: Fortress.

Winterbottom, Michael, ed., 1974. *Seneca the Elder: Declamations.* 2 volumes. Boston, MA: Harvard University Press (Loeb Classical Library).

Winterling, Aloys, 2011. *Caligula,* trans. Deborah Lucas Scheider, Glenn Most, and Paul Psoinos. Oakland, CA: University of California Press.

Ziolowski, Theodore, 2004. "Seneca: A New German Icon?" *International Journal of the Classical Tradition,* 11, 47–77.

ART CREDITS

Figure I.1   BPK, Berlin/Antikensammlung, Staatliche
              Museen/CoDArchLab/Art Resource, NY.
Figure 1.1   © Shutterstock.
Figure 1.2   © Courtesy of the British Museum.
Figure 1.3   Erich Lessing/Art Resource, NY.
Figure 1.4   © Manfred Heyde.
Figure 2.1   Erich Lessing/Art Resource, NY.
Figure 2.2   Album/Art Resource, NY.
Figure 2.3   Album/Art Resource, NY.
Figure 2.4   Scala/Art Resource, NY.
Figure 2.5   © Ethelwulf, The Megalithic Portal.
Figure 3.1   Album/Art Resource, NY.
Figure 3.2   Foto Marburg/Art Resource, NY.
Figure 3.3   © Shutterstock.
Figure 3.4   Scala/Art Resource, NY.
Figure 3.5   Jewelry: Album/Art Resource, NY. Cup:
              © Shutterstock.
Figure 3.6   © Shutterstock.
Figure 3.7   © RMN-Grand Palais/Art Resource, NY.
Figure 4.1   Scala/Art Resource, NY.
Figure 4.2   © Shutterstock.
Figure 4.3   © Shutterstock.
Figure 4.4   © Shutterstock.
Figure 4.5   BPK, Berlin/Alte Pinakothek, Bayerische
              Staatsgemaeldesamm)/Peter Paul Rubens/Art
              Resource, NY.

INDEX

Academy (Platonic school), 11, 18
Acte, 119, 141
Actium, Battle of, 8
adiaphora. See indifferent things
adoption, 117
Agrippina ("the Younger"), 20, 33, 78, 79,
      95, 99, 100, 104, 105, 108, 109, 113,
      118, 119, 120, 121, 141–142, 143,
      144, 148, 149, 151
Alexander the Great, 12–13, 14, 38, 93, 176
Alexandria, 62
Anicetus, 142
aphorisms, 9, 197
   see also Seneca: style
Apollo, 113, 172
asceticism, 12, 32, 51, 52–53, 164, 186,
      189, 200
ataraxia (tranquillity of mind), 13, 93, 218
Athens, 116, 163
Attalus, 52, 101
Atticus, 5
Augustine, 106, 217–218
Augustus, 8, 48–49, 62, 64, 82, 112, 149
aunt, Seneca's, 33, 48, 61, 62, 63
authenticity, 8, 192, 210, 226
   See also hypocrisy *and* Seneca (the
      Younger), relationship of life to work

Boudica, 151–152
Britain, 21, 30, 77, 113, 131, 151–152
Britannicus, 99, 108, 109, 113, 120, 123,
      126, 138
Burrus, Sextus Afranius, 108, 109, 113, 114,
      115, 119, 120, 121, 142, 143, 154,
      155, 162, 181, 225

Caligula, 10, 66, 67, 68, 69, 76, 89, 94, 100,
      104, 108, 112, 126
Canus, Julius, 66
Castiglione, 220
Cato the Elder (Cato the Censor), 44
Cato the Younger, 125, 171, 205
Chrysippus, 13–14
childhood, Roman, 72
Christians, 203, 216, 217, 221
Cicero, 5, 9–11, 25, 36, 38, 43, 44, 51–52,
      116, 219
   daughter of, Tullia, 11
   Tusculanian Disputations, 11
   On Duties, 11
   On Ends, 11
   Pro Murena, 11
civil wars, Roman, 29, 35, 36
Claudius, 10, 76, 77, 78, 79, 80, 87, 88, 99,
      100, 104, 108, 109, 110, 112, 113,
      115, 128, 130, 149
Collins, Suzanne, 228
Columella, 25, 29, 188
consulation, as literary genre, 34, 69–70, 84
consumerism. *See* luxury
Corduba, 24, 26, 27, 28, 29–30, 48
   See also: Spain
Cordus, Cremutius, 70, 71
Corneille, Pierre, 225
Corsica, 5, 82, 83, 84, 85, 86, 87, 100, 112
   See also exile
Crates the Cynic, 13
Crispus Passienus (husband of
      Agrippina), 79
cursus honorum, 10, 62–63, 116–117
Cynicism, 12, 18

death, 1–4, 9, 18, 19, 57, 58, 72, 89, 93,
        153, 158, 163, 174, 177, 181, 194,
        202, 203, 205, 208, 210–212, 219,
        221, 227, 228
declamation, 36–42, 51
Descartes, Renée, 107, 222
Diderot, 223
Dio, Cassius, 6, 78, 79, 80, 88, 110, 111, 120,
        128, 131, 141, 206, 207, 208, 215
Diogenes the Cynic, 12
dissimulation, 66, 67, 143, 154, 170, 184
doctors and medicine (literal and
        metaphorical), 32, 58, 61, 62, 95,
        109, 162, 189, 193, 197, 209, 211,
        213, 222
Domitian, 125

eclecticism, philosophical, 11, 14, 18, 55,
        136, 193
ecpyrosis (destruction of world by fire), 14, 71
education, moral, 16, 73, 95, 96, 107, 123,
        159, 160, 175, 192–193, 196–197,
        198, 208–209
Egypt, 61, 62, 65, 118, 127, 142
Eliot, T. S., 226
elite, Roman, 8, 13, 21, 24, 29, 35, 38, 50,
        51, 65, 78, 92, 117, 122, 188–190
    see also social mobility *and* status *and*
        inequality
empire (*imperium*), 7, 13, 20–21, 199, 202,
        203, 206, 207
    see also kingship and power
Epicharis, 206
Epicureanism, 11, 13, 18, 74, 116, 132
Epictetus, 17, 155–157, 164, 227
equestrian class, 10, 35, 115, 117
Erasmus, 219
Euripides, 225
exile, as punishment, 82
    Seneca's attitude towards, 82–83, 84
    See also, Seneca, Lucius Annaeus (the
        Younger): exile

Fabianus, 42–43
fear, 18, 65, 66, 89, 91, 93, 122, 159, 166,
        167, 176, 182
flattery, 88, 89, 122, 123, 124, 184, 207
    See also dissimulation *and* theatricality
fortune, 9, 132, 138, 149, 150, 198
Foucault, Michel, 227

freedom, 9, 14, 16, 132, 152–154, 177, 189,
        200, 205, 213, 216
freedmen, 115, 128, 184, 213
Freud, 58–59

Galerius, Gaius (Seneca's uncle), 61, 62
Galba, 213
Gallio, Junius, 117
Gaul, 28
Germanicus, 79
gifts, 138, 144, 145, 146, 147, 148, 198,
        201, 209
    and Emerson, 144–145
    see also gratitude; Seneca (the Younger):
        On Benefits
gladiators, 154, 155
God, 90, 132, 179, 181, 218, 221, 222, 223
Goulart, Simon, 221
gratitude, 120, 148–151, 200, 209
Great Fire (64ᴄᴇ), 202
Greece, 26, 38, 44, 51, 93, 100
Griffin, Miriam, 155
Greek, 51

happiness (*eudaimonia*), 13, 17
hedonism, 18, 132
Helvia (Seneca's mother), 20, 29, 30,
        32–35, 36, 61, 72, 73
honesty, 26
Horace, 24, 167, 168
Hostius Quadra, 178–179
Hughes, Ted, 226
hypocrisy and inconstancy, 6, 100, 123, 129,
        131, 133, 134, 135, 136, 139, 196,
        212, 221, 226
    see also authenticity; theatricality;
        dissimulation

I, Claudius (Robert Graves and BBC), 77
impulse, involuntary, 1, 218
indifferent things, 15–18, 51, 72, 74, 75, 83,
        95, 129, 133, 137, 188, 216
individuality, 93, 220
inequality, 20–21, 127–128, 139, 147, 228
    see also: status; social mobility; elite,
        Roman
informers, 65, 130

James I, 220
Jefferson, Thomas, 222

Jerome, 217
jewelry, 120, 129, 134
Jews, 118, 216
Julia Livilla, 33, 78, 79, 80, 81, 82, 99, 112
Julio-Claudian family, 8, 78, 142, 215
Julius Caesar, 10, 29, 35, 62, 124, 171
Jupiter, 14, 15
Juvenal, 33, 40, 140–141, 228

kingship and power, 9, 116, 124, 125, 126,
    132, 182, 200, 219, 220

Latin, as language for philosophy, 11, 19,
    51, 69
Latro, Porcius, 38, 40
law, 94, 113, 130
Liberalis, Aebutius, 145
Lipsius, Justius, 221, 225
Livia (wife of Augustus), 108
Loyola, Ignatius, 106–107
Lucan, 25, 45, 73, 116, 118, 125, 157, 164,
    171, 172, 206, 213
Lucian, 16
Lucilius, 52, 58, 83, 90, 179, 181, 182,
    192, 195
luxury, 9, 13, 21, 51, 53, 54, 55, 85, 90, 128,
    131, 133, 134, 135, 175, 177, 186,
    189–190, 198–199, 200, 206, 228

Machiavelli, 220
Mark Antony, 9, 10
marriage laws, 76
Martial, 25, 129
masculinity, 8, 15, 41, 44, 80, 87, 91, 222
Mela, Annaeus Seneca (younger brother),
    42, 44–46, 47, 52, 116, 117,
    118, 213
Messalina, 78, 79, 88, 99, 115
Middle Ages, 218–219
Milton, John, 150, 182, 222
money-lending. See usury
Montaigne, 107, 220
Monteverdi, 220
More, Thomas, 219
mushrooms, 53–54, 109, 183
Musonius Rufus, 15, 156, 164, 213

Narcissus, 79–80, 99, 128
Nashe, Thomas, 224
Nazism, 226

Nero, 1, 2, 7, 11, 19, 20, 54, 73, 83, 91, 95,
    99, 100, 104, 105, 107, 108, 109,
    110, 111, 112, 113, 114, 115, 116,
    118, 119, 120, 121, 122, 123, 126,
    128, 130, 131, 141, 148, 149, 154,
    155, 157, 158, 159, 168, 169, 170,
    172, 173, 175, 178, 180, 183, 184,
    185, 192, 200, 202, 206, 207, 212,
    213, 214, 216, 219
Newton, Thomas, 224
nobility (nobilitas), 24, 116
    see also social mobility; status
Nomentum, 29, 185, 190, 191, 197, 206
Novatus, Annaeus Seneca, (Gallio), 42, 45, 46,
    47, 87, 92, 117, 118, 131, 190, 216
    daughter, Novatilla, 73

Octavian. See Augustus
Octavia, 76, 99, 108, 119, 121, 184, 215
Octavia, 73, 215, 216
Otho, 141, 184
Ovid, 24, 39–40, 82, 87, 88, 117, 137
    exile poetry, 5, 87

Pallas, 113, 120, 128, 184
Panaetius of Rhodes, 17
paradox, 16
passions, 92, 94, 95, 96, 222
patronage, 140–141, 148–149, 167, 215
Paul (apostle), 118, 216, 217, 219, 221
Paulina, Pompeia, 1, 74, 116, 134, 190, 191,
    208, 209
    see also Seneca, Annaeus Lucius (the
    Younger), wife and Seneca, Annaeus
    Lucius (the Younger), On Marriage
Paulinus, 165
Peripatetics, 18
Petronius, 40, 130, 172, 173, 174, 213
philosophy, Roman, 44, 51, 52, 56, 58,
    93, 132
physics, 14
    see also, Seneca, Natural Questions
Piso, Gaius, and Pisonian Conspiracy, 1, 184,
    205, 206
Plato, 11, 87, 115–116, 136, 150, 178
    Phaedo, 1, 209
    Gorgias, 42
Pliny, 28, 29, 40, 61, 62, 87, 176, 184
poison, 41, 97, 109, 121, 127, 149, 162, 183,
    185, 203, 205

Pollio, Gaius Assinius, 48
Polybius, 88, 115
Pompey, 29, 35, 171
Poppaea Sabina, 141, 184, 213, 215, 220
Praetorian Guard, 76, 108, 109, 110, 162,
    206, 213
pragmatism, 55, 75, 105, 119, 209–210
providence, 12, 15
Pythagoreanism, 18, 55

Quintilian, 25, 38, 216

Racine, Jean, 225
reason, 15
retirement from public life, 18, 63, 89–90,
    141, 162, 163, 165, 166, 168–169,
    177, 181, 196, 201, 202
rhetoric, 9, 10, 36, 38, 39, 40, 42–43, 51,
    105, 121, 206, 210, 226
Roman Principate, 8, 10, 21, 77, 94, 115
Roman Republic, 8, 10, 21, 70, 77, 94,
    124, 171
Rome, 48–49, 50, 57, 87, 94, 100, 101, 103
Rousseau, 222
Rubens, "The Death of Seneca", 2, 211
Rufus, Rutilius, 83
Rusticus, Fabius, 140, 208, 215

sapiens. See Wise Man
Saturnalia, 111
Scipio, 30, 185
self-examination, 106, 107, 227
Sejanus, 63–64, 70
Senate, 8, 76, 111, 112, 115, 124, 143, 153
Seneca, Lucius Annaeus ("the Elder"), 20,
    24, 35–46, 48, 58, 90, 117, 128
    Controversies (Debates), 25, 36, 37, 41, 42
    Suasoriae (Persuasions), 36, 41
Seneca, Lucius Annaeus ("the Younger"),
    passim
    adultery scandal of, 34, 76–82, 130
    and affairs with boys, 141
    bathing and exercise habits of, 53,
        186, 187
    birth of, 23
    body of, 54, 186–187
    childhood of, 30–33, 50–51
    consulship of, 116
    diet of, 1, 32, 53–54, 56–57, 81, 187,
        189, 203

death of, 1
education of, 51–58
exile of, 5, 78, 82–99, 130
health of (especially chronic lung
    problems), 1, 32, 57, 61, 62, 68,
    186, 203
as political advisor, 105, 109, 110,
    114–116
praetorship of, 100, 104
property of, 127, 128, 168, 169, 185
quaestorship of, 62
relationship of life to work, 5, 19, 76,
    86–87, 134, 194 (and passim)
son of, 72
as speechwriter, 105, 109–110, 111
style of, 69, 216, 219, 224, 226
suicidal impulses of, 57, 190–191, 219
as tutor to Nero, 105
wealth of, 3, 7–8, 127–141
    See also wealth and luxury
wife of (mother of son), 72, 73,
    74, 86
wife of, identity unknown, 106
will of, 3, 209
women and, 33, 68, 74
works of
    Agamemnon, 9, 103
    On Anger, 66, 84, 92–96, 105–106,
        126, 218
    Apocolycyntosis, 111, 112, 123
    On Benefits (De Beneficiis), 23, 64, 65,
        83, 100, 140, 143–151, 175
    On Clemency (De Clementia), 64, 121,
        122, 123, 124, 125, 126, 191, 215,
        216, 220, 221
    On Constancy, 7, 17, 31, 90, 91
    epigrams (pseudo-Senecan), 29–30,
        85, 86
    Epistles (Letters to Lucilius), 2, 18, 6, 29,
        1, 3, 4, 35, 7, 31, 50–51, 52, 54, 56,
        57, 61, 83, 116, 155, 163, 184,
        185–205, 218, 221
    On the Happy Life, 131–139, 222
    To Helvia, 34–35, 47, 72, 80, 84,
        85, 87
    Hercules Furens, 9, 101, 153
    On Leisure (De Otio), 165, 166
    Letters to Lucilius, see Epistles
    lost works, 5
    To Marcia, 69, 82

On Marriage, 74–76

Medea, 9, 96–97, 101

Natural Questions, 14, 47, 68, 69, 80, 105, 163, 170, 174–183, 210

Oedipus, 59

Phaedra, 9, 223–224, 225

Phoenissae, 126

To Polybius, 80, 84, 88–90, 112

On Providence, 4, 15, 90

On the Shortness of Life, 2, 165

Thyestes, 9, 66, 126, 135, 150, 158, 159, 160, 161, 162, 216

tragedies, 96, 97, 98, 99, 105, 125–126, 157–158, 179, 223–224, 226

On Tranquility, 66

Trojan Women, 9, 126, 127

Serenus Annaeus, 90, 91, 117, 119, 181, 183, 184

Sextianism, 18, 42, 54–55

Skepticism (philosophical school), 11, 13

slaves and slavery, 41, 87, 111, 127, 134, 155, 178, 187, 188, 189, 190, 196

social mobility, 25, 26, 76, 113, 116, 117, 135, 186, 195

Socrates, 1, 2, 3, 12, 139, 148, 209, 210, 211, 223

Sotion, 54–55, 195

Spain (Hispania), 20, 24, 26, 27, 28, 29, 30, 48, 180

status, 13, 45, 106, 135

Stoicism, 4, 11, 12–19, 38, 44, 52–53, 55, 74, 75, 84, 91, 93–94, 96, 105, 116, 124, 125, 129, 132, 136, 164, 165, 171, 175, 179, 183, 216, 218, 219, 222

Suetonius, 38, 69, 104, 105, 109, 120, 171, 213

suicide, 19

Suillius, Publius, 130, 131, 147

Tacitus, 1, 2, 4, 40, 46, 56, 99, 100, 105, 108, 109, 111, 113, 114, 115, 116, 118, 119, 120, 126, 130, 131, 142, 168, 169, 170, 171, 183, 184, 206, 207, 208, 209, 212, 222

Tertullian, 217

theatricality, 66, 67, 95, 105, 153, 154, 155, 173, 195, 202, 212

Thrasea, 125, 153, 184, 213

Tiberius, 10, 63, 64, 65, 66, 82, 104, 108, 120

Tigellinus, 183, 213

toga, 49–50, 108

United States and Europe, 21, 72, 117, 128, 227

usury, 130–131, 138, 151–152

vegetarianism, 55, 56

view from above, 92, 173, 178, 179, 180, 183, 194

Vincius, Marcus, 79

Virgil, 24

virtue (*virtus*), 8, 9, 12, 16, 91, 94, 124, 132, 135–137, 161, 200, 212, 222

see also masculinity

viticulture, 29, 128, 185, 197–198

wealth, 117, 120, 126, 127–141, 148, 168, 169, 184, 189, 190, 198, 199, 212

see also luxury

Webster, John, 224

Wise Man (in Stoicism: *sapiens*), 12, 15, 55, 72, 83, 84, 132, 137–138, 161, 201, 218

as king, 54, 101, 201

Wolfe, Tom, 227

Zeno, 13, 87